D0893413

SOCIAL HOUSEKEEPERS

WOMEN SHAPING PUBLIC POLICY IN NEW MEXICO

1920 – 1940

SOCIAL HOUSEKEEPERS

WOMEN SHAPING PUBLIC POLICY
IN NEW MEXICO
1920 – 1940

SANDRA SCHACKEL

UNIVERSITY OF NEW MEXICO

ALBUQUERQUE

Library of Congress Cataloging-in-Publication Data
Schackel, Sandra.
Social housekeepers : women shaping public policy in New
Mexico, 1920–1940 / Sandra Schackel. — 1st ed.
p.   cm.
Includes bibliographical references and index.
ISBN 0–8263–1324–8
1. Women social reformers—New Mexico.
2. Women volunteers in social service—New Mexico.
3. Women social workers—New Mexico.
4. New Mexico—Social policy.   I. Title.
HQ1438.N55S33   1992
305.42′09789—dc20   91–26105
                                                        CIP

To my support team
Greg, Christi, and Angie

CONTENTS

ACKNOWLEDGMENTS

Although this book carries the name of a single author, many people have contributed to the finished product. In the process of creating a dissertation then shaping it into a readable, and I hope meaningful, book, I have incurred many debts. Now comes the satisfying task of conveying to those people my deep appreciation for their efforts.

My first debt is to Donald Cutter, my earliest academic supporter and mentor. From Cutter, I witnessed firsthand the excitement and satisfaction that comes from pursuing history through research and writing, and eventually the pleasure of transferring that knowledge through the classroom experience. My only hope of reducing my debt to him is to try to pass on to others the love of history that he generated in me.

Others followed Cutter in shaping my professional character, five of whom served unstintingly on my dissertation committee. Most importantly, my thanks go to Jane Slaughter, the "intellectual mother" of this study, who shaped my views on gender and history in a profound way. While I appreciate the professional support she provided, I especially treasure the mutual respect and friendship that has evolved. Richard Ellis continually prompted my interest in the American West and kept me focused on the goal of "getting published." Richard Etulain provided not only superb editorial assistance but continually asked questions that stretched my thinking, not only on this topic but throughout my graduate experience. I am grateful to Joan Jensen for the foundation of scholarship she has created on the lives of rural women in America which helped me shape my ideas about rural New Mexico women. Helen Bannon provided not only intellectual balance but gender support as well, a commodity often in short supply. To all the members of this committee, my heartfelt thanks for all the readings and rereadings, the criticisms and questions, and especially the moral support that sustained me throughout the project.

A book is more than the sum of its parts, however, and many thanks go to the persons and institutions that contributed to the whole. I am especially grateful to the New Mexico women who invited me into their homes and shared their stories with me. K. Rose Wood was an invaluable source not only for oral history contacts but for her insights and experiences during the New Deal and after. Elinor Galvin of the Santa Fe Woman's Club and Mary Carter of the Albuquerque Woman's Club were more than generous in allowing me access to club records. Austin Hoover alerted me to the oral histories of rural homemakers in the Rio Grande Historical Collection at New Mexico State University. Janet Johnson, archivist in the University of New Mexico Medical Library, provided me with a first-rate photo as well as research material on health issues. At the State Records Center and Archives in Santa Fe, archivist Al Regensberg patiently fulfilled my requests for one box after another of source material and for photographs. In an eleventh-hour situation, Jean Holliday, Assistant to the Curator in the Seeley G. Mudd Library at Princeton University, produced two files of wonderfully rich material on the nurses who worked among the Navajo and Pueblo Indians.

The somewhat intimidating and perplexing nature of the National Archives in Washington, D.C., was made "kinder and gentler" through the able assistance of Aloha P. South in the Judicial, Fiscal and Social Division and Robert Kvasnicka in the Scientific, Economic and Natural Resources Division. In Denver, Eileen Bolger provided me with Bureau of Indian Affairs materials at the National Archives Branch in that city. I thank the personnel in the Photoduplication Department of the Library of Congress for many of the photos reproduced here and Arthur Olivas and Richard Rudisill, photoarchivists at the Museum of New Mexico, for their assistance in locating other images.

To my editor, Barbara Guth, my heartfelt appreciation for her skills, tact, and patience. When other tasks threatened to interfere, she was there to remind me of our mutual goal—press time.

Writing a book entails both time and money and I am grateful to Boise State University for providing me with a Faculty Research Grant that allowed me to finalize the last stage of this project.

Finally, loving thanks go to my parents and my children, who were always there for me and to whom I continually turn for renewal and reinforcement. And most of all, thanks to Bill Tydeman, who has provided me with steady encouragement and loving support, along with unlimited intellectual excitement.

INTRODUCTION

The noonday sun was rapidly approaching its zenith in a bright blue New Mexico sky when the two women sat down to talk on a late summer day in 1986. The younger woman listened intently as her new friend began to describe the human landscape of fifty years earlier, desperate years when the rains did not fall and the soil blew away, leaving the land barren and dry. The older woman was then a newly graduated social worker, looking for a place to be needed. After placing a map of the United States on the floor of her Minnesota home, K. Rose Wood blindfolded herself and chose a spot at random; her hand fell on Santa Fe. Within ten days, Wood was on a bus enroute to this sleepy, dusty small town of just over 11,000. A single phone call to the New Mexico Department of Public Welfare had assured her she was indeed needed in a state whose meager resources were spread thin among a diverse and needy population.

Wood quickly found her place in the social welfare community in New Mexico. She was one of many women who entered and benefited from the rapidly growing field of social welfare work in the years between the two world wars. Bounded by two watershed events—the passage of the suffrage amendment in 1920 and the outbreak of war in 1941—the decades of the 1920s and 1930s proved to be rich in opportunities for women in social welfare reform.[1]

During this period, women's social welfare activities in New Mexico both replicated and differed from reform activities of women nationwide. Like women elsewhere, New Mexico women focused on issues of family and children, particularly health. By doing so, they fit their reform efforts into the existing social order, developing public power that allowed them to influence social welfare policy. The impact of gender on the nature and direction of welfare reform is the major theme of this book.

New Mexico Counties and County Seats, 1925

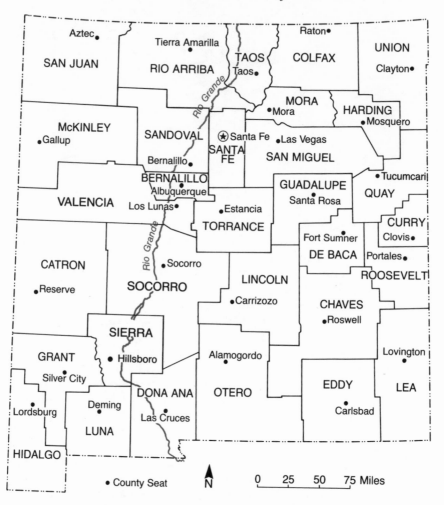

1. New Mexico Counties and County Seats

1. Corn and chiles, traditional fare, drying in the New Mexico sun. Courtesy of Museum of New Mexico, neg. no. 31509.

Equally important is the impact of class and ethnicity on the state's social welfare structure. Here, the New Mexico case differs from other areas since reformers were forced to adjust their programs to a multicultural population that included Hispanics, Anglos, Native Americans, and blacks. Female reformers were most successful when they modified or ignored strict gender and racial prescriptions, consequently forcing authorities to alter their concepts of social welfare reforms.

Although New Mexico was one of several impoverished and economically depressed Western states in the interwar years, certain characteristics set that state apart from the others. In 1920, when the federal census announced that, for the first time, more people nationwide lived in urban than rural areas, New Mexico was 82 percent rural. This rural population—295,390 of 360,350—was scattered over 122,000 square miles, the fifth largest state in the nation. Long distances and poor roads further contributed to New Mexico's isolation. Even more central to the state's uniqueness was its cultural diversity: 60 percent of the population was Hispanic, 33.4 percent Anglo, 5 percent Native American, and 1.6 percent black. Repeatedly, this cultural mix affected social welfare policies in unexpected ways and forced reformers and administrators to adjust their ideas and concepts accordingly.[2]

There were 169,894 women in New Mexico in 1920. A demographic profile of one of these women would show her to be rural, young (median age nineteen), married, likely to have many children and to see many of them die in infancy. Most of these women would be Spanish-speaking, live on a farm of fifty acres or less, and engage in subsistence farming. The majority of Hispanic families lived in the small mountain villages of northern New Mexico or in the southern portion of the state, particularly the Mesilla Valley, although many lived in larger towns and cities as well. By 1920, economic circumstances had forced Hispanic men to leave livestock raising for wage labor in the beetfields and coalfields of southern Colorado or the agricultural valleys in southern New Mexico. The result was the growth of regional communities in which the role of Hispanic women in village life increased in importance.[3]

Hispanic women frequently have been stereotyped as submissive, dependent wives and mothers locked in a rigidly patriarchal social system. This distorted vision does a disservice to women and their families, for whom the wife, mother, daughter, sister, aunt, and grandmother were pivotal figures in daily life. Significantly, women reinforced the ties of kinship that provided the basis of Hispanic community life. They also entered the community as individuals, performing communal labor and religious services for the entire village. Central to community life, women also helped sustain it. The Hispanic women addressed in this study provided mutually supporting networks that went beyond subsistence to include community issues such as health and childcare. They frequently took jobs outside the home to provide for their families.

The lives of Native American women differed from their Anglo, Hispanic, and black sisters in ways that were determined long before they came into contact with Euro-Americans in the Southwest. The Pueblo people lived a settled agricultural life clustered in villages primarily along the upper and lower Rio Grande, while the Navajo were scattered on reservation lands that extended from western and northwestern New Mexico into central and northeastern Arizona. Indian women numbered 9,363 of the 19,512 total Native American population of New Mexico in 1920. Like women of other cultural groups, Indian women were responsible for domestic tasks that included childcare and food production and preparation, but, in addition, many were engaged in perpetuating or relearning Indian arts, especially pottery-making and weaving. With the Indian Reorganization Act of 1934, which encouraged the development of Indian arts and crafts (and not incidentally the Anglo pursuit of tourism), many Indian women became economically important to tribal survival. At the same time, they and their usually large families suffered poor health, lived in crowded conditions with poor sanitation, and generally fared badly by all socioeconomic measurements. For the most part, when Anglo caregivers interacted with native women, such as the Public Health nurses of the New Mexico Association on Indian Affairs, they were received with interest and cooperation.

Black women in New Mexico numbered even fewer than Indian women: 1,140 of a total black population of 5,733. Albuquerque showed a small black population of 213, many of these men working for the Santa Fe Railway. Raton, in the northeastern corner of the state, listed 136 blacks, most of them employed in the coal mines of that region. The majority of the rest of the black population lived in southern and southwestern counties where they worked in the cotton fields and on agricultural farms in the Mesilla Valley. The 110 black women who made Albuquerque their home in 1920 lived lives much like their white middle-class counterparts. While some were employed as teachers, others were active in women's clubs, church affairs, and other civic and social concerns. Although they did not share in the empowerment that some Anglo women experienced during the New Deal years, black women, like Hispanic and Indian women, were central figures in shaping family and cultural life.[4]

Central to this study are women's efforts as volunteers and as paid workers. Examining their activities raises the question: Were women able to influence the nature and direction of social welfare policies, and if so, how? Earlier research demonstrates that women were instrumental in providing services that communities might not have afforded otherwise, services that embraced health, education, housing, labor, and other aspects of social welfare.[5] This study focuses on how New Mexico women achieved those ends within the private and public spheres of their communities.

The concept of separate spheres has long been a tenet of feminist theory, but scholars are now calling into question the utility of the public/private dichotomy as a model for Western industrialized societies.[6] The separation of work from family, the domestic from the public, denies the interdependence and interconnectedness of the two realms. In fact, the distinction between public and private spheres has rarely been precise, since women have often played significant roles in public life. Equally important is the degree to which the public/domestic relationship has shaped the concept of gender and how, in turn, women's actions "continue to restructure and redefine ideology, social structure, and power relationships."[7] This study reaffirms the more realistic model of a blurring between the domestic and the public spheres. New Mexico women, like other women, did not abruptly leave the home and suddenly appear in the public arena. Instead, by focusing on traditional issues of women and children, they became both public and political. A major avenue to the public sphere was voluntarism.

Voluntarism has been a major force in the lives of many women since early in the nineteenth century. Primarily a function of white middle- and upper-class women, who had leisure time and the means to become involved in community service, volunteer organizations allowed women to move freely between private and public spheres. The earliest efforts began with charity work in the churches, where, as long as women remained docile, subservient, and nonthreatening, their benevolent activities were acceptable.[8] Gradually, however, some women moved beyond religious societies and became active in major nineteenth-century reform movements, including abolition, temperance, and suffrage. Sociologists Marilyn Gittell and Teresa Shtob, who have studied women's roles in urban reform, note that though women were excluded from the centers of urban power, they successfully led urban reform movements.[9] They did so through voluntary associations, which they used as a channel for their interests and energies. For example, in the 1830s, women in New England and New York set up moral reform societies aimed at abolishing prostitution, gambling, and profanity. These public, morality-based societies allowed women to move beyond the rigidly prescribed roles of wife and mother, confined to the home. In the process, they enlarged their sphere of homelike duties to encompass the community, a concept that has become known as "domestic feminism."

Historian Daniel Scott Smith coined this phrase in 1974 to describe the activities nineteenth-century women used to justify their departure from the home.[10] Drawing on the supposedly "natural" traits of ladyhood—moral superiority, compassion, and sensitivity—women gradually won a place for themselves outside the home by using their domestic credentials.[11] This idea was especially prevalent in the woman's club movement that began in 1868 and was formalized in 1890 with the creation of the General Federation of Women's Clubs. Initially established as literary clubs, these "culture clubs" provided a training ground in which women could nurture and expand their intellectual and social skills while retaining their "ladylike" qualities. At the same time, domestic feminism reinforced the belief that a woman's first obligation was to her husband and children. Stocking the pantry with pies and getting supper on the table remained standard female behavior and met male expectations.[12]

Quite naturally, a second phase of domestic feminism developed that capitalized on women's perceived special moral qualities. Known as "municipal housekeeping," this concept applied women's domestic skills to the community at large as women turned to civic reform around the turn of the century.[13] Drawing on their abilities to create healthy, happy homes, clubwomen sponsored civic projects that included, among other things, building libraries, beautifying streets and parks, and promoting pure milk campaigns. One man, Clinton Rogers Woodruff, tidily summed up their Progressive reform sentiment: "Women by natural instinct as well as by long training have become the housekeepers of the world, so it is only natural that they should in time become effective municipal housekeepers as well."[14] Thus, the movement of women out of the private sphere into the public arena marked a turning point in the late nineteenth century, as clubwomen began to apply domestic solutions to community issues.[15]

By the early twentieth century, the government had taken over many of the functions of the home, especially in the areas of education and health care. Social policy, formerly the province of women's voluntary work, became public policy. Historian Paula Baker sees this change as an important transition in women's political experience and the history of national politics. Women's clubs continued to be an important avenue through which to initiate social change, but, increasingly, women found that their efforts at "public motherhood" were not enough; the help of the state was needed. As the population increased and society became more complex, social problems multiplied and were not always solvable at the local level. For example, women's goal to prevent poverty, rather than to aid poor people, demanded solutions beyond the abilities of local charities. So, they turned their efforts toward securing legislation that would alleviate social problems—laws to compensate victims of industrial accidents, to require better education, to provide adequate nutrition, for example. Women passed on to the state the problems they found unmanageable. Increasingly, then, government took on the burdens of social and moral responsibility formerly assigned to the women's sphere.[16]

How did this transformation affect women and social policy in New Mexico? In particular, how did ethnicity shape the nature of social welfare? To begin with, voluntarism, which dominates much of this study, is a concept that varies among different cultural groups. The voluntarism discussed here is primarily white, middle-class, based on the nuclear family, and individualistic. On the other hand, voluntarism in Native American and Hispanic populations is less formal and institutional because it is inherent in the family, community, and even religious structures. Among the Pueblo people, for instance, traditional village life centers around the concept of the "gia" (synonymous with mother), in which the nurturer provides the central focus for the community's social, political, and religious systems.[17]

Recent works by Richard Griswold del Castillo and Sarah Deutsch on Hispanic families illuminate some of the above themes. Prevalent throughout these works is the strong sense of and dependence on the family that characterized this ethnic group in the 1920s and 1930s. In *La Familia*, Griswold del Castillo examines the popular mythology associated with the Mexican-American family—the large, tight-knit, male-dominant, female-submissive family—and how the process of assimilation has altered these stereotypes. Yet inherent in the twentieth-century Hispanic family is the ability to combine older traditions with newer ones as the family adapts to modern American life. Drawing on a heritage from the past, "la familia" still promises love, self-respect, personal dignity, hope, and caring.[18]

Sarah Deutsch echoes this theme of the primacy of the family in her study of Hispanic communities in northern New Mexico and southern Colorado. Anglo notions of gender behavior and race strongly affected Hispanic traditions and the influence of female community builders. From missionaries to agricultural extension agents to WPA directors, middle-class Anglo women sought to transform Hispanic women into ideal domestic servants and housewives. Deutsch argues that Anglo reformers were unable to integrate Hispanic women into positions "in the new society that would match the power of their village roles." Both Hispanic men and women suffered a loss of status, but for women, "full integration and assimilation into the Anglo community would not remedy that loss." [19]

The rate of assimilation varied among Hispanics, particularly between the Mexican-American immigrant population in southern New Mexico, primarily in the Mesilla Valley, and the Hispanic population in northern New Mexico villages. For those families in the southern part of the state, the immigration experience forced them to adapt quickly to American customs and attitudes, thereby weakening traditional ties to their extended families. In the north, where the assimilation process was slower, family solidarity remained of primary importance, much of it reinforced by the Catholic church. These differing patterns determined how Hispanic women reacted to social welfare reform attempts.[20]

Among black women, social welfare needs were met largely through voluntary activities. The nature of voluntarism among blacks falls somewhere between that of Anglo women and of the Native American and Hispanic populations. Generally, middle-class black women acted much like Anglo women. There are important differences, however. Racism was a significant factor in that black women were always operating as a racial minority and therefore were placed in a defensive position, giving them a less positive relationship with the existing power structure. Black middle-class women, furthermore, often adopted rigid gender roles of ladylike behavior because of the stereotypical view of them as less moral than white women. Victorian womanhood and motherhood were legitimizing mechanisms in very different ways for white women and black women.[21]

Women's social welfare activities in the 1920s and 1930s in New Mexico serve as a good test of national patterns in which (a) the institutional reformers are a fairly homogeneous group while the target population is much more heterogeneous; and (b) supposed recipients of reform efforts, instead of being simply passive victims, negotiate with their "benefactors" to meet self-defined needs and goals.[22] In this context, welfare reform is a reciprocal relationship between recipients and those who structure the reforms.

Few accounts in Western history address such issues, although in the past decade the body of literature that incorporates the roles of women into the history of the American West has increased appreciably. Several journals have devoted special issues to new interpretations and approaches, and numerous historiographical articles have appeared that chronicle the direction, and the omissions, in the field.[23] In a ground-breaking essay in 1980, historians Joan Jensen and Darlis Miller called for a multicultural approach examining women's lives across a wide spectrum including ethnicity, class, region, and time.[24] Little mention was made of the twentieth-century West, however, except to note a need for further study of the modern period. In mid-1988, Elizabeth Jameson published a comprehensive companion piece to "Gentle Tamers," chronicling the expansion of the field since 1980.[25] As the history of the West continues to be written and revised, women's history must also be included to provide a fuller understanding of the field as a whole.[26]

Within the many subdivisions of twentieth-century Western history, social welfare has generally been neglected. The omission is significant given the impact of the Great Depression and the creation of massive social welfare programs in the New Deal years. Current literature on the twentieth-century West focuses primarily on political and economic aspects and only briefly, if at all, includes women.[27] Exceptions are Julia Kirk Blackwelder's study of San Antonio in the Depression era, Sarah Deutsch's examination of Hispanic/Anglo interaction in northern New Mexico and southern Colorado, Richard Griswold del Castillo's study of Chicano families in the urban Southwest, and Suzanne Forrest's recent work on New Mexico Hispanics and the New Deal.[28] The absence of extensive secondary material makes synthesis and conclusions difficult.

This study marks a modest beginning. There are significant areas and organizations I have not considered, such as the work missionary women carried out, particularly in northern New Mexico, or the contributions of national organizations such as the Red Cross or YWCA. Of the numerous women's clubs that engaged in social welfare work, I have focused on those clubs within the state's General Federation of Women's Clubs, singling out the work of two: the Woman's Club of Albuquerque and the Woman's Club of Santa Fe. Although numerous women's clubs were organized in smaller communities around the state, they, too, were urban-based organizations of which these two clubs are representative. For rural women, I have drawn on the work of home demonstration agents of the Agricultural Extension Service. It was not my intent to discuss women and politics because that is a topic worthy of a separate study; however, some discussion of women's role on the New Mexico political scene is integral to the fuller picture.

With these caveats in mind, the study is limited to a handful of public and private organizations involving women active as volunteers and as paid workers at local, state, and national levels. The research trail led from the New Mexico living rooms of oral history respondents to papers of several governors in the State Archives and Records Center in Santa Fe to numerous record groups in the National Archives in Washington, D.C. and in Denver. Particularly fruitful were the records of the Children's Bureau, the Works Progress Administration (WPA), and the Federal Emergency Relief Administration (FERA). At the heart of this study, however, are the voices of the women who lived through this period of social welfare reform and were willing to share their experiences and recollections with me.

The study opens with a topic of major interest to New Mexico women—health reform. This opening chapter examines women's roles in establishing the state's public health structure and how that process contributed to the "domestication of politics." The second and third chapters focus on health as well: how women carried out maternity and infancy work under the provisions of the federal Sheppard-Towner Act, and the role of a private organization, the New Mexico Association on Indian Affairs, in securing nurses to work among the state's Native American population.

Voluntarism and the power women accrued within the existing political structure are the subject of chapter four. The urban-based women's clubs of Santa Fe and Albuquerque form the core of this chapter. In contrast to the urban experience, chapter five focuses on the Agricultural Extension Service and its effect among rural women, pointing to the issues of cooperation among various institutions and the process of adaptation. And, finally, chapter six looks at a variety of New Deal programs and their empowerment of women, both as providers and as recipients of services. One important result in this era was the movement of some women into county and state jobs, providing varying degrees of power and authority. In each chapter, where appropriate, regional, racial, and cultural variations are discussed.

Overall, the study examines the movement of women between the private and public spheres and the effect of that movement on the social welfare of New Mexicans between 1920 and 1940. As a small piece in the cultural quilt of social history, this work will, I hope, increase our understanding of gender, class, and ethnicity in the twentieth-century American West.

1

HEALTH PROMOTION, DISEASE PREVENTION

CREATING A PUBLIC HEALTH STRUCTURE

On January 6, 1912, a delegation from New Mexico gathered at the White House to witness the signing of the bill that allowed New Mexico to become the forty-seventh state to enter the Union. Affixing his signature to the proclamation, President William Howard Taft turned to the delegation and said, "Well, it's all over now. I am glad to give you life. I hope you will be healthy."[1]

Despite the president's wish for good health, New Mexico was in a paradoxical situation. Touted as a health-seeker's refuge as early as 1877, New Mexico attracted thousands of newcomers between the 1880s and the 1930s, many of them suffering from tuberculosis.[2] On the advice of physicians in the East, they sought to take advantage of the sunshine, fresh air, and high altitude in the West. Yet at the same time, the New Mexico population was not especially healthy. Communicable diseases such as diptheria and typhoid, as well as tuberculosis, caused high numbers of deaths. In addition, the infant mortality rate was the highest in the nation.[3]

In the first decades of statehood, then, health issues were a primary concern of both public and private groups. These were issues in which New Mexico women, through various women's clubs and organizations, played a major role. Much of their effort was channeled through voluntarism, uniting public and private efforts toward the shared cause of the health of New Mexico residents. In the process, women's groups developed a base of social power that allowed them access to the formal, male-dominated political structure and ensured that women would influence subsequent health reform, if on a limited basis. As with reform efforts elsewhere, change was imposed from the top by white middle-class reformers anxious to impart Progressive era values to a multicultural population.

Prior to statehood, little had been done to meet public health needs. Several factors account for this lack of organized health care. Most important, health facilities were simply too few and too scattered because of the size of the state and its sparse population. There were vast areas, in fact, where trained physicians were not available. In addition, most people could not afford the one dollar per mile charge for a doctor to make a home visit. As a result, health care was often the province of local *curanderas* and midwives, women usually untrained in modern health and hygienic methods. In the years immediately following statehood, local citizens and state officials took the first steps toward regulating and improving health care on a state-wide basis.

A major health concern was the extremely high infant mortality rate, an important indicator of a society's well-being. In the words of Dr. S. Josephine Baker, first director of the Bureau of Child Hygiene in New York City: "The infant mortality rate is the most sensitive index of municipal housekeeping of a community. It is more than that; it is an index of civic interest, cooperation, consciousness, and worth."[4] Although New Mexico was slow to initiate civic interest and cooperation, sensitivity was not lacking. New Mexicans were genuinely concerned that their state led the nation in the 1920s and 1930s in mortality rates for infants under one year. In 1929, the first year for which the state compiled statistics, 140 babies died in the first year of life for every 1,000 born. This figure was more than twice the national rate of 61 per 1,000, and it continued to rise in the 1930s before dropping to 96 per 1,000 in 1940.[5]

Throughout these two decades, health issues were a major concern of both private and public organizations at federal, state, and local levels. A concerted effort between local groups, such as women's clubs, and state agencies like the Bureau of Public Health addressed these issues. Together they made significant improvements in the quality of New Mexico's health care. Those efforts have been one of the most significant changes affecting New Mexico in the twentieth century, and women played a major role in the process. For example, the genesis of the Child Welfare Service in 1919 was the result of the determination and dedication of women's club members throughout the state between 1910 and 1919. The creation of the Department of Public Welfare in 1921 was their second major success.

The creation of the Child Welfare Service is testimony to New Mexico women's initial efforts to instigate social reform through legislation. Using this volunteer organization as a mouthpiece, clubwomen continued to lobby for a child welfare department within the state structure. They cited the increase in child welfare and maternity work in official health agencies and voluntary welfare organizations across the nation and around the world. Using New Zealand as an example, the women pointed out that that nation had cut its infant mortality rate by more than half and, in 1921, had the lowest rate in the world.[6] Improved maternity and infant care was achieved through the regulation of the training and practice of midwives and nurses, establishment of maternity hospitals, and the supervision of child placement. New Mexico women saw no reason why such practices could not be established in their state, thereby reducing the high infant mortality rate to a more "acceptable" level. The Child Welfare Service, wisely administered, would be an example of advanced welfare legislation typical of the Progressive era.[7]

Generally, New Mexico had been slow to implement modern health practices. Although a Board of Health and Medical Examiners existed during the territorial period, its activities were restricted to licensing candidates to practice medicine. Not until the ravages of the influenza epidemic of 1917–18 brought to light shockingly inadequate conditions did New Mexico create a public board of health. World War I played a part in the drama as well, for the armed services rejected many young men because of poor physical condition, and of those who served, many returned with syphilis and tuberculosis. These issues became even more critical when the American Medical Association made a comparative study of various state health departments in 1916 and found New Mexico to be the only state lacking such an agency. When Julia Lathrop, chief of the Children's Bureau in the Department of Labor, requested that New Mexico join with other states in a nationwide campaign to save the lives of 100,000 infants in 1918, the state could not participate because it lacked the bureaucratic machinery and money to carry out the campaign. Nor could the state qualify for federal funds under the national rural health act of 1919 for the same reasons.[8]

Governors Washington E. Lindsey (1917–19) and Octavian A. Larrazolo (1919–20) supported the movement to establish a department of public health. But a private citizen, John Tombs—a Canadian who came to New Mexico as a tuberculosis patient—was responsible for creating publicity and support for the implementation of a formal structure for public health care.[9] In 1917, Tombs organized the New Mexico Public Health Association, an affiliate of the National Tuberculosis Association. Its major objective was to convince state officials to create a state department of health. To aid in those efforts, the Association repeated in press releases, letters, and other printed materials a statement that boldly declared New Mexico's situation: "It is unfortunate that a state with a population which now numbers nearly half a million should do

2. A typical scene in New Mexico villages in the 1920s; drawing water from the well in the village plaza. Photo by T. Harmon Parkhurst, courtesy of Museum of New Mexico, neg. no. 31630.

nothing whatever for public health. It is the only state of which this can be said."[10] Drawing on his organizational skills and his background as a journalist, and using the results of several health surveys, Tombs became a major figure in the effort to create a state department of health.

The influenza epidemic of 1918–19 finally propelled citizens and officials to take concrete action. Influenza appeared in New Mexico late in 1918, despite the claims of some that the state's "salubrious . . . atmosphere" and great distance from the nation's disease-ridden ports and big cities would prevent a visit from the "epidemical malady."[11] The malady did appear and exacted a painful toll—more than 15,000 cases resulting in 1,055 deaths.[12] Even with the cooperation of private citizens, civil authorities, physicians, and nurses, the structure and machinery for coping with an emergency of this magnitude were lacking. In Tombs's words:

The outstanding feature of the situation was our absolute lack of health
preparedness. . . . We will never know how many friends, relatives,
and fellow citizens . . . were sacrificed as a result of the lack of an
official health organization, linking up the counties and towns of our
state for efficient health protection and the prevention of disease.[13]

The flu epidemic, while not the only health problem of that period, highlights the precarious condition of public health conditions in New Mexico.

In mid-1918, Governor Lindsey requested that the United States Public Health Service carry out a survey of New Mexico health needs; in September, Surgeon J. W. Kerr arrived from Washington, D.C., to do so. Reacting to the flu epidemic, Kerr established an emergency health department staffed largely with Public Health Service personnel. Fourteen physicians were sent to the most critical areas of the state, including Taos, Rio Arriba, and Torrance counties. Tombs, as liaison officer for the Red Cross, brought in nurses to help in the emergency effort.[14] Kerr also helped carry out the survey, conferring with state and local health authorities, making inspections and studies in several cities, and analyzing existing laws. The resulting report to the surgeon general on November 15, 1918, was well received in New Mexico and elsewhere and formed the basis of the bill introduced to the fourth regular legislature in 1919. On April 25, Governor Larrazolo signed into law the bill that created New Mexico's first public health agency.

Although male public officials were responsible for formally creating the health care structure, women's influence did not go unrewarded. Nina Otero-Warren, prominent Santa Fe citizen and member of the politically influential Otero family, was appointed to the first Board of Public Health along with John Tombs and Oliver Hyde, medical director of Albuquerque's St. Joseph Sanatorium. While Otero-Warren would go on to become a leader in the field of education in New Mexico, her work in public health made her a valuable member of the board. When she tendered her resignation in December 1921, the members of the board— Mrs. Max Nordhaus, Mrs. George Prichard, Charles Lembke, and F. G. Shortle—prevailed upon Governor Merritt Mechem not to accept it, "if there be any way to avoid it." The governor did refuse it, citing her "tireless [work] in getting the public welfare legislation passed in the recent legislature," and Otero-Warren agreed to remain on the board.[15]

The board's first act was to ask the governor to request the loan of an officer from the U.S. Public Health Service. The governor

3. Nina Otero-Warren, member of the first Board of Public Health. Courtesy of Bergere Family Collection neg. no. #21252, State Records Center and Archives.

complied with the request, and in July, 1919, Dr. Clifford E. Waller arrived to staff and organize the agency. He remained as director until 1921. Waller set up an administrative plan that created the following divisions: vital statistics, preventable diseases, sanitary engineering and sanitation, and public health education. The first three regulations Waller proposed included the most basic of public health requirements—the reporting of births and deaths; the disposal, interment, and disinterment and transportation of the dead; and the reporting of notifiable diseases. For the first time, it was mandatory that vital events be reported on a statewide basis.[16] In a massive volunteer effort, women, especially midwives, took on the task of reporting births in towns and communities throughout the state.

Centered in Santa Fe, the Bureau of Public Health was organized around work at the county level, a method proven effective in other states. County health officers would be responsible for overseeing the reporting of vital statistics, monitoring sanitation needs, supervising public health nursing, and conveying general health information to the public. The largest problem facing the necessary and demanding health work, however, was funding, a problem that dogged the bureau into the 1930s. Indeed, the entire budget for the Bureau of Public Health in 1919 was $13,000, barely enough to open the doors and staff the office.[17] Ten years later, funding had risen to $104,000, which was less than that allocated to the Department of Fish and Game and a fraction of the more than five-million-dollar Highway Commission budget.[18]

Because of this inadequate funding, New Mexico was forced to secure support from both private and public sources to augment the state's meager resources. Three private foundations, the Rockefeller Foundation, the Commonwealth Fund, and the Milbank Memorial Fund, along with the federal government, kept the health department afloat during these difficult years.[19] Private organizations, such as the New Mexico Association on Indian Affairs and various women's clubs, supplemented these funds even further in a joint public-private push to improve overall health conditions in New Mexico.

The most important boost to state coffers for the important work of infant welfare and maternal health came in 1921 with the passage of the Federal Maternity and Infancy Act, popularly known as the Sheppard-Towner Act. Throughout the 1910s, Julia Lathrop, head of the Children's Bureau, and many others worked hard to secure federal funds for maternity and infancy work. To this end, in 1917, Lathrop recommended that federal aid be given to the states to provide for maternity and infancy care much as the Smith-Lever Act of 1914 provided matching funds for county agricultural extension agents. Representative Jeanette Rankin of Montana, the first woman elected to the United States Congress, introduced the proposal in July 1918, but neither President Wilson nor Congress was enthusiastic about the measure until after the full enfranchisement of women in 1920. In the fall of that year, Senator Morris Sheppard (D-Texas) and Representative Horace Towner (R-Iowa) submitted the bill to the Sixty-Sixth Congress, where it passed the Senate but died in the House in December.

Resubmitted in April 1921 in a special session of the Sixty-Seventh Congress, the maternity bill finally passed in August. President Warren Harding signed the bill on November 23, 1921, and women across the nation rejoiced in the knowledge that their pleas finally had been heeded.[20]

A major intent of this piece of Progressive legislation was to provide assistance for widowed or incapacitated women with small children to raise. As early as 1911, several states had pioneered in these mothers' assistance programs, or "mothers' pensions," as they became known. The programs caught on and became so successful that a report issued in 1925 asserted, "Motherhood has been lifted out of its long association with pauperism and the stigma of dependency has been removed from children who have lost a father's support."[21] Although many social workers initially opposed mothers' pensions because they viewed them as a step away from charity and toward entitlement, by 1930 such assistance was viewed as a proper public assumption of responsibility toward those burdened through no fault of their own. Instead of providing assistance after the mother was forced to seek employment outside the home, the pension allowed her to remain in the home to care for her children.[22] This policy dovetailed nicely with prevailing cultural attitudes that recognized a mother's place as in the home with her children, not in the labor force.

The passage of the Sheppard-Towner Act was a major victory in the struggle to provide child welfare at the national level. Julia Lathrop was partially responsible for this development. Her bureau sponsored numerous studies between 1909 and 1921 that showed "clear correlations between infant mortality and ill health, on the one hand, and low wages, crowded housing, parental ignorance on the other."[23] As a result, a program of federal grants-in-aid to the states was proposed to Congress in 1919 and 1920, but was not successful until the passage of the Sheppard-Towner Act in 1921.

Sheppard-Towner provided for setting up public health centers, prenatal clinics, and hygiene and child-welfare divisions in all the states. This funding, approximately $16,000 yearly (allocated on population percentage and a matching fund basis), was a godsend to New Mexico. The additional dollars allowed the state to initiate work in the all-important areas of child and maternal health. Sheppard-Towner funding remained in place for eight years until congressional inaction allowed the bill to lapse on June 30, 1929. Between that date and the passage of the Social Security Act in 1935, New Mexico was once again on its own in funding child-health programs. Nevertheless, the Sheppard-Towner Act set precedents for child and maternal health and welfare that served as a basis for future programs, particularly Title V of the Social Security Act.[24]

The initial disbursement of Sheppard-Towner funds created gender conflict in New Mexico, however. Under the provisions of the federal act, funds would be dispensed through the child hygiene division of the state Bureau of Public Health, which C. E. Waller directed. As noted earlier, women's organizations throughout the state had lobbied successfully between 1910 and 1919 to get the Child Welfare Service established; therefore, they expected to have a measure of control over child welfare work. Bertha Nordhaus, a prominent Albuquerque clubwoman and chair of the Child Welfare Service Board, was especially adamant that Sheppard-Towner money be administered through the Child Welfare Service. Waller just as staunchly believed that the funds should be dispensed through his agency. To reduce competition between the two agencies and resolve the dispute—a power struggle between a male public health official and a female health reformer—the fifth New Mexico legislature in 1921 created the Department of Public Welfare. This department served as an umbrella agency under which the work and funds would be divided between the bureaus.[25]

With this legislation, the Child Welfare Service and the Child Welfare Board were discontinued and merged into the state Department of Public Welfare. Especially important was the gender makeup of the new board: not less than two nor more than three of the five-member board were to be women. Among those first women appointed were Nordhaus, Mrs. R. P. Donohoo, and Nina Otero-Warren; the latter had served on the first Board of Public Health created in 1919. The board then created and organized the Bureau of Child Welfare and continued the Bureau of Public Health. By law, the director of Child Welfare was to be a woman of experience and special training in child welfare work. The lawmakers' recognition of this qualification was testimony to women's newly developing political expertise in the business of health and welfare.[26]

The first appropriation of Sheppard-Towner funds in 1921 allotted $6,600 to the Bureau of Public Health and $10,830 to the Bureau of Child Welfare.[27] The minuscule amount appropriated to the Bureau of Public Health was intended to cover the handling of vital statistics, help control preventable disease, aid in general sanitation efforts, provide for the regulation of midwives, and cover medical exams for school children. On its limited budget, the Bureau of Child Welfare was to investigate and improve conditions of dependent mothers and children and investigate all welfare conditions with regard to maternity, infancy, and childhood. In some respects, the functions of the two bureaus overlapped, especially in maternity and infancy work. This duplication of services would lead to further squabbles and another reorganization of departments in 1924.

The Child Welfare Service, established two years before the passage of Sheppard-Towner, had its eye on that funding from the beginning. At the suggestion of the Child Welfare Service board, the state Federation of Women's Clubs undertook as one of its special activities in 1920 the purchase of a child welfare home in Santa Fe.[28] Once Sheppard-Towner legislation was passed, this house was placed at the disposal of state and federal agencies designated to carry out the provisions of the bill. The building, on seven acres within the northern city limits, became the administrative headquarters for child welfare and maternity work. While the house was not large enough to serve as a general maternity hospital, it did provide facilities for office work and laboratories for physical and mental examinations, child welfare and maternity institutes, model clinics, model baby health centers, and the care of mothers and children as demonstration cases.

Once the state federation decided to buy the property, women's clubs throughout the state worked to raise the purchase price of $40,000 as well as funds for the operation of the home. Consequently, numerous clubs organized fundraising campaigns that included raffles, bridge parties, bake sales, and community dances. Monetary contributions were in addition to other charitable projects such as sewing clothing for needy clients, making layettes for expectant mothers, and serving as volunteers at well-baby clinics the Child Welfare Service sponsored. Overall, the state Federation of Women's Clubs played a key role in getting New Mexico's health projects off to a good start.[29]

Club programs during those years indicate that women were well informed about current health issues. Child welfare, for example, was a frequent topic at monthly meetings, covering such subjects as school lunches, the delinquent child, and the tubercular child.[30] On other occasions, health officials appeared on club programs, including Waller of the Bureau of Public Health and Margaret Reeves, director of the Bureau of Child Welfare. When legislation concerning health care was pending, women's clubs gave their support. The Woman's Clubs of Albuquerque and Santa Fe were especially active in urging their members to support passage of the Sheppard-Towner bill, the Child Welfare bill, and other proposed laws relating to the health of women and children.[31] In other states, women's clubs also pushed for improved health care linking New Mexico with a nationwide effort.[32]

Although New Mexico, a low population/highly rural state, differed from heavily populated urban regions, the philosophy underlying its health programs closely resembled the underpinnings of public health programs across the nation. The act that established the Child Welfare Service in March 1919, for instance, was predicated on the values of white middle-class Americans during the Progressive era, especially their feelings about nativism. Nowhere is this tendency more evident than in the introductory remarks published in an agency bulletin in 1921. Commenting on the nation's excessive infant mortality rate while referring to the high rate of immigration in the past two decades, the author declared:

> The safest way to guard America for Americans . . . is to increase the number of Americans. Pure American stock is not so prolific as it used to be. If America is to remain American despite the foreign strains pouring into her arteries, we must have more Americans.[33]

Americans, in this context, referred to native-born, white Anglo-Saxons. In New Mexico, where the population was divided unevenly between Anglo, Hispanic, and Indian people, such remarks reinforced policies and ideas formed in the East and transferred to the West. Despite cultural diversity, Indian and Hispanic traditions were not taken into consideration. The state agencies and bureaucracies that were created in the 1910s and 1920s instead reflected mainstream middle-class American values. Hispanics, Indians, and blacks were also Americans, but their values were not those of the dominant culture in 1920; hence they were, if not invisible, then ignored. When reformers did attempt to transmit public health values to these groups, with little knowledge of their customs and values, a clash of cultures was inevitable.

The goals and objectives of the Child Welfare Service confirm this reality. Although created within the state educational system, the service was not devoted entirely to public school work, but placed maternity and infant care first on its program as the starting point for "race betterment." Santa Fean Edgar Hewett, board member of the Child Welfare Service, likened the growth and development of young lives to agriculture in a bulletin distributed by the Department of Public Welfare:

> It [the Child Welfare Service] aims to reach the sources of human life and so protect them that a better race is as inevitable as is the im-

provement of our crops of fruits and grains and our livestock when we
apply the simple biological laws which are familiar to every intelligent
farmer and stockgrower.[34]

The farmer (or stockgrower) responsible for planting the "seeds" of good health and "right behavior" was a woman, the child welfare organizer. It was her task to link the home with the school as much as possible and "change, direct or control" conditions there. Like other institutions, such as schools and churches, the Child Welfare Service was a "coercive" organization that served as an agent of moral and social order.

In this capacity, the child welfare organizer, through home visits, would soon "learn the true conditions of the individual home that are making or breaking it" and introduce the "ideals of right living." Her tasks might include anything from demonstrating personal hygiene to correcting faulty ventilation to explaining compulsory education laws. Drawing on psychological theory, the woman worker would recognize unhealthy behavior in the children of the home and plan effective follow-up work. She would see how parents lost the control and confidence of their children, and in the case of the "foreign home," she might "be able to educate the home and the children together." She would become school guidance counselor and social worker, adjusting school programs to individual children, guiding boys and girls toward wise vocational choices. In gaining their confidence, the social welfare organizer would have opportunities to direct young people away from questionable places and amusements, and learn how to influence street children, therefore improving street conditions. Obviously, these comprehensive and lofty guidelines were adopted for immigrant, urban areas, not the rural landscape of New Mexico.[35]

This was a tall order for the social welfare organizer, but not out of line with Progressive goals and the objectives of social workers around the country at the time. In the first two decades of the twentieth century, the nature of social work underwent a transition, moving from cure to prevention. "This is the age of prevention," wrote a Boston social worker in 1911. "In medicine, sanitation and the conservation of natural resources, the theories of prevention are rapidly gaining precedence over the theories of cure."[36] Prior to 1900, social reformers sought to correct the behavior of individuals who failed to live up to society's expectations. Moral judgments affected (and infected) much of the work. But with the advent of the Progressive era and a rising social consciousness, the emphasis shifted, by turns, from modifying the individual to altering the environment to preventing trouble by

4. Children do their part in carrying water for domestic use. Taos County, 1941. Courtesy of National Archives, neg. no. 41585.

overcoming its causes. Poor housing, ill health, and other social ills once considered the result of individual failure became the province of publicly organized relief—social evils to be eradicated through governmental decree. In other words, the emphasis in social work evolved from "humane care, the correction of abuses and neglect, to preventive measures." Observing firsthand the effects of bad housing, lack of recreation, tuberculosis, and child labor, Progressive reformers sought to eradicate evil and injustice through social reform.[37]

Reform in New Mexico, however, required an adaptation of traditional social service goals to existing conditions in a large rural state. The largest problem was geographic—New Mexicans were so scattered that it was difficult to reach them efficiently. It fell to the agencies and organizations, therefore, to take their programs to rural areas as much as possible. This approach entailed great expense and personal hardship given the existing condition of the roads and highways, particularly in the mountainous areas of northern New Mexico. Many nursing reports detail the difficulty of reaching families tucked away in mountain communities, nearly inaccessible except by horse or on foot. Red Cross nurse Augustine Stoll, reporting on her work on the Jicarilla Apache Reservation in November 1922, wrote that "roads are often almost impassable" due to mud; "it clings and defies mere shaking off!" To keep a healthy attitude, Stoll suggested, "It helps a bit to keep your gaze fixed on the beauty of the mountains and the blue blueness of the sky."[38] Bureau of Indian Affairs nurses on the Navajo reservation faced similar difficulties. Drifting snow, blowing sand, lack of roads at all—"much of the way we leave the road and bump across the desert"—added a dimension to health work that increased the challenge.[39]

A second more important factor was a clash of cultures as reformers sought to impose Anglo systems on Hispanic, Indian, and black people with little knowledge of those cultures or their languages. In matters of sanitation, nutrition, and hygiene, Anglo bureaucrats were repeatedly frustrated. For example, field agent E. W. Prothro of the U.S. Public Health Service complained that "the sanitation, customs, and superstitions of the natives, especially of the Spanish-American and scattered Indians, are such that the work is very slow and results often apparently unsatisfactory."[40] Regarding diet, the agent castigated all three cultures in the following comment: "Neither [sic] of the three groups of people mentioned are [sic] informed. The Anglos live primarily out of tin cans. The Spanish-Americans largely upon their highly seasoned foods, and the Indians upon mellons [sic], refuge [refuse] and other unwholesome foods."[41]

The agent's remarks reflected his lack of understanding and disdain for the dietary habits typical of the three groups at the time. Until well into the 1930s, most Native American and Hispanic diets included foods preserved through drying, such as corn, melon, squash, chile, beans, and meat. Among the Navajo, processed food was seldom purchased, although traders began to stock canned foods around 1910. Home canning was introduced early in the twentieth century as part of Progressive era reform in Anglo kitchens, but did not reach Hispanic and Indian women until the 1930s. Prior to that time, they continued to use traditional drying methods. For various reasons, dietary changes did not occur easily or quickly, part of Prothro's lament.[42]

Nor did other cultural changes imposed by reformers take root easily. As we will see in future chapters, female health reformers were most successful when they were able to mold middle-class Progressive ideas to conditions in New Mexico. By taking their programs to the people and developing a sensitivity to cultural differences, the reformers were better able to disseminate health information. Their ability to be adaptable facilitated their role in public health reform, in turn providing varying degrees of social power to individual women and to women's clubs and organizations.

Overall, the cultural differences among New Mexicans, the isolation, and the general impoverishment contributed to the state's poor health record. Health care reformers, with women's club members leading the way, worked hard to create a formal health structure that could begin to attack the immediate problems, especially the high infant and maternal mortality rates. By 1921, the state structure was in place and Congress had passed legislation providing federal funding for maternity and infancy work. New Mexico women, empowered by their success, saw a bright future of health reform ahead. The next chapter examines how women continued to influence health reform through maternity and infancy work among New Mexico's different cultural groups and the challenges and rewards their efforts brought.

2

BETTER MOTHERS, BETTER BABIES

THE EFFECTS OF MATERNITY AND INFANCY WORK

Public health programs in New Mexico experienced marked improvement during the 1920s, primarily as a result of the Sheppard-Towner Act and the implementation of the state public health structure.[1] Sheppard-Towner provided the framework and the money that contributed to a significant decline in infant and maternal mortality rates. This funding allowed New Mexico, as well as other states, to provide infant and maternal health care to the far reaches of the state, supplemented meager county resources, and authorized public health nurses to set up programs of health care that rapidly expanded in the 1920s and 1930s. In addition, New Mexico was able to employ more public health nurses, raising their number from four in 1920 to thirty-five in 1930, thereby increasing the effectiveness and visibility of public health work and women's influence in shaping health reform.[2]

Two facets of the work were especially important in New Mexico: (1) carrying maternal and infant care information to New Mexico's mothers and (2) finding, training, and regulating midwives. Leading these efforts was a cadre of capable women including Janet Reid, Margaret Tupper, Amanda Metzgar, and Agnes Courtney. These Anglo women, and others like them, were committed to health care reform at a time when some elements of Progressive reform, namely political reform, were waning in other areas of the country. Nevertheless, reform efforts in social welfare in New Mexico, along with other states, escalated in the 1920s as a result of federal funding and the state's newly created public health structure. This political activism on the part of women influenced the nature of politics in New Mexico as it did nationally, contributing to the "domestication of politics." As women transferred their domestic interests to the public arena, they became empowered as social housekeepers, their efforts reflecting the best interests of families, especially.[3] The Children's Bureau, a Progressive reform agency at the federal level, was one of their earliest achievements, and its role in maternity and infancy work made a significant impact on New Mexico.

At the turn of the century, social reform focused on the family, particularly on children. Implicit in reform efforts was the newly developed status of the child. Children were no longer to be perceived as "miniature adults"; instead it was acknowledged that they passed through distinct developmental stages that parents and teachers should study and respect.[4] This new emphasis on children and their value to society as unique individuals, rather than as exploited laborers, meshed well with Progressive reform that stressed the unity and stability of the family as one response to industrialization, urbanization, and immigration.[5]

Implicit in the new emphasis on the child was the importance of the mother's role. Traditionally, motherhood has been central to being female, and, as mothers, women have been responsible for the moral and physical well-being of children. During the Progressive era, the essentially private nature of the mother-child bond underwent a change that redefined specific maternal responsibilities. The concern over the high infant mortality rate involved women in public aspects of matters that had previously been private. The idea that the federal government was responsible to some degree for child welfare added a public dimension to the private, individual experience of motherhood, although it did not supplant traditional beliefs; mothers retained primary responsibility for their children's welfare. Progressive reformers now focused on this private situation through public means such as women's clubs, civic organizations, mother's associations, and the Children's Bureau.[6] When Congress passed legislation creating the Children's Bureau on April 9, 1912, a major federal attempt to initiate social reform had begun, two decades before the formal appearance of the welfare state in the New Deal years.[7]

The Children's Bureau worked in several ways. It was, writes historian Nancy Weiss, "something like a national settlement house with a specialty in children."[8] For example, it served as counselor to the nation on proper methods of child-rearing through its infant care publications. Moreover, using sociological techniques, the bureau gathered and disseminated data on infant mortality, maternal death rates, child labor, juvenile delinquency, illegitimacy, and dependency. And the bureau had a practical effect as well, eliciting public action on birth registration, well-baby clinics, and maternal and prenatal health care. Through the bureau, the public was made aware of the special problems of some children: those without family to care for them, those with handicaps, and those considered delinquent. In the vision of its Progressive-minded progenitors—Jane Addams, Lillian Wald, Florence Kelley, Julia Lathrop, and Grace Abbott—the Children's Bureau would compile data, circulate reports, and suggest solutions. Although the federal government could investigate and report, it would fall to the power and conscience of local communities to take the necessary action. In other words, the data would be used to affect social change, a typically Progressive vision.[9]

The earliest efforts of the Children's Bureau involved "baby-saving studies" that were geared to education and prevention: infant mortality studies, infant care pamphlets, and maternal mortality reports. Discovering that the rate of infant deaths differed from community to community, researchers for the bureau concluded that environmental conditions were an important factor in child health. Babies died when the home was overcrowded, sanitation was poor, wages were low, and the parents (especially the mother, since she was presumed to be the central caretaker) were generally uninformed about scientific health and hygiene. These conditions did not reflect well on the nation's level of social progress, of which its rate of infant mortality was an important indicator.[10]

In 1918, the United States ranked seventeenth of twenty nations in maternal mortality and eleventh in infant mortality. Unfortunately, New Mexico contributed to this low ranking: infant mortality for 1929, the first year that New Mexico qualified as a Birth and Death Registration state, was 140 deaths per 1,000 live births, while the maternal mortality rate was nine deaths per 1,000 live births.[11] Two factors contributed to this alarming situation: the lack of prenatal care and the link between poverty and mortality rates. To reduce these rates nationally, Julia Lathrop proposed a two-fold solution: provide pre- and post-natal care and help poor families achieve an adequate income, hence, raising their standard of living. The former proved easier to achieve and was made possible with the passage of the Sheppard-Towner Act.

New Mexico was eager to participate in the new program and had already laid the groundwork by creating the state Bureau of Public Health in 1919. The state's share of Sheppard-Towner funding in the first year, 1921, amounted to $17,430 and was divided between the Bureau of Public Health and the Bureau of Child Welfare.[12] These funds made possible the hiring of two full-time nurses whose exclusive assignment was maternal and child health-care nursing. Given New Mexico's fledgling health-care program, Sheppard-Towner funding was crucial, for it allowed the state to

5. Waiting to see the doctor at the traveling clinic at Chamisal, New Mexico, 1940. Photo by Russell Lee, Library of Congress, USF34-37144D.

establish fundamental patterns of public health work that continued throughout the 1920s.[13]

Rural areas and small towns especially benefited from this important piece of social reform legislation. For several reasons, maternal mortality rates in rural areas were higher than those of the United States as a whole. For instance, farm wives, unable to afford or obtain domestic help, had heavy farm and home duties which sapped their strength and often contributed to poor health. In addition, health facilities were fewer and scattered, and where available, were more costly than city services.[14] In all, Sheppard-Towner seemed tailor-made for New Mexico since the state was overwhelmingly rural in 1920.[15]

Initially, only one nurse, Amanda Metzger, worked in rural communities, but in 1921 two more nurses, Teresa A. McGowan and Beatrice A. Rees, were hired with Sheppard-Towner funds.[16] Three public health nurses in the fifth largest state were hardly adequate to meet New Mexico's health needs. However, the successes of McGowan and Rees were proudly touted as a "tribute to the work of these pioneer nurses and to the ready spirit of the people," in a state with few people and many counties as large as the state of Massachusetts.[17] These nurses, and others that followed, were instrumental in educating New Mexico mothers in the care of their infants and children, as well as in the importance of prenatal care.

Logically, women would be the ones to carry out health-care work. Women had traditionally been active in social welfare issues as an extension of their work in the home. Municipal or social housekeeping, as their work in the community came to be called, allowed women to take an active role in community affairs without threatening the prevailing social structure.[18] This role was as true for New Mexico women as it was nationally. Their activism was demonstrated in chapter one, where women were a major part of the effort to create the state public health structure. Nina Otero-Warren and Bertha Nordhaus, for example, were important figures in establishing child welfare work. In addition, much of the impetus for this work came from the General Federation of Women's Clubs, an important avenue through which to initiate social change.

At the national level, this organization was instrumental in helping gain passage of the bill to establish the Children's Bureau and later provided an unpaid work force that gathered statistics for the bureau's early birth registration and infant mortality studies.[19] At the local level, women led campaigns in their communities and cities to establish municipal bureaus of child hygiene and baby health stations to educate parents about child health care. By their actions, they demonstrated that the prevention of illness had both a private and a public dimension; maternal concerns translated to citizen action. Furthermore, as part of Progressive reform, the protection of health had become a duty of the state, and Sheppard-Towner incorporated this judgment as well.

Because Sheppard-Towner was concerned with preventive health care, it was not a threat to the physicians who treated those already sick. Hence, women were welcome in the public health field and were not seen as competition to the medical profession. Physicians, as a whole, were not interested in public health work, considering it outside the services they offered their private patients. This attitude changed during the 1920s, as the American Medical Association belatedly realized an opportunity they could claim for professionals. But initially their reluctance allowed women to occupy the public health arena in large numbers.[20]

For women physicians, public health service offered opportu-

6. Dr. Janet Reid, first director of the Bureau of Child Welfare. Courtesy of New Mexico Board of Medical Examiners.

nities that private practice did not. As a result, bureaus of child hygiene and public health departments employed women physicians in disproportionately high numbers. Once Sheppard-Towner was in place, women also filled staff and director positions. By 1927, sixteen female physicians served as directors of Sheppard-Towner programs in forty-three states. Of the eighty-nine full-time physicians, forty (45 percent) were women.[21] In New Mexico, doctors Florence Janet Reid, Evelyn Fisher Frisbie, Nancy Campbell, and Marion Hotopp were all active in public health work, and some maintained private practices as well. Reid, a tubercular specialist, served as director of the Bureau of Child Welfare in the 1920s. Frisbie maintained an active obstetrics/gynecology practice in Albuquerque as well as serving as medical consultant to the isolated people of western New Mexico in the 1930s. Campbell, too, was an obstetrician/gynecologist specialist, in Santa Fe, who took part in the midwife training programs among the Pueblo people in the same period. And Hotopp, though she came to New Mexico later than the others (1945), was especially effective as director of the Maternal and Child Health Division. For these women, public health work proved to be a satisfying component of their professional lives as well as a source of empowerment.[22]

Esther Van Pelt was typical of women caught up in maternity and infancy work. Van Pelt and her husband, Paul, both doctors of osteopathy, came to the Estancia Valley, an agricultural and livestock area east of Albuquerque in Torrance County, in 1936. There they established what Esther described as a "ranch practice," tending the medical needs of ranchers and their families within a fifty-mile radius of the small community of Willard (population 500). No other physicians, osteopaths, or nurses resided in the immediate vicinity, so all major health care fell to the Van Pelts. Esther cared most, however, about the maternity cases.[23]

Although midwives served many of the women in this half-Spanish, half-Anglo community, Van Pelt estimated that she and her husband delivered 250–300 babies during a four-year period. Their practice was unique in that they encouraged the mother to come in for at least one prenatal visit, something previously unheard of among the people. "We delivered a baby for twenty-five dollars," said Van Pelt, "and did an aftercall which they had never had before. And they liked the idea of a woman doctor coming out. They had never had two doctors for the price of one." Both the prenatal and postnatal visits were well received and helped reinforce the importance of having health care prior to and after delivery.[24]

Public health nursing also attracted large numbers of women. In the 1920s, the public health nurse was a combination health-care and social worker. Trained at a school of social welfare, she then usually served on the staff of a settlement house or a municipal department of child hygiene, or she worked for a public school. The public health nurse was not a member of a hospital team, preferring to remain in public rather than private health care.[25] Many of the health-care workers New Mexico employed came from other states where they had previously been engaged

7. The young women and mothers of a Home Hygiene class held in Vallecitos in Rio Arriba County, 1938. Courtesy of the National Archives, Record Group 200.

in similar activities. For instance, Margaret Tupper, the first director of the Division of Child Hygiene and Public Health Nursing, an agency within the state Bureau of Public Health, was a Vassar graduate trained as a public health nurse and had many years' experience as a medical social worker.[26] Similarly, Helen Fenton, who followed Tupper as director in 1923, was a graduate of the public health course at Simmons College and of the Boston Instructive District Nursing Association. Additional nurses came to New Mexico from the Children's Bureau, and some were recruited from public health and nursing programs in other states.

The nurses who came to New Mexico had to be adventurous and flexible to carry out the provisions of the Sheppard-Towner Act. Given a sparse population scattered over great distances, efficient organization was necessary. Using the county as a unit, Tupper proposed that a demonstrating nurse for maternal and infant hygiene spend three months in each of four adjoining counties. The nurse would seek out mothers-to-be and instruct them in prenatal care, conduct well-baby clinics, and make use of exhibits and other material in educational campaigns. After three months, she

8. A student of Home Hygiene classes with her baby "whom she gives nice care." Rio Arriba County, 1938. Courtesy of the National Archives, Record Group 200.

would move on to another group of counties, continuing in like manner until the state was covered. This method required a great deal of traveling, so the work was, of necessity, time-consuming, because the more remote communities were those that needed help the most.[27] The state continued this form of organized maternity and infancy work until all counties were covered to some degree.

In 1922, the Bureau of Health's biennial report noted the satisfaction that maternal and infancy work provided. It read: "The most appealing phase of health work is maternal, infant and school hygiene, for it is here that we come into the most intimate contact with the home and have the greatest opportunity to influence the future generation of citizens."[28] Here was "hands-on" work for the nurses, carrying information to mothers who could not get to the larger population centers. Since group conferences were not effective because of the scattered population, the nurses visited individual homes, advised mothers on basic health care and hygiene, instructed local midwives, and gave physical examinations to young children.

While the Sheppard-Towner nurses from the Bureau of Public Health carried out maternity and infancy work, their sisters in the Bureau of Child Welfare, which Dr. Janet Reid headed, also engaged in a wide variety of health-care projects. From the beginning, the directors of the two bureaus, G. S. Luckett and Reid, agreed to "keep off each other's heels" in order not to duplicate services, though this situation was difficult to avoid.[29] While the public health nurses were charged with primary health-care tasks such as physical examinations, weighing and measuring of school children, and administering innoculations, their work load was much larger. They were also responsible for holding prenatal and infant care classes, instructing midwives, securing birth registration, and distributing health literature. Within the Bureau of Child Welfare, the nurses and staff members, with help from local nurses, worked closely with county health physicians in conducting weekly clinics. They, too, held classes for mothers, registered births, and provided literature the federal Children's Bureau distributed. The Bureau of Child Welfare made it a point, however, not to carry out maternity and infancy work in localities where the Bureau of Public Health was spending Sheppard-Towner funds on the same activity. These funds had to be administered through a county health unit and, since only eight full-time units were in operation by 1923, plenty of room existed for both bureaus to operate.

Central to the work of the Bureau of Child Welfare were the volunteer efforts of local women's clubs. In this regard, close links were established between the New Mexico Federation of Women's Clubs and the bureau after its creation in 1921. Although women's clubs were typically organized in urban areas, New Mexico's population centers were so small that issues in rural areas easily became objectives for town clubwomen. To meet bureau objectives, each local club established a child welfare committee responsible for

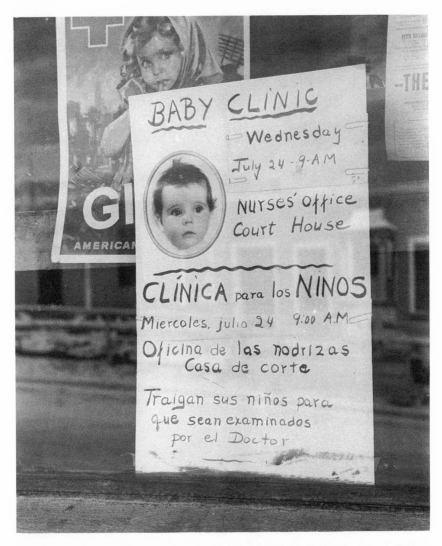

9. Sign in a post office window in Taos, July 1940. Photo by Russell Lee, Library of Congress, USF33-12849-M3.

organizing and coordinating projects within its communities. The director of the bureau then visited individual clubs and furnished plans for financing and organizing the work locally. In towns where nurses held mother's classes, members of the women's club assisted in transporting mothers to and from classes and provided care for babies and children while the mothers attended classes. Often, the local club also sponsored educational campaigns that

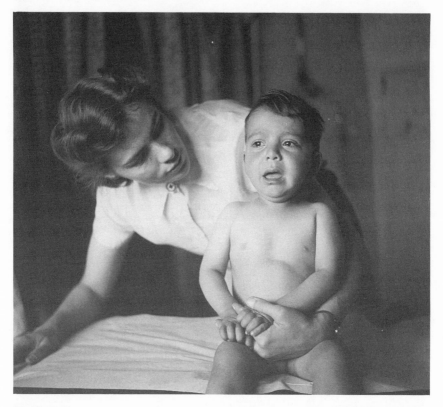

10. Red Cross nurse comforting small patient at a baby clinic in Peñasco, New Mexico, 1943. Photo by John Collier, Library of Congress, USW3-14589.

focused on infant care. Many of these events, such as Baby Weeks, were modeled after similar activities in Eastern cities, including New York, Chicago, Pittsburg, and Detroit. City health departments often promoted Baby Week events designed to educate the public concerning infant welfare work.[30]

Typical of these events was a Baby Week in June 1921 that the Woman's Club of Santa Fe held in cooperation with the city health department. Local physicians and nurses weighed, measured, and examined seventy-eight children, finding about one-half of them underweight. Publicity efforts included daily newspaper notices, announcements by ministers, and the use of posters and exhibits in merchants' windows.[31] The volunteer efforts of women at the local level aided immeasurably the state organizations, which were limited in funds and staff.

The close connection between women's clubs and the Bureau

of Child Welfare allowed the bureau to hold activities at the Child Welfare House in Santa Fe. In particular, the bureau regularly held its Little Mothers' Club classes in the home. These classes followed the model introduced in New York City in 1908, which the Children's Bureau continued to recommend. The movement began in the public schools, where older girls were instructed in the care of babies and young children. Soon, boys became interested as well, prompting the creation of Junior Health Leagues for adolescent boys. Physicians, nurses, and teachers provided instruction to students who often were responsible for younger siblings when not in school themselves.

In New Mexico, children caring for children was commonplace where large families were the norm in the Hispanic population. The classes evidently were popular, for in July 1923, nearly two hundred young girls were enrolled in Little Mothers' Club classes at the Child Welfare House in Santa Fe.[32] The girls attended two classes a week, learning the importance of nursing, how to keep a home clean and hygienic, and how to care for infants. Included in their training were instructions on "infant feeding with methods of milk modification."[33] This last topic referred to bottle-feeding, an alternative to breast-feeding when mother's milk, the preferred and prescribed method, would not do.

When the girls completed the course, their mothers were invited to graduation exercises. To demonstrate their newfound skills, one girl carried out the practical work while a second girl explained the steps in English and a third girl explained the work in Spanish.[34] New Mexico mothers apparently were amenable to having their daughters learn child care, as the following quote indicates:

> Mothers tell us that the children that have taken "Little Mothers' Club" work come home and insist that the younger children and infants be taken care of as taught by the nurse. They teach their mothers the proper way to bathe the baby and dress it, the right foods and the correct health habits. The mothers are usually so proud of their children for knowing these things that they do not take offense.[35]

In this instance, crossing cultural boundaries could be successful when daughters facilitated the process.

The instructions came to mothers via the publication department of the Children's Bureau in Washington. From the beginning, the bureau pamphlets were in great demand. For example, *Infant Care*, *Child Care*, and *Prenatal Care* topped the best-seller list of government publications in the late 1910s. In its first year of publication, *Prenatal Care* went to 30,000 households, and the bureau could have sold (at twenty-five cents each) twice that many. In 1922, the bureau printed 600,000 pamphlets and could not keep up with the demand. In 1955, *Infant Care* became the government's biggest seller, surpassing even the always popular agricultural bulletins.[36]

Obviously, the booklets touched a nerve among American mothers, who had genuine concerns and questions about child care. The literature of the Children's Bureau provided answers based on certain American values and served as "a weather vane of modern middle class views on child-rearing techniques."[37] The authors of the material (and women of the Children's Bureau) clearly saw the mother as central to the well-being of the child. In their publications, her role was clearly defined and imbued with great importance. The booklets also presumed certain standards, such as rest and adequate food, and a standard of living that allowed women to conserve their strength for the family. Much of the prescribed behavior was predicated on the authors' own standards and values. For example, the pamphlets insisted on breast-feeding and warned of the dangers of using nursemaids to substitute for mother's attention. In particular, the use of lower-class and immigrant girls as caregivers was especially discouraged. Clearly, the material did not recognize cultural differences. Instead, conformity to a specific social norm was implicit in the advice. Although the pamphlets were printed in many languages, the message remained essentially middle-class and mother-oriented. Overall, bureau literature was intended to influence women, especially immigrant women, "to conform to the American mainstream through the avenue of their little ones."[38]

Designed to reach immigrant populations in Eastern urban areas, the material had to be adapted to New Mexico's rural Hispanic population. One adjustment was to print the pamphlets in Spanish, though reports are inconsistent regarding numbers. Between July 1925 and June 1926, for example, the Bureau of Public Health alone distributed 15,039 pamphlets on prenatal, infant, and child care, yet the record is silent on how many were printed in Spanish.[39] Figures for six month's work in 1924, however, suggest that both Spanish and English-speaking mothers received literature, although distribution was uneven. For instance, 1,040 copies of *Infant Care* in English went out, while just 173 copies in Spanish were distributed. On the other hand, 704 pamphlets of *Leche* and 544 copies of *Sugestiones a las Madres* were mailed.[40]

In its early years, the state Bureau of Public Health produced mixed results. For example, when Dr. G. S. Luckett reported on the quality of health care in New Mexico in late 1922, he was pleased to note that in the three years since the Bureau of Public Health had gone into operation, its continued progress compared favorably with other state health departments. Heroic efforts were being made, yet health service remained sketchy: only about 35 percent of the population was then receiving moderately adequate service.[41] Only eight of twenty-four counties, for instance, had full-time health units in operation: Bernalillo, Chaves, San Miguel, Santa Fe, Union, Eddy, Doña Ana, and Valencia. Most of these counties had a full-time public health nurse; others had only part-time nursing care. As Luckett noted, the hardest part was ahead— reaching the less progressive and less prosperous counties that were in even greater need due to poverty and a lack of knowledge regarding good health-care measures.

By January 1924, ten full-time county health units reached nearly one-half the state's population of 360,000. The increasing success of public health work was attributed to the support and cooperation of local communities. Once made aware of the work of the Bureau of Public Health and the Bureau of Child Welfare, people requested help and advice. For instance, in Quay County, child welfare headquarters were established at Tucumcari in the Masonic hall with help from local merchants, physicians, and bankers.[42] For those who could not get to Tucumcari, the health team visited adjacent communities and held conferences in family homes. Other counties reported a willingness to cooperate as well.

San Miguel County was a special success, thanks to strong support from the child welfare departments of the women's clubs in that county. The outstanding feature of the work was the creation of the Child Welfare Association of Spanish-American mothers, with a membership of fifty-six. A Hispanic nurse conducted classes in maternity and infancy work that 615 women regularly attended in 1924.[43] That the county was able to provide not only a Spanish-speaking nurse but also one of Hispanic descent surely encouraged the enthusiastic support of the Hispanic mothers in San Miguel County.

Anglo missionary women were another source of support in promoting public health work. For example, Alice Blake, a Presbyterian medical missionary, served for nearly thirty years in Trementina, a tiny Hispanic community sixty miles southeast of Las Vegas in San Miguel County. There, Blake served as teacher, nurse, and "Jill of all trades" from 1901 to 1930. Initially greeted with suspicion and distrust, she gradually won over the people, campaigning all the while for improved health care. Blake willingly cooperated with county health officials in matters of health education and was successful in convincing the Presbyterian mis-

11. Mothers and their children waiting to be seen at the Taos County Co-operative Health Clinic, 1943. Photo by John Collier, Library of Congress, USW3-18135-E.

sion board to establish a small hospital there in 1915. Blake became a much-revered figure in the community until drought and the Depression caused the medical mission to close in the mid-1930s.[44]

Alice Blake was just one of many female medical missionaries active in New Mexico in the first half of the twentieth century. These women provided an important link in the chain of health care because they were willing to go to remote areas and face cultural differences head-on. Others among the Presbyterians were Dora Fish, who established a small hospital at Dixon, later served by Dr. Sarah Bowen; Ruth Herron, nurse-midwife in Rio Arriba County; and Mary MacKenzie, also an R.N. who staffed the Brooklyn Cottage Hospital at Dixon for many years. As a result of the efforts of these early missionaries, the people were much more accepting of maternity and infancy work when it was introduced in the 1920s.[45]

The situation was less encouraging in Taos and Rio Arriba counties. Only four physicians practiced in the two counties, severely limiting health care. Because the towns were small and inaccessible, the nurse and director (Reid) traveled from village to village, holding conferences in district schoolhouses. In Rio Arriba County in 1924, they weighed, measured, and examined 754 children. In this county, many families who attended the conferences belonged to the religious sect known as the Penitentes, which added another dimension to bureau efforts. When Reid remarked that "they are very superstitious and with their many religious rites may well belong to the dark ages," she displayed an ethnocentrism that sometimes crept into public health reports. In this case, health-care reformers were uncertain how effective their work was among the Pentitentes.[46]

Gradually, however, the efforts of Sheppard-Towner nurses and county health teams produced results. In 1925–26, home visits totaled 10,500, and 3,900 babies and 24,900 school children were examined. Nearly one-half the children were found "defective in some way"; in those cases, health officials sent seven thousand notices to parents and visited five thousand homes. Overall, nurses made 29,700 visits and traveled nearly 130,000 miles.[47]

Reducing the infant mortality rate was the overriding challenge. While no precise statistics on infant mortality were kept until 1929, the state board of health estimated the infant mortality rate at 125 deaths per 1,000 babies born, higher in some counties than others. A maternity and infancy report for 1927–28 put the situation in perspective:

> When you consider the poverty, isolation, especially during winter months, age old superstitions, ignorance of modern methods of infant care, lack of medical attention and inadequate housing among our Spanish American people, it is not surprising that our infant mortality rate is high. It will take years of intensive M and I [maternity and infancy] work to achieve great results but we are getting more requests for literature and advice each year.[48]

The Bureau of Public Health nurses logged many miles and a multitude of experiences getting public health work established. The first public health nurse hired in New Mexico, Amanda Metzger, began work in Santa Fe County in 1919, just six weeks after the state agency was created. She carried on both city and county school health work until 1921, when Elizabeth Duggan took over the city schools. Metzger was quick to praise city and county school officials—including Nina Otero-Warren, superintendent of Santa Fe County Schools—and the local women's club for making public health work a success. "The hardships endured, the walking, riding in rickety wagons was made worthwhile," Metzger reported. The greetings she received in the villages especially touched her. "We are poor, but the best we have is yours while a guest in our house" was the cheerful welcome she frequently heard. The cooperation between the schools, women's clubs, and the bureau was a crucial link between the agency and the people.[49]

Metzger was an adventurous, lively woman, leaving Santa Fe County in January 1923—"as it seemed too tame by that time"— for the Dawson coal mining camp in Colfax County. There she encountered hardships, discouragements, and a "different class of people—Negroes, Itallians [sic], Austrians, Slauvish [sic], Polish and Old Mexico Mexicans." Nevertheless, despite cultural differences and new obstacles, she managed to organize prenatal and maternity classes and Little Mothers' Clubs. Considering her efforts in Colfax County successful, Metzger again felt a "wanderlust for greener pastures" and went to Oregon, where she took up public health work once more.[50]

In less than three years, Metzger returned to New Mexico, this time to Los Lunas in Valencia County. This county was "controlled absolutely by politics—the welfare of the masses was not considered," she complained, and after two years, she left the county to join the Indian Health Service. Assigned to Old Laguna in the early 1930s, Metzger initiated many public health projects among the Pueblo people, where she found a great deal of interest and support for the work.[51] Overall, Amanda Metzger typifies the women who found New Mexico to be both a challenging and satisfying place in which to work—challenging because conditions there were so demanding, and satisfying because their efforts produced results.

Dorothy Anderson, chief of the Division of Child Hygiene and Public Health Nursing in 1926, credits women like Metzger for New Mexico's high success rate in maternity and infancy work. Despite the drawbacks of isolation, limited funding, and inadequate facilities, nurses responded to the great need for the work and appreciated that even the most uninformed attempted to follow directions, though in doing so they "had to give up some age-old superstitions." Anderson noted as well the special spirit of cooperation between the state Bureau of Health and the individual nurse, each sharing in the other's successes. To those endowed with the "pioneer spirit" and a sense of adventure, coupled with self-reliance and common sense, New Mexico "offer[ed] the most wonderful opportunity for real service that [could] be found."[52]

Particularly demanding but equally rewarding was the work done among the midwives, a major part of the maternity and infancy program. Like other areas of the country, such as in the South and Midwest, and earlier in immigrant neighborhoods in Eastern cities, midwives delivered many babies in New Mexico. In 1929, when reliable statistics were first available, New Mexican midwives delivered 29 percent of births and doctors 57 percent, leaving 14 percent of births "unattended." Nationwide, midwives assisted in 15 percent of births, a decline from the turn of the century when midwifery was at its peak.[53]

Unlike other parts of America, however, the decline was slower in New Mexico. First of all, among Hispanic families, which were 60 percent of the state's population, a strong cultural preference existed for women to care for women during pregnancy and birth. Equally important, many families could not afford to pay a doctor to deliver their babies. And, finally, professional medical care was simply not available in many areas of New Mexico. Midwives, then, were depended on because they were preferred, they were affordable, and doctors were unavailable. For these reasons, attitudes in New Mexico regarding midwives differed significantly from other parts of the United States, and this fact deserves some discussion.

Midwifery has been practiced in America since the first colonists settled on the Atlantic seaboard. Gradually, however, the custom declined. Early in the twentieth century, the medical establishment initiated a vigorous campaign to force midwives out of business. Two motives prompted this activity. First was the realization that infant and maternal mortality rates were no better among physicians than among midwives, prompting medical schools to recognize obstetrics/gynecology as a specialized field of study.[54] Second, physicians feared the competition midwives represented and quickly moved to end that competition by moving into the business of delivering babies and providing all the services that process required. Midwives were at a distinct disadvantage when matched against the powerful American medical profession. Because they had no professional organization to support them, they lacked any voice in setting training guidelines and establishing regulations. As a result, doctors were able to wage a successful anti-midwife campaign that peaked between 1910 and 1920. After that time, deliveries attended by midwives declined nationally.[55]

One result of the debate was the rise of nurse-midwifery, a compromise between the lay midwife and the obstetrician. Those

12. A group of "typical" Hispanic midwives, ca. 1935–1940 in Taos County. Photo by James Valentine, Library of Congress, USZ62-72219.

who recognized midwifery as a "necessary evil" conceded that a graduate nurse could be trained in six months or a year to learn the rudiments of midwifery. Proponents believed that the "nurse-midwife would prove to be the most sympathetic, the most economical, and the most efficient agent in the case of normal confinements." [56] And, it may be added, they would be under the control of male doctors.

The first nurse-midwifery program, the Maternity Association of New York City, was established in 1918. Seven years later, a second important program was begun in the mountains of Kentucky. There, Mary Breckinridge, a graduate nurse trained in England, created the Frontier Nursing Service. Breckinridge believed that if a successful nurse-midwifery program could be established in the remote and poverty-stricken mountain areas of Kentucky, similar work could be performed anywhere in the United States. Breckinridge was right; the service flourished, bringing maternal and child health care to women and children throughout 250 square miles of Kentucky terrain. Several nurse-midwives who acquired experience at the Frontier Nursing Service—including Jean Egbert, Anne Fox, and Olive Nicklin—later practiced in New Mexico. In 1942, a similar program was established in Santa Fe. Staffed by nurse-midwives, the Catholic Maternity Institute provided maternity care primarily for women who could not afford a private physician or hospitalization. In 1945, New Mexico became the first state to formally recognize nurse-midwifery. It was the only state to do so until 1959, when New York adopted similar legislation. [57]

Unlike many other states, New Mexico viewed midwifery pragmatically. To its credit, the medical profession in the state was generally supportive of midwives, primarily because doctors recognized the realities of the situation—distance, economics, and cultural preferences. Public health officials believed the infant and maternal mortality rates would be reduced if midwives were properly trained and regulated; therefore, they were willing to work for rather than against the midwives. Not everyone in the state's medical community agreed with such a commitment. Some believed that no training programs or regulations could ever raise midwives to acceptable standards. The health department persisted, however, despite the criticism. [58] Between 1920 and 1950, state health officials carried out numerous successful programs designed to improve and regulate midwifery while reducing high infant and maternal deaths. From a high of 140 infant deaths per 1,000 live births in 1929, the figure dropped to 104 per 1,000 in 1939 and to 65 deaths per 1,000 by 1949. [59] Improving and regulating midwifery played a large role in this decline.

When doctors Esther and Paul Van Pelt arrived in Torrance County in the mid-thirties, midwife training had not yet reached that area. Dr. Esther, as she was called, often acted as teacher to those who were present at a birth. Although her husband nearly always delivered the babies and she kept in the background, delivering the anesthetic—"I thought that was wiser because that was the period when the males were dominant"—she took over once the baby was born. "I took it to the kitchen where it would be warmer, and cleansed it with oil. You always used oil, and silver nitrate for the eyes. I always had spectators, talking in Spanish. Or if they were Anglos, asking questions and I was answering them. Then I turned the baby over to them to dress as they wished." In the four years the Van Pelts spent in the Estancia Valley, they provided a crucial service, crossing cultural boundaries to introduce good health habits and information to a needy population.[60] Much of their success was due to Dr. Esther's sensitivity to the valley's Hispanic culture.

Women caring for women had long been a tradition among Hispanic families, as it was among black families. For example, nearly 80 percent of American midwives were black "grannies" practicing in the South.[61] Similarly, in northern New Mexico where the Spanish population was highest, people counted on the *partera*. In 1936, a decade after midwife training programs were begun, midwives in San Miguel County continued to deliver 95 percent of the babies. In neighboring Taos County, midwives were present at 71.5 percent of births.[62]

One such partera was Jesusita Aragón of Las Vegas, who began delivering babies in the Las Vegas area in the late 1920s. By 1980, at the age of seventy, Aragon had delivered over 12,000 infants. She was representative of the many traditional female healers (*curanderas*) who were counted on in the harsh environs of northern New Mexico. Within the village, the partera was an important person and served as a counselor and confidante to many. Mothers looked up to the partera and sought her out for advice and help with child-rearing problems. Like other midwives, Aragon took a life-long interest in the babies she delivered, following their activities into adulthood. Aragon was significant in that she was also the last of the traditional parteras to be licensed in this area as part of the state's program for training midwives in the 1930s.[63]

Typically, the partera was a neighbor, relative, or older woman in the community who had learned her skills from another woman. Most were untrained by modern standards, and while some knew and practiced safe hygiene, many others did not. County nursing reports are peppered with discouraging descriptions of many midwives, characterizing the women as illiterate, dirty, ignorant, and superstitious. For example, a study carried out in 1924 showed that midwives attended nearly 90 percent of births in Taos County, "most of them [the parteras] ignorant, unskilled, and dirty."[64] Or, from a weekly report made in 1928: "The midwives interviewed this week were simply impossible. They were all very old and crippled up as well as ignorant."[65] The nurses minced no words in expressing their disapproval of the partera's methods, a disapproval tinged with racism and class consciousness.

Other reports continued the litany of complaints. Sometimes the parteras were hearing and/or sight impaired, as was one woman in Valencia County who continued to deliver babies four years after going blind. Some were so feeble they could hardly see to cut the umbilical cord. Moreover, health officials often found their equipment crude and unsanitary. For example, Promitiva García of Seboyeta, near Laguna Pueblo, practiced for twelve years without carrying any equipment, sometimes using a carving knife to cut the baby's cord. In some homes, string from tobacco sacks was washed and saved until needed as umbilical tape because it was "stronger than twine." Another woman cauterized the umbilical cord with a hot coal, believing it prevented hemorrhaging.[66]

Dirt and superstition, however, did not cause natal deaths. The high infant mortality rate was a result of several complex factors that included poverty, inadequate prenatal care, and the capability of the birth attendant. Because doctors and government officials, in their reports, were quick to condemn midwives as "ignorant" and "dirty," these women became scapegoats for high mortality rates associated with childbirth. These were the midwives the health department wished to "weed out" through training and regulation.[67]

With Sheppard-Towner funding, New Mexico was able to devise programs for training and regulating midwives, a process not without problems. The first step was to locate as many midwives as possible. As with the maternity and infancy work, the task was farflung, time-consuming, and often met with resistance. Once in a community, nurses and staff members sought out doctors, priests, mission teachers, sub-registrars (local citizens responsible for recording births and deaths), and home demonstration agents for names of women who were delivering babies in the neighborhood. Often, the nurses were greeted with suspicion or denial from the midwife, who sometimes feared legal consequences or that a cost was involved. Husbands could be an obstacle, too; some were suspicious of the nurse and sometimes refused to allow their wives to attend the classes. One nurse reported that "it was impossible to locate some of the midwives as they are very much afraid of anyone they think represents the law, and as soon as a nurse arrives in their vicinity, they hide out in the hills until she is gone."[68] In some villages, rumors were started, and only at the completion of a course were some skeptical midwives convinced that they, as well as their clients, received the benefits.[69]

Language could be a barrier as well. Unless the nurse spoke Spanish, Hispanic midwives sometimes refused to understand or respond in English, though they were able to do so. This situation made it imperative for the Sheppard-Towner nurse (almost always Anglo) either to learn the language or obtain an interpreter. Often a young girl or woman in the community offered to serve in that role. For instance, Rafaelita Alberico of Lumberton, near Dulce on the Jicarilla Apache Reservation, was especially valuable as a translator because she also "knew well all the trails through the canyons."[70] To their credit, most of the nurses either spoke Spanish or quickly learned the language, which lessened the initial resistance they often encountered.

Agnes B. Courtney was one who quickly became a Spanish speaker. From Indiana, Courtney was a registered midwife and a public health nurse who had trained in Cincinnati. By 1924, she had completed three years of nursing in Colorado and New Mexico and understood the special problems in the Southwest. At her suggestion, the Children's Bureau developed a syllabus of instruction in Spanish tailored to the needs of New Mexico parteras. Courtney proposed that the instructions the bureau had created for black midwives in other states be adapted to midwives in New Mexico, who seemed "to present a problem somewhat similar to the negro midwife, with an added handicap of a language barrier."[71] Courtney had several recommendations for the syllabus, among them how to correctly deliver the placenta. Common practice was to "tie the cord to the leg, give the woman pepper on her tongue or tickle her nose with a feather to make her sneeze, thinking this will cause expulsion."[72] Courtney also provided suggestions that a midwife could carry out in problem cases, while waiting for a doctor to arrive. A syllabus would provide a guide for midwives to refer to when necessary and increase the chances the information would be remembered in an emergency.

Eventually, the Children's Bureau forwarded to the New Mexico Bureau of Public Health a manual for midwives that a physician had prepared who was then teaching black midwives. Not only did it need to be translated into Spanish, but the use of a local translator was suggested, since the women spoke Spanish that was "somewhat different from the classical."[73] This remark

13. Unidentified Hispanic midwives in Mora County, 1932. Courtesy of New Mexico Medical History Program, Medical Center Library, University of New Mexico.

referred to an archaic form of Spanish spoken in northern New Mexico, settled by Spaniards whose roots lay in the northern provinces of Spain. On at least one occasion, Courtney was suspect because the midwife did not believe an Anglo could speak Spanish as well as she did.[74]

The translation issue raised two problems. First, Luckett, of the Bureau of Public Health, did not think translation was necessary because so many of the midwives were illiterate and apparently would remain so.[75] He stressed the importance of verbal instruction and detailed demonstration rather than the printed word. In the same letter, however, he noted that the state provided the midwives with a pledge in Spanish to be signed and filed with the county health officer upon successful completion of the training course. A second issue for Luckett was the matter of paying for the translation. He wanted the Children's Bureau to fund the project, not the state of New Mexico. How the dilemma was resolved is not clear, although records show that much of the literature was rewritten and revised in both Spanish and English between 1926 and 1927.[76]

Once midwives were located in a community, a nurse arranged for classes to be held in a woman's home, a school, or another central location. Within a week or ten days, the nurse would begin a series of ten classes. Attendance was always uncertain. Perhaps only two or three women would appear at first, but usually ten or twelve would eventually enroll. Often, however, the older or more feeble midwives dropped out after a session or two. Instruction was both verbal and practical, consisting of demonstrations that allowed each woman the opportunity to repeat the action being demonstrated. At the ninth and tenth sessions, women demonstrated what they had learned throughout the course and were given oral examinations. Those who qualified were awarded certificates bearing the signature of the county health officer, and they took the midwife's pledge. The health department then compiled a list of the "graduated midwives" that was sent to each doctor in the county, urging him or her to call upon these authorized midwives rather than on those who had not received training. Periodically, health department officials checked with midwives to see that they were keeping their pledges. In this way, New Mexico was able to train and regulate midwives in a manner that met the standards of the health profession.[77]

Basically, the midwives were taught standard obstetrical techniques, procedures for dealing with the most common complications encountered in delivery, and fundamentals of the care of the newborn with emphasis on the importance of cleanliness and on calling the doctor at the first sign of real difficulty. State regulations enacted in 1922 included a lengthy list of "do's and don'ts" and required each midwife to take a prescribed set of items to all confinement cases. Once the delivery was completed, the midwife was required to fill out the birth certificate within ten days and mail it to the county health office.[78]

State regulations required a midwife to keep certain items ready for immediate use. This equipment included a freshly washed and ironed apron or cotton dress, Ivory soap, a nail brush, Lysol (for scrubbing her hands and arms), two clean towels, four ounces of Wesson oil, a jar of Vaseline or fresh, clean lard, cord dressing and tape, a pair of blunt point scissors, 1 percent solution of silver nitrate (for the baby's eyes), and sterile cotton and dressings. The midwife had specific instructions to keep this equipment in a special bag with a washable lining or towel that was to be washed and boiled before each case. These medical kits were unique, for they were designed by a Santa Fe woman for the use of midwives in northern New Mexico and provoked admiring comments in Washington at the Children's Bureau. Eleanor Roosevelt was especially intrigued with this item while visiting one of the WPA sewing rooms in Santa Fe in 1938.[79]

To initiate midwife instruction, the Children's Bureau "loaned" instructors to the various states as needed. In New Mexico, Agnes Courtney served as midwife-instructor from February 1, 1925 to February 1, 1926. Her monthly reports detail some of the trials and tribulations of the work, of which distance was always a consideration. For instance, one project covered a five-county area including Dōna Ana, Valencia, McKinley, Bernalillo, and Eddy counties. Within this area, Courtney made 367 home visits, located a total of 198 midwives, and granted certificates to 135.[80]

In some counties, the women had had midwife instruction prior to her visit and were anxious to have more; she found this was true in Doña Ana County, where midwives were present at 50 percent of reported births. There, Courtney located fifty-five active midwives. In McKinley County, thirty-eight midwives were willing to learn and showed great interest during the course; twenty-seven earned certificates. In Bernalillo County, the midwife was still a necessity, wrote Courtney, because of impassable roads in wet weather, because doctors were unavailable, and because many poor families simply depended on the midwife. Fifty-one women were practicing midwifery in that county; thirty-eight became certified.[81]

In May of 1925, Courtney reported to the Children's Bureau on conditions in New Mexico.

> *The work is such a new thing to the people. . . . They do not grasp ideas quickly so it takes a little time for them to comprehend the fact that the Government is providing instruction for midwives. They are usually timid and have some fear that a charge is to be made or that they should not attend classes because they cannot read or write. The fact that a law governs the practice of midwifery means little to those who have lived in the isolated districts and practiced without having received any instructions or restraint. It has been gratifying to find that some of the midwives have appreciated the help we are trying to extend.[82]*

She added that midwife classes would help eliminate the less capable women, either because the responsibilities were too great or because their neighbors or patients would want a competent midwife and would "refuse to call those who [were] old and feeble or known to be dirty."[83] That, of course, was the intent behind the regulation of midwifery as determined by the state medical structure.

In 1936, the state established a rural demonstration unit in San Miguel County to improve maternal and child health. Initially, the Children's Bureau funded the demonstration unit; later, money from Title V of the newly enacted Social Security Act supplemented bureau resources. Ten nurses were hired to work at the unit, including eight public health nurses and one nurse-midwife. Using portable equipment, they and other staff members established clinics in communities throughout the county. In some isolated areas, "outside" visitors arriving in an automobile were a novelty, and everyone came to "*la clínica*." That the women appreciated the service was clear, for many were willing to walk long distances or ride for miles over rough roads in primitive vehicles to attend the clinics.[84]

One public health nurse working on the unit was Edith Rackley, who regularly conducted midwife classes, graduating Jesusita Aragon from one session. Aragon proudly recalled the things she learned from Rackley: to keep her fingernails short and clean, to have a clean white apron ready, to teach her patients to have blood tests done when necessary; she also expressed her pleasure at receiving her home nursing pin upon completion of the classes.[85]

At this time (mid-1930s), between 700 and 800 midwives were practicing throughout the state, most of them in northern New Mexico and most of them as yet unlicensed. Since midwives attended 701 of 972 live births in San Miguel County in 1936, the lone nurse-midwife instructor was in great demand. To ease her burden, a second nurse-midwife and an obstetrician joined the demonstration team in 1938. In an ambitious effort to reach as many parteras as possible, midwives throughout the state were brought to the demonstration area in Las Vegas for classes and supervision of deliveries. The program continued until 1944, when improved roads and increased use of cars reduced the isolation of scattered communities. Maternal and infant mortality rates had been substantially reduced as well. With this improvement, the Children's Bureau decided the county and state should assume more financial responsibility for public health work.[86]

Although the majority of New Mexican midwives were Hispanic, Anglo midwives were also at work, especially in Bernalillo, Valencia, and McKinley counties. Courtney located seven Anglo midwives in the Mormon community around Ramah and one Slavic woman, Julia Radosevich, practicing among her Slavic neighbors forty miles west of Gallup. Doña Ana County listed

14. A state-trained midwife in the 1940s, carrying her equipment and supplies in a suitcase provided by the Department of Health. Courtesy of State Records Center and Archives, Health and Social Services Division, no. 10022.

eighteen "foreign" (Hispanic) midwives and nine Anglo-Americans. Generally, Hispanic and Mexican midwives predominated in the New Mexico-Mexico border area and in the heavily Hispanic communities of northern New Mexico.[87]

At times, midwifery cut across cultures as well, as when Courtney found Hispana Severa Armenta of Chilili working in Isleta Pueblo.[88] Customarily, Indian women preferred to be delivered in their homes rather than in a hospital, when available, because of certain ceremonies they carried out after the birth of a child. Health officials in the Bureau of Indian Affairs (BIA), however, were insensitive to this cultural digression from Anglo birthing methods. A private group, the New Mexico Association on Indian Affairs, was much more attuned to Native American preferences and, as a result, by the mid-1930s, a successful program of midwife training had been established among the Pueblo people that took into consideration their special birthing customs.

Basically, health authorities agreed that normal births should be cared for in Pueblo homes, but that Indian midwives should be taught to recognize abnormal conditions that required hospital care. Two physicians, Nancy Campbell, an obstetrician/gynecologist in Santa Fe, and Gertrude Light, a general practitioner in Ranchos de Taos, conducted midwife classes in the northern Rio Grande Pueblos and among the Zunis, Navajos, and Apaches in western New Mexico.[89] Maternity and infancy work was an integral part of the private practices of both women, bringing personal as well as professional satisfaction. More important, their success indicates the impact of gender influence on health-care reform among the Pueblo Indians.

Light, who began Sheppard-Towner work in 1924, was especially sensitive to cultural differences, a sensitivity apparent in her observation of health conditions among the western Indian groups. Reporting to the Children's Bureau, she noted:

> In the matter of the Indian, I think we shall have to carry on the Sheppard-Towner work as the experience of local conditions suggest and with constant and delicate appreciation of the reflection in their minds of their body of birth taboos about which we really know so little. Their interest in their babies is genuine and delightful. One sees it everywhere.[90]

Light recognized there would be problems, but was hopeful that, with the cooperation of the Bureau of Indian Affairs, Sheppard-Towner work would be effective among the Native Americans. "At best, it will be slow work and scattered work," she wrote, "but the Indian has had such a rough deal that I would like him to feel the hand of the Government from a new angle—possibly a shade gentler!"[91]

Cultural differences such as these finally forced Anglo health care reformers to readjust their methods in light of New Mexico's diverse population. To be successful, they were forced to adapt their notions of modern health practices to existing Hispanic and Native American customs and values. In addition, the rural nature of New Mexico—great distances, poor roads, few doctors, scattered medical facilities—made their work even harder. When assessing their progress in mid-1937, the Bureau of Child Welfare grudgingly noted:

> We have come to the reluctant admission that in view of the small size and the remoteness of the rural communities, the customs of the people, the bad roads, and the lack of telephones, many women will have to continue to depend on the Spanish-American midwives living in their neighborhood for help at the time of delivery. . . . It is a cherished though distant hope that all women in the state may have at least one medical examination during pregnancy.[92]

Cultural differences reflect one facet of health-care work in the 1920s and 1930s. Despite other obstacles, such as limited funds, great distances, and language barriers, female health-care reformers produced results. From an estimated high of 145 deaths per 1,000 births in the mid-1920s, the infant mortality rate dropped to 100 deaths per 1,000 births by 1940.[93] While this figure continued to be well above the national average of 47 deaths per 1,000 births, it marked the beginning of modern health-care reform in New Mexico.

Clearly, gender influences shaped the nature of maternity and infancy work in New Mexico. The enlightened attitudes of physicians Light and Campbell, for example, influenced the way Anglo caregivers provided aid to Native American women. Women made other adjustments as well, adapting health reform to the needs and requirements of the population. They were permitted to do so within the male-dominated political structure because the needs of the state meshed with their desire to effect change. In addition, the early health-care reformers—Reid, Tupper, Van Pelt, Courtney, Rackley, and the local Hispanic and Anglo health-care practitioners who worked with them—were an important link between the Progressive reform movement of the early twentieth century and New Deal reforms in health and welfare in the 1930s. With the support of the Children's Bureau and federal funding through the Sheppard-Towner Act, female health-care reformers played a major role in producing "better mothers and better babies" in New Mexico. In the private sector, their counterparts played an equally important role in introducing health-care reform among the Native American population.

3

"THE TALES THOSE NURSES TOLD!"

PUBLIC HEALTH NURSES AMONG

THE PUEBLO AND NAVAJO INDIANS

When I came here . . . I soon realized that the Navajos hereabouts expected to find me antagonistic to their religious customs and were slow to consult me about illness until the medicine man had failed to help, but gradually they are showing more confidence in my good will and often notify me that they are having a sing [a healing ceremony] and invite me to attend. Sometimes I am invited to practice medicine with the medicine man, sometimes I am asked to wait until the conclusion of the sing so as to be on hand to take the patient to the hospital. I am surprised and gratified to find my medicine men friendly and often cooperative.[1]

Elizabeth Forster's gratification at becoming an accepted member of the Navajo health community marked just one of the many emotions that the public health nurse experienced during her stay among these Southwestern Indians in the early 1930s. As part of a unique public-private effort to improve health conditions among the Southwest's Indian population, Forster was one of a handful of health-care reformers participating in fieldwork in the 1920s and 1930s. As employees of the New Mexico Association on Indian Affairs (NMAIA), a private organization created in Santa Fe in 1922, the women played an important role in the development of social welfare policy at the state and national levels.[2]

It was not unusual that women were the backbone of reform efforts among the Indian population in New Mexico and Arizona. Like their sisters across the nation, Southwestern women had been active in their communities for decades. Like women elsewhere, their activities fell within traditionally female patterns that focused on concern for others. Nursing, for example, was an acceptable field for women because it reflected qualities considered essentially female—compassion, sensitivity, nurturance, and supportiveness. In this sense, the women who became involved with Indian issues in the Southwest continued in a traditional role— that of nursing—but did so in very nontraditional ways and circumstances. A major component of their work was the ability to cross cultural boundaries effectively.

In other ways, the nurses were like other middle-class white women who interacted with non-whites. Essentially they were culture-bearers, attempting to transmit their ideas of proper gender roles and values to Indian families. Like missionary women before them and home demonstration agents and social workers later, they faced possible rejection and resentment from their health-care recipients. While a few of the nurses proved unsuited for field work among Native Americans, the majority of the women were able to adapt to less-than-perfect working conditions as well as meet cross-cultural challenges successfully.[3]

Equally important is the degree of cooperation between public and private agencies and how this interaction allowed female health-care reformers to determine social welfare policy. Technically, the Bureau of Indian Affairs (BIA) was responsible for the health and welfare of Native Americans, but the bureau's efforts were sporadic and relatively ineffective in providing adequate medical care. One of the root problems was the bureau's focus on relief of the sick rather than prevention and eradication of disease. Contributing to the situation were low salaries and inadequate medical facilities that failed to meet even minimum scientific standards.[4] As a result, many reservations lacked adequate health-care personnel, and in some cases, such as at Zuni in eastern Arizona, BIA officials showed a decided disinterest in doing much for the Indians. Professional and jurisdictional jealousies frequently impeded bureau efforts, as well.[5] The major problems facing the Indians, however, were extreme poverty, an inadequate supply of food, and poor sanitation and hygiene. Aware of BIA shortcomings, the NMAIA hoped to ameliorate some of the problems through their field service program.

This offer of cooperation between a private organization and a public agency was typically American; voluntarism had long been a part of the national character. As so often happened when state or federal funds were limited or lacking, local groups provided the difference. Gradually, social welfare agencies came to depend on city and county help to meet human needs, particularly during the Depression years. The NMAIA was one such organization.

Although the NMAIA was formed around the political issue of the Bursum Bill, its scope was twofold, embracing political and humanitarian action, and it was the women of the associa-

15. Making chile ristras, San Ildefonso Pueblo, ca. 1935. Photo by T. Harmon Parkhurst. Courtesy of Museum of New Mexico, neg. no. 5144.

tion who supported welfare issues, particularly health care.[6] Frequent visits to the pueblos and reservations had disclosed serious health problems. A chronic state of malnutrition existed among the Pueblo people in the early 1920s; tuberculosis was common and trachoma, a highly infectious eye disease, was widespread, especially among children. For example, the Catholic priest at Laguna Pueblo, Father Schuster, reported that 33 percent of the children there had trachoma. In addition, an epidemic of measles and whooping cough caused many deaths at Zuni Pueblo in 1924. One eyewitness account reported "the village cemetery was so filled that the little bodies had to be buried on top of one another." To make matters worse, a drought during 1922–23 caused an acute shortage of food for people as well as livestock, especially in the northern pueblos of San Ildefonso and Tesuque. The NMAIA was instrumental in supplying food and fodder through the winter until the government finally made these items available, but this was only a stopgap measure at the time.[7]

Because trachoma was so widespread, the association focused

first on this problem. Conditions were critical at the Indian schools in Santa Fe as well as in several pueblos. Forty-six percent of the children at the Santa Fe Indian School, 48 percent at Saint Catherine's School in Santa Fe, and 50 percent of the people at Tesuque Pueblo had trachoma, but no government specialist was assigned to care for them. The disease was likewise out of control among the Navajo population. So the association appealed to noted Boston eye specialist and summer resident of Santa Fe, Francis I. Proctor, who offered his services free during his summer visits. Proctor was able to persuade the BIA to establish a school among the Navajo where contagious trachoma patients could be segregated to prevent further spread of the disease. In this way, their education could be continued along with medical treatment. Proctor's idea of segregated schools became a model for the BIA, and by the time of his death in 1935, four boarding schools had been established for the treatment of trachomous children.[8]

Nursing care was also lacking or nonexistent except where BIA field matrons possessed nursing skills. Field matrons, first utilized in the 1880s, were expected to do far more than provide health care, however. Their usefulness was based on the idea "that any good woman could teach some good women what all good women should know."[9] The field matron, woman as "civilizer par excellence," would be able to enter the Indian woman's separate sphere and reshape it to fit the accepted (white) American model. She would teach housekeeping duties, nurse the ill and the old, serve as a model and confidante for young girls, and attempt to impart attitudes and skills white America deemed necessary in a civilized world. The only qualifications for the job were subjective, unmeasurable qualities. The most important priorities to the BIA were that the field matron possess character and personality and the ability to understand and get along with Indians. Admittedly, these requirements covered a wide, even vague, spectrum. For example, the BIA defined personality as innate kindness tempered with firmness, patience, tact, and motherly instinct. Specialized skills, such as nursing, were not required, nor did the bureau demand any sensitivity to cultural differences.[10]

The overwhelming nature of the tasks expected of the matrons quickly proved apparent. The field matrons, often the wives of the agent, missionary, or trader on the reservation, were untrained generalists in situations often calling for specialists. In addition to domestic duties, matrons spent a great deal of time dispensing health care. The demands went beyond lessons in first aid and the preparation of bland diets, and included helping patients follow a physician's orders, teaching basic infant care and feeding, and emphasizing sanitation and prevention of disease. These were reasonable tasks, but nursing a community through an epidemic went beyond reasonable expectations and abilities, a burden that weakened an already inadequate system. Clearly, competent health-care specialists were needed among the Indians, and it was logical for public health nurses to take over many tasks initially assigned to field matrons.[11]

During the nineteenth century, the concept of woman as civilizer had been expanded beyond the home to include "social housekeeping chores" within the larger world of political and social service work. By the 1920s, many women had professional careers; specialization was becoming the norm. Where one woman (the field matron) had previously filled a variety of roles, the BIA began to employ home economics agents, day-school teachers, social workers, and nurses. When these new types of workers became more numerous, the field matron program was phased out.[12] Seeing an opportunity to introduce nurses among Native Americans, the NMAIA, with the tacit approval of the BIA, began an experimental field nursing program among several northern New Mexico pueblos in 1924.[13]

The task of selling public health nursing to the various superintendents in the BIA fell to Elinor Gregg, a public health nurse from Brookline, Massachusets. In August 1924, Gregg was appointed supervisor of public health nursing in the Medical Division of the BIA, at a salary of $2,600 a year plus $5 per diem.[14] She immediately set out on a fact-finding tour, spending three months visiting pueblos and reservations in the Southwest. Her findings convinced her that field matrons were sadly inadequate for the job.

In the eight pueblos of the Southern Pueblos Agency in New Mexico, including approximately 5,500 people, field matrons reached perhaps 3,000 Indians. It was impossible to hold clinics for tuberculosis, trachoma, or infant welfare because field matrons could not carry out the required follow-up work. At Isleta and Jemez pueblos, both matrons were burdened with invalid husbands. In addition, the matron for Sandia and Santa Ana pueblos was in poor health and interested only in cooking and sewing. While Gregg noted that the limited ability of the matrons was not to their discredit, she nonetheless recognized the restricted value in continuing field matron work.[15]

No field matrons were assigned to the Northern Pueblos Agency, composed of nine pueblos and approximately 3,400 Indians. Among these people, tuberculosis and trachoma were chronic diseases, along with those of infancy and childhood, such as measles, mumps, and chicken pox. Conditions were especially dif-

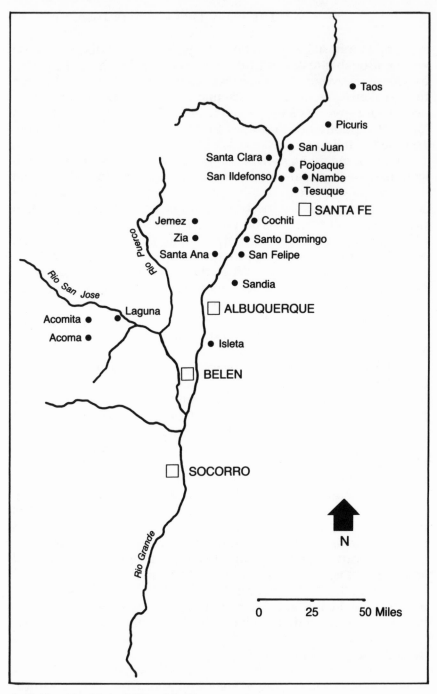

2. Indian Pueblos of New Mexico

ficult in Taos and Picuris pueblos, seventy-five miles from the nearest BIA physician, in Santa Fe. As a result, nursing care was nonexistent in those pueblos. In addition, the road between Santa Fe and Taos was then under construction and the road between Taos and Picuris often impassable by auto during the winter months. Nor was there telephone service between Taos and the agency in case of emergencies. Gregg's recommendations included establishing a field nurse position for these northernmost pueblos and providing an automobile. Her assessments meshed well with the plan the NMAIA devised to provide public health and child welfare work among the Pueblo and Navajo Indians of New Mexico and Arizona.[16]

A volunteer group, the NMAIA represents both the importance and the influence voluntarism can command at local, state, and national levels. The group was composed primarily of middle- to upper-class Anglos, and members were a colorful, flamboyant lot. The group included writers and artists who had drifted into New Mexico after World War I, settling in Santa Fe and Taos where they found escape from the conventions of society they had come to find constraining. They were searching for an "American place," free of the stress of the urban-industrial world. What could be more "American," they thought, than taking up the cause of the American Indian? Others came to New Mexico for reasons of health or leisure, and some were already members of Santa Fe society. The membership was fairly evenly divided between men and women. Former territorial governor Miguel A. Otero was the only Hispanic member of the organization in the early years. There were no Indian members, although records indicate that Pueblo people often attended association meetings.[17]

Shortly after the NMAIA organized, a group of like-minded citizens on the East Coast formed the Eastern Association on Indian Affairs (EAIA). Many of the influential and wealthy members had ties with New Mexico, some as part-time residents. For instance, Amelia and Martha White, daughters of Horace White, editor of the *New York Evening Post*, were active in the EAIA as well as benefactresses of the School of American Research in Santa Fe. The EAIA supported Indian groups all over the nation in addition to the Pueblo Indians and often provided funding for programs undertaken in the Southwest. In Erna Fergusson's words, "The New Mexico Association had found a big-sister association back east where the money grows." The two groups continued to affiliate until the early 1930s when financial and jurisdictional disagreements led to a formal separation.[18]

Recognizing that joint action between federal authorities and private agencies was needed, the NMAIA proposed that the pueblos be divided into districts of 1,500 to 2,000 people and a competent public health nurse assigned to each district. A full-time trachoma specialist with two nurses to assist with operative cases was also recommended. To help meet expenses, the NMAIA suggested eliminating contract physicians, allowing the public health nurse to call in a doctor in critical cases. Like the BIA, the NMAIA recognized the inefficiency of the field matron program and supported its elimination. Overall, the New Mexico group saw the benefits to the Indians as invaluable and believed the experience the NMAIA acquired would furnish a working base for their future plans for expansion under government auspices. History proved them correct.[19]

Over the next decade, the NMAIA employed several competent nurses—Hilda George, from Massachusetts General Hospital, was the first. George's initial report indicated plenty to do in all the pueblos, and the reports of the nurses that followed her echoed her remarks. In addition to unsanitary conditions and disease, the nurses encountered distrust of Anglo medicine, indifference of government doctors, great distances, and inadequate equipment. "The tales those nurses told! And the things they did!" exclaimed one writer.[20] These tasks demanded a cultural sensitivity that included fortitude, determination, and patience, qualities not lacking in the women who pioneered public health nursing among the Southwest's Indian population.

George proved to be a good choice to inaugurate public health nursing in the northern pueblos of New Mexico. Headquartered in Española and provided with an automobile—a professional necessity—George was able to spend all her time in the field. Described as gentle, flexible, and determined, George was particularly effective among small children with trachoma. In fact, hers were the only trachoma records at the time that gave any indication of the value of certain methods of treatment. In tandem with the pueblo agency doctor, George was a conscientious and devoted worker and earned the praise of Gregg and the NMAIA.[21] Others quickly followed George in task and example.

Her replacement, Augustine Stoll, a Red Cross nurse, began work in the spring of 1926. At San Juan Pueblo, Stoll initiated a program of training native girls as assistants, which proved highly successful and was expanded to other pueblos. Stoll also established a laundry and bath house at San Ildefonso that became a model for other pueblos and for the Navajos. The Indians' idea of cleanliness, however, contrasted with that of the Anglo nurse and others who more clearly recognized the connection between poor hygiene and disease. One Indian woman told Stoll, "We are not dirty, because some things you consider so, we do not." Nevertheless, the weekly baths became so popular that the BIA had facilities installed at other pueblos and on the Navajo reservation. The Indians took great pride in the government-installed laundry and bathing facilities and looked forward to weekly hot baths.[22]

Stoll's nursing report for 1926–27 detailed other small but significant breakthroughs. Calling it "slow up-hill work," Stoll nonetheless noted improvements in treating trachoma, tuberculosis, malaria, and physical defects, and in educating Indian mothers about infant welfare and nutrition. Regarding the introduction of fresh vegetables into their diet, Stoll remarked, "The carrots have been distributed with this perplexing result: all the children want them!"[23] In the Anglo culture, where children often turned up their noses at such a common dietary item, this response provoked amusement and the mistaken cultural assumption that what is disliked in one culture will also be rejected by another.

Poverty and an inadequate supply of food were two major factors contributing to Indian medical problems. Indian diets were not well balanced and, as a result, malnutrition was a serious problem. The standard daily fare consisted of watermelon, muskmelon, squash, chile, meat, beans, tortillas, and coffee; the poorest Indians lived on a monotonous diet of potatoes, tortillas, and coffee. Milk was not a part of their daily dietary intake, and, hence, it became a goal of health officials to introduce this important food into the Indian diet.[24]

Introducing new cultural attitudes and customs was not always easy. In matters of illness, for example, the Indians often sought out their medicine man or woman. The thought of being taken from their pueblo or reservation to a hospital often provoked outright resistance or at least uneasiness. A lack of cross-cultural awareness on the part of reformers could jeopardize well-meaning efforts. Tact, patience, and persuasion were necessary to convince Indians that Anglo medicine could provide a safe alternative to traditional health practices. Reshaping attitudes was a delicate process at best, one in which many dominant Anglo attitudes and values were gradually superimposed over Indian customs. While many Indians preferred the ways of their medicine men and women, they did not object to seeking hospital care once the traditional methods had been tried. Over time, automobiles, schools, and gradual change in BIA policies combined to lessen resistance to Anglo ways in some, but certainly not all, aspects of Native American life.

Tonsillectomies provide an example. Considered a routine

procedure for the children of middle-class Americans (at least until the 1960s), tonsillectomies were not easily accepted in the pueblos. Yet, given time and careful explanation, many Indian parents became convinced of the efficacy of the surgery and trusted their children to the nurse's care. Within a year, Stoll was successful in persuading parents in the northern pueblos to send their children to Santa Fe for the operations. Some resistance persisted among the elders, however. Stoll cautiously approached Santiago Naranjo of Santa Clara to convince him that the two underweight grandchildren living with him needed the operation. When finally the Indian elder agreed and asked, "When?" Stoll quickly replied "tomorrow," for she had learned "never to allow much time between the consent and the departure."[25] Hesitation on her part might allow a change of mind, which she hoped to avert.

Stoll, and others after her, devised various approaches for introducing new ideas to the Indians. Because the importance of maternal influence was inherent in the prevailing ideology of domesticity, they focused their efforts on the women, who in turn taught the children.[26] Using posters, songs, and poems as teaching aids, nurses directed their efforts at mothers and children. Simple songs often made an impression on young minds. Included in Stoll's report are a few lines of verse she composed while traveling among the pueblos. Set to the tune of "Tramp, Tramp, Tramp, the Boys are Marching," the ditty celebrates the benefits of a tonsillectomy:

> *We have had our tonsils out.*
> *Yes, we have had our tonsils out.*
> *If you watch, you see us growing very stout.*
> *We are eating carrots too, hard tack, milk—*
> *that will do.*
> *If we do it day by day, we'll surely gain.*
> *Chorus:*
> *Watch, watch, you'll see us gaining—*
> *Come on, Comrades, fall in line.*
> *Let the doctor take them out.*
> *You'll be sure to gladly shout:*
> *We have had our tonsils out,*
> *our tonsils out!*[27]

Other messages in this childlike verse included good dietary habits (eating carrots, drinking milk) and coming around to the Anglo (doctor's) point of view.

Attempting to cross cultural boundaries in mundane matters such as bathing and diet was a common challenge to health reformers in the 1920s and 1930s. By 1931, BIA directives focused on health education, introducing ideas of cleanliness and demonstrating the advantages of sanitary measures.[28] Nearly all the nurses that worked in the Southwest, whether Red Cross, public health, or private, were Anglo women. As a result, they were not always welcome in the pueblo communities, for the Indians correctly perceived that the white women were trying to change Indian ways. Only a nurse with tact, patience, and understanding could integrate herself and her ideas into these communities, and then only if the Indians allowed it. Most, though not all, were successful, and the nurses' efforts were significant in improving overall health conditions in the Indian population.

The nurses who followed George and Stoll were singularly outstanding and quickly made inroads where health care had been absent or inconsistent. In the spring of 1925, the NMAIA sent Elizabeth Duggan, former Santa Fe County health nurse, to Zuni, where conditions were unusually bad and the BIA doctor appeared indifferent to the sufferings of the Indians. In this community of 2,000, the Indian agent took little or no interest in the Indians as well, creating a special challenge for the overburdened nurse. The doctor's attitude is clear in his remark that "the Indians would not follow instructions anyway, so why should he bother." In spite of this indifference, Duggan was especially effective in reforming conditions at Zuni. Backed by her reports, the NMAIA appealed to the BIA, and the doctor and agent were soon replaced.[29]

Shortly after her arrival, Duggan reported that tuberculosis was the "scourge of this reservation, and terrible epidemics of whooping cough and measles" attacked the people with dreadful regularity. At Duggan's request, future NMAIA chairwoman Margretta S. Dietrich witnessed the effects of the whooping cough epidemic in 1924 that filled the village cemetery. Duggan's hard work and determination to improve conditions at Zuni resulted in the establishment of a sanatorium for tubercular children at the Zuni boarding school at nearby Black Rock. She also was responsible for encouraging the BIA to dig new and deeper wells to provide safer drinking water, and as a result, the death rate declined. When Duggan left Zuni in the spring of 1928, she could point with modest pride to her accomplishments there.[30]

A third nursing experiment began late in 1927 when the NMAIA assigned Molly Reebel to Jemez Pueblo. The nearest doctor was sixty miles away in Albuquerque and no telephones connected the pueblo to the city. The association, therefore, provided her with an automobile to allow her to reach medical facilities. At first, the people were unaccepting of the white woman and her

16. Jemez Pueblo woman tending her cooking pot over an indoor fire, ca. 1940. Photo by Ferenz Fedor. Courtesy of Museum of New Mexico, neg. no. 101994.

ways—for it was "not easy to convince the [Jemez Indians] that there is any good in white man's ways"—and it might have been a discouraging process, but Reebel persisted and, through patience and kindness, gradually gained their trust.[31]

Reebel was especially successful in introducing milk into the diet of the Jemez people. Babies and small children were particularly vulnerable to sickness and disease once they were weaned from mother's milk. As soon as a baby produced a tooth, the child was considered able to manage the food of grownups, often the sacred food, *atole*. A thin blue cornmeal mush, atole was an irritant to young intestines and produced diarrhea, a leading contributor to the infant mortality rate. To counter these problems, the government supplied four goats that provided a regular, healthful source of milk for the pueblo.

Reebel then devised a dairy with a cooler and small icebox in an Indian home. At first the children had to be coaxed to drink milk, but they soon came to like it, and the infant mortality rate began to decline. Only one baby died at Jemez in the summer of 1929, "instead of the usual large proportion." Eventually, the government built a model goat dairy in connection with a new day school. When fresh milk was unavailable, powdered or canned milk served as a substitute. The introduction of milk into the children's daily diet was a significant breakthrough and became a regular component of maternity and infant work in the Southwest.[32]

Elizabeth Duggan, meanwhile, spent a brief time among the Navajos at Nava (now Newcomb, in western New Mexico); then the BIA hired her as nursing supervisor for the Southwest. She continued in this position into the 1930s, her reports detailing a decade of health work among the Indians. By September 1931, Duggan could report positive responses to six years of health education among the northern pueblos. Trachoma and venereal disease clinics were in place, young mothers were readily bringing their children to infant and child welfare meetings, and the improved appearance of pueblo homes (window screening, outdoor toilets) showed the positive effects of health teaching. By 1941, the most common request among the Pueblos was for more outdoor privies.[33]

Still, stumbling blocks persisted. In Taos, for example, bad roads continued to hinder public health work. In addition, Duggan regretfully reported that the Taos Indians were reluctant to use their new hospital at the pueblo, "the people being apparently quite indifferent when not antagonistic to 'white medicine.'" Duggan correctly perceived that the BIA contract doctor and field nurse assigned to this area were not as effective as the situation demanded. The doctor, recorded only as "Dr. Martin," had a busy private practice as well as county health work to do. Duggan cited the nurse, "Donovan," as "perhaps not suited in personality to the pioneer field work still required in this community" and recommended that the nurse be assigned elsewhere and another nurse brought in. In this case, the nurse's ineffectiveness, coupled with the contract physician's inattention, slowed public health work at Taos.[34]

Turning to the southern pueblos of Isleta, Jemez, San Felipe, Laguna, Mesita, and Paguate, Duggan reported in 1931 that "the work . . . [had] been carried on long enough to show results and in most of the pueblos . . . [was] very satisfactory." The work at Isleta, moreover, was more than satisfactory because of Louise Kuhrtz's presence there. A Red Cross nurse who spent thirty years at Isleta, Kuhrtz became a much-loved and respected figure in the pueblo. Her field work also included the pueblos of Sandia and Santa Ana, respectively fifteen and twenty-five miles north of Albuquerque, with a population of 1,500 Indians. Counting trips to the hospital in Albuquerque and twice-weekly trips to Sandia and Santa Ana, Kuhrtz traveled an average of 2,000 miles a month. She remained enthusiastic and interested in her work despite long hours spent traveling difficult roads.[35]

Initially lacking a dispensary and living in crowded quarters at Isleta, Kuhrtz, according to Duggan, still had "the ability to accomplish her work with a minimum of friction." Possessing tact, patience, and a genuine desire to help the Indians, Kuhrtz was especially successful in convincing the Indians of the importance of immunization. In 1934, she could count among her successes the vaccination of two of the village medicine men. In maternity and infancy work, the infant mortality rate steadily declined from twenty-four deaths (under four years old) in 1927 to just four in 1933. Moreover, she soon gained the trust of the head midwife of the village, who came to her for supplies and advice. Similarly, Kuhrtz's efforts in nutrition introduced new foods into Indian homes. Where chile, beans, and tortillas had been the daily diet, Kuhrtz added fresh fruits and vegetables, cereals, milk, and butter. As a result, the proprietor of the local trading post was forced to stock these items in greater supply over the years.[36]

Other nurses among the southern pueblos reported progress as well, but noted that their efforts had to accommodate Native American schedules. Generally, they were successful in persuading mothers to bring their babies to infant welfare clinics, establishing venereal disease clinics, treating trachoma, teaching home and personal hygiene, and encouraging gardening and food preservation. The nurses quickly learned, however, not to schedule their child welfare clinics during periods that took mothers away from the village, such as at harvest and wheat threshing time. For example, the Laguna Pueblo field nurse, Zola Brewer, found the mothers "so busy plastering their houses, white washing and cleaning, that they have not had time to bring their babies to be weighed." [37] Adapting the work to Indian lifestyles was important to the success of public health nursing.

Health work progressed slowly but steadily among the southern pueblos. By 1934, Duggan believed the Indians were ready to take more responsibility in developing health programs for themselves, both in groups and as individuals. Among her immediate requests were a car for the Isleta field nurse and typewriters and nursing journals for all stations.[38] Overall, the field nursing experiments the NMAIA had established among the Pueblo people proved effective. The successes of Stoll, George, Duggan, and Reebel had already helped bring down the infant mortality rate and introduce good health, hygiene, and nutrition to the Indians. In the 1930s, BIA gradually assumed more responsibility for health care among the Pueblos, allowing the NMAIA to turn their attention to yet another neglected group, the Navajos.

The needs among the Navajo were immense. The people numbered approximately 45,000 in the 1920s and were scattered over an area of 15 million acres in New Mexico and Arizona. At that time, the Navajos were divided among six agencies: the Southern Navajos at Fort Defiance, the Western Navajos at Kayenta, and the Leupp and Keam's Canyon agencies, all in Arizona; the Northern Navajos at Shiprock, and the Eastern Navajos at Pueblo Bonito, both in New Mexico. This scattered population, however, suffered from many of the same social ills.

In 1924, Elinor Gregg had investigated conditions among the Indians in the Southwest, and her report painted a grim picture. Recalling the ramshackle hospitals she found at Shiprock and Pueblo Bonito, Gregg described the practice of medicine and surgery as "archaic" and the services as limited. The best the hospitals could do was provide "warmth, food, cleanliness, and aspirin." Just getting to the hospital was difficult because of the vastness of the reservation and poorly maintained roads. In addition, government cars were old and worn-out, yet necessary because of great distances. Communication by telephone, a two-wire system strung on fence posts, was also unreliable.[39]

Social problems were many, and Gregg saw them repeated all over the reservation. Bigamy was not uncommon, law enforcement was erratic, and alcoholism was increasing. These disorders contributed to a family life that was less than stable. Most children attended boarding schools, which seemed to weaken the family unit. Families also moved to spring and summer sheep camps; Gregg assumed this forced mobility was disruptive as well. Despite the problems, however, she was convinced that public health

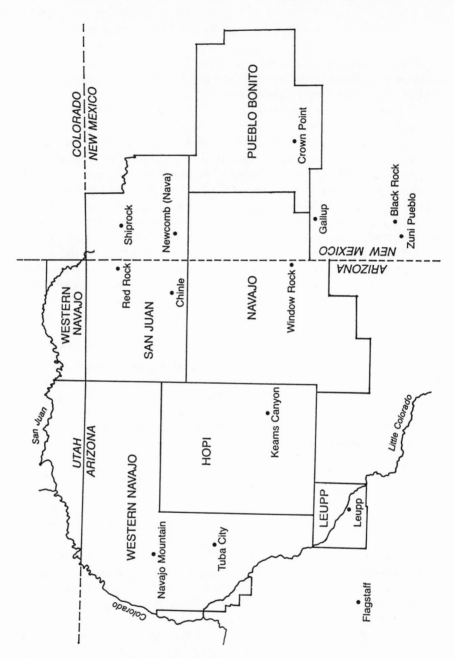

3. Jurisdictional Boundaries of the Navajo Reservation to 1927

nursing among the Navajos was possible and would be not only challenging but rewarding. The nurses who subsequently worked among the Navajos found the experience to be exactly that.[40]

Elizabeth Duggan introduced the first nursing program among the Navajos at Nava in the spring of 1928. Little was accomplished, however, until the arrival of Mrs. Wade Nickolds in May 1929. While Nickolds was unable to make much headway in such a vast area, she did establish dispensaries at a number of outlying trading posts. Because Nickolds visited each place on the same day of the week, the Indians came to expect her on a regular basis, providing some continuity of health care.[41] Yet much work remained untouched, at least by Anglo hands. As they had done for generations, the Navajos depended on the healing skills of their medicine men and did not readily accept the field nurses. Altering or modifying traditional Indian customs tested the sensitivity of both the care givers and their Indian recipients.

In 1930, the NMAIA sent two more nurses to the Navajo reservation. Upon the recommendation of the senior medical officer at Shiprock Indian Hospital, Elizabeth Forster was assigned to Red Rock, a trading post thirty-five miles west of Shiprock, New Mexico, and Molly Reebel, formerly at Jemez, was transferred to Newcomb (then Nava), fifty miles south of Shiprock. Conditions proved difficult for both women, and, as in some of the pueblos, the nurses were not readily accepted. At Newcomb, the Indians were unwilling to use Reebel's services until she proved she could cure their animals. When her ministrations to horses proved successful, the Navajos began to trust Reebel to treat them.[42]

Both nurses lived a nomadic lifestyle, fashioned after that of the Navajos. In the spring, families moved their sheep from overgrazed areas around the villages to greener pastures in the mountains, where summer hogans awaited them. In the fall, the families returned to their villages. Only by visiting the temporary camps could the nurses treat the sick and introduce better health-care practices. Finding this unusual routine to be of benefit to the Indians, the association used the "mountain clinic" experiment as a basis for constructive recommendations to the BIA on the feasibility of nursing in Navajo country.[43]

For Elizabeth Forster, the challenge came at just the right time. Head of the Visiting Nurse Association in Colorado Springs, Colorado, for seventeen years, Forster was ready for a change. A chance happening a year earlier played a part in her decision. In the fall of 1930, Forster and her companion, photographer Laura Gilpin, had made an auto camping tour through the Navajo reservation to allow Gilpin to photograph the people and their surroundings.

When the women ran out of gas twenty miles north of Chinle, Arizona, curious and helpful Navajos quickly appeared and befriended them. The experience made a deep impression on both women, so that when Forster heard a year later that the NMAIA was looking for a nurse to send to Red Rock, she eagerly applied for the position and was hired. In mid-September of 1930, Forster and Gilpin made a brief scouting trip to Red Rock to see what awaited the new field nurse.[44]

The small community of Red Rock in the remote northeastern section of the reservation was without medical attention. The Presbyterian Medical Mission there had recently shut down and turned the buildings over to the government. The BIA decided to use the Shiprock agency as an experimental field and had called on the NMAIA to provide a nurse at Red Rock. Packing her old Chevrolet with warm clothes, books, a radio, and a game of checkers, Forster arrived in the community in October. Despite the superintendent's promise to have quarters and buildings ready for occupancy, nothing had been done toward that end. Nevertheless, Forster cheerfully installed herself in two small adobe rooms—with no cook stove and only a small heating stove for warmth—and began treating ill Navajos.[45]

Because of bad roads and snow, she could not visit many hogans that winter, but reported that as many as ten Indians a day came in for help and treatment. In December, she held four clinics and treated 138 cases—including appendicitis, frostbite, tuberculosis, and trachoma—and delivered a baby at home. She was pleased that the clinics were well attended (because she served soup to her patients, she wondered?) and remarked, "I am finding my place in the community." Gradually, her niche expanded beyond nursing. She coached a basketball team, assisted with funerals, dispensed personal and legal advice, organized Christmas parties, and opened her small home to all who wanted or needed her services and friendship.[46]

Forster's annual report to the NMAIA for 1932 captures in colorful detail the nature of her work at Red Rock. Noting the hazards of travel over poor roads in bad weather—snow that "drifted and redrifted"—she nonetheless remained energetic and pleased in her situation. Her description of Christmas day is both poignant and compelling, for although the government provided food for a feast for the Indians,

> thru bad management the food was spoiled and the poor Navajos who travelled thru the cold and snow were sadly disappointed. My heart was sore for them and how I wished that I might stretch my small

Christmas to include them all! I had invited a few intimate friends to dinner and a few more to a tree. My ten dinner guests were invited to a six o'clock dinner but to my horror they arrived about one to find me struggling with pumpkin pies and turkey. From then on my day was a hectic one with small Navajos under foot and into everything. The feast, when it was finally accomplished, was worth the struggle. Never have I seen such quantities of food disappear with such dispatch. Table manners (or rather floor manners, for we dined Navajo fashion) were excellent but enjoyment was so evident that I was well repaid for my effort. For the tree I had invited about twenty guests but found myself receiving some forty-odd.[47]

Events such as these endeared Forster to the Red Rock Navajos and they to her.

As these activities reveal, Forster was a remarkable woman. She possessed the ability to fit in among the Navajos without being presumptuous or condescending. Also a hard worker, she remained open to new ways and customs, a trait that endeared her to the Indians. She was able to laugh at herself and some of her "civilized" customs that seemed inappropriate in the Navajo world. For example, Forster believed in the efficacy of established (Anglo) medicine, but remained open to the ways of the medicine men. Occasionally she was invited to a healing sing and sometimes was asked to take the patient to the hospital afterward. Such action was gratifying, for it showed the trust the Navajos put in Forster's medicine, while maintaining their traditional beliefs. To Forster's credit, she never overestimated her ability to make profound changes in their long-established way of life.[48]

The measure of trust the Navajos placed in Elizabeth Forster clearly shines through in several of Laura Gilpin's photographs. Because the Indians trusted and respected Forster, they extended the same graciousness to "the nurse's friend," which allowed Gilpin to photograph the Navajos so appealingly. Gilpin occasionally accompanied Forster on her daily visits to the hogans and sometimes asked to be allowed to photograph a scene. On one occasion, while Forster administered digitalis to an elderly man lying on a sheepskin blanket with his wives sitting peacefully on the floor beside him, Gilpin pondered whether to ask permission to take a picture. "To my surprise," she later wrote, "they seemed pleased that I wanted to, which was one more evidence of their confidence in their nurse." Thirty years later, when Gilpin and Forster visited Red Rock for the last time, they were given a heartwarming welcome, a reminder of the friendships created during Forster's nursing days.[49]

17. Elizabeth Forster and Navaho Women, 1932. © 1981 Laura Gilpin Collection, Amon Carter Museum, Fort Worth, Texas.

Unfortunately, Forster's ability to get along so well with the Navajos, particularly the medicine men, played a part in her dismissal in 1933. By this time, the BIA superintendent in Red Rock, E. R. McCray, had become unhappy with Forster's attitudes toward traditional Indian medicine and no longer wished to work with her because she worked "hand-in-hand" with medicine men. McCray and many of the doctors at the Shiprock hospital saw the local healers as an impediment to bringing modernization to the reservation. Grounded in precise scientific training, Anglo doctors were unwilling to recognize the spiritual and psychological aspects of traditional Indian medicine. Often, abrupt and thoughtless remarks or impersonal interactions retarded health education. Not until the 1960s did medical training take into account the importance of combining traditional Indian medicine with Anglo medical practices.[50]

In the situation at Red Rock, the local Presbyterian missionary also acted as an obstructionist. By arrangement with the government, he was required to supply the dispensary and living quarters with light and water. But as he became more and more unhappy about Forster's congenial relationship with the Indian healers, the light and water became less and less dependable. He also locked the one available bathroom for weeks at a time. Jealousy was clearly a factor, as "she had so many more Indians at her clinics than he did at his prayer meetings." Finally, Superintendent McCray notified Forster that her dispensary would be turned into a dining room for a day school and she was to move her belongings out immediately. Hoping for a change in the BIA medical administration, the NMAIA considered moving Forster to Crystal, New Mexico. But when officials at Shiprock failed to provide support for the nurse's work, the NMAIA reluctantly let her go. In April 1933, Forster returned to Colorado Springs. With her departure, the Southwest health-care field lost a valuable and effective nurse, and the Navajos lost a caring and concerned friend. In broader terms, Forster was a casualty of the government's lack of cross-cultural sensitivity in a situation where they could have been effective. The larger loss, of course, fell upon the Native Americans.[51]

Although the Association was not able to save Forster's position, they kept Molly Reebel among the Navajos. Her job was rescued through a "friend," probably Martha or Amelia White of the Eastern Association on Indian Affairs, who committed $150 a month to continue Reebel for one year. While the salary was sufficient, Reebel knew it would not cover the costs of keeping an old car running over bad roads and long distances. She also knew "that her Indians would never understand if she refused to answer calls as she had in the past and that on $150 a month, the value of her work would be so curtailed it would not be worth undertaking." So the NMAIA, in consultation with its sister organization, the EAIA, agreed to provide an auto allowance of $50 a month. With that, a one-nurse program among the Navajos was back in operation by fall of 1933, and Reebel returned to Nava.[52]

At Nava, and later at Navajo Mountain in the remote northwestern section of the reservation, Reebel continued to hold the mountain clinics she and Forster had jointly developed. Following the Indians to their mountain sheep camps meant traveling by horseback long distances and camping out, but this proved worth the hardships incurred. By May 1934, Reebel had established clinics in summer camps at Cottonwood Pass above Sheep Springs and in the Say Nos Tee Mountains, and she was happily contemplating a third:

> Have taken my bedroll with me on these mountain trips. Held clinics
> until late in the afternoons then put my bedroll in a wagon close to a

hogan and spent the night, returning to Nava the following afternoon.
Have held clinics in the tents in each of these places, Cottonwood Pass
and Say Nos Tee Mountains. The third one at Toadlena is to be set
up for me and will be ready for clinic on the 6th [June]—one more
dream come true.[53]

When Reebel requested three more tents for her clinics, the association gladly complied.

After July 1934, Navajo nurse aides were available to assist the field nurses. Commissioner of Indian Affairs John Collier devised a plan for training young Navajo women to serve as aides to local nurses. In May 1934, Collier appointed Elinor Gregg, supervisor of nurses for the BIA, to organize a nurse institute in Santa Fe. From June 11 to July 11, ninety-six Navajo women, ranging in age from fifteen to thirty-five, attended the institute.[54] Collier was emphatic about the purpose of the institute: to train the students how to treat trachoma, which required irrigating the afflicted eyes daily. Some instruction in infant care and family hygiene was included, but their primary training was on the treatment of trachoma.

The following year, however, the emphasis shifted from training nurse aides to furnishing instruction to "future wives, mothers, and neighbors so that they may be better able to prevent sickness, and promote health." One hundred Indian girls from the Southwest who had graduated from high school in 1933, 1934, or 1935, attended the four-week Health Institute at the Santa Fe Indian School. While a few Navajo students were selected as nurse aides, unlike the institute held in 1934, there was no effort to concentrate on training all the students as nurse aides. Instead, the BIA deemed it more advisable to train the young women for their future roles as wives and mothers, roles that presumed a minimal knowledge of nursing expertise while also presuming they would all become traditional wives and mothers.[55]

Two of the young Navajo women trained at the institutes assisted Molly Reebel: Mary Gould at Nava, and later Ida Nathan at Navajo Mountain. At Nava, Reebel and Gould made specific efforts to reach the people on a personal basis. To interest the women, Reebel requested and received a sewing machine from the Tuba City agency. It helped draw the women to her home, where she could initiate friendships. Many Indians also enjoyed coming to her tent to look at magazines, especially *National Geographic*, whether or not they could read. She was almost always welcomed on her hogan visits; only once or twice did she meet with opposition. That these isolated Indians were receptive to her made work easier and more satisfying.[56]

On the other hand, poor roads, isolation, and bad weather were ongoing problems that made the work difficult. Snowstorms, sandstorms, and sudden rainstorms took a toll on existing roads, making travel hazardous if not impossible. In April 1934, Reebel reported, "Chaco clinic would only be held twice this month, sand making the Chaco Wash impassable." On two night trips that same month, her car became stuck in the sand, and she had to walk to the mother and baby who needed her. In November, in cold, snowy weather, women and children traveled "barefoot in the snow or with their feet tied up in rags." Reebel persisted, and, like Forster, had great compassion for the Navajo, believing that "if only one could persuade these people to take care of themselves and conserve what strength they have, we could save them. Their endurance is remarkable." Her zeal may sound like the rhetoric of others who wanted to "save" the Indians, but the plea made sense, for, at the least, a healthy population could better tolerate epidemics, disease, and other health problems.[57]

In August 1934, Reebel was transferred from Nava to Navajo Mountain, "a wild, beautiful and extremely remote section of the Navajo country about 200 miles from the railroad." Navajo Mountain was eighty-five miles north of Tuba City, Arizona, on a difficult road, "the last thirty miles of which is the worst possible road." The nearest telephone was sixty miles away, the nearest hospital at the Tuba City agency. Despite the remote location, the NMAIA was determined to demonstrate to the BIA that an effective health program could be carried out through their field nursing program.[58]

Reebel's reports, like Forster's, are full of colorful details of her work among the Navajos. But they also reveal economic, social, and cultural aspects of a population far removed from urban areas and modern ways. Shortly after arriving at Navajo Mountain, Reebel wrote to the association describing the timidity of these isolated people compared to other reservation Navajos. The work was, of necessity, slow and some had never been in a trading post. "Practically all of the women and children go barefooted all the while and many of them run and hide if a white person approaches," she reported. Working slowly and patiently, with Ida Nathan to assist her, Reebel gradually gained the trust of the people as they came to depend on her and her "white medicine ways."[59]

Reebel's first six months at Navajo Mountain found her dealing with epidemics of whooping cough, measles, and influenza. December and January were especially difficult months among the forty families of the community. In December, when an outbreak of flu was added to whooping cough and measles, Reebel noted sickness in all the families. She visited thirty different hogans and discovered at least two people sick in each one. When a second wave of measles hit in January, she described the appalling situation:

> We were called one morning to go and see Yellow Salt's family who they reported were all sick. Wish I could adequately describe the situation we found. This family consisting of three wives and thirteen children have just gotten over the worst of whooping cough from which they lost one baby. Then some of them had flu. Now this morning we find them, eleven children and the youngest wife, down with measles. The second wife and Grandmother with tonsilitis, and the Grandfather also suffering from a terrific sore throat—trying to take care of them all—temperatures ranging from 100 degrees to 103½ degrees.
>
> In the adjoining Hogan—the oldest wife with her two oldest children—one with pneumonia and the other with tonsilitis, both very ill. I believe it was the most pitiful thing I have ever encountered.[60]

Calling December and January a nightmare, Reebel reported ten deaths among adults and children—six from measles and four from flu. Dispensary cases for just these two months totaled 258 and hogan calls 126. Because some hogans could not be reached by car, Reebel walked to them. Yet she thought the epidemics brought her into a closer relationship with the Indians than six months of normal health care could have done. As she noted, the medicine men were cooperative and, "in the midst of a sing, have allowed us to take care of the sick." Her Navajo nurse aide was well liked and competent, which facilitated Reebel's efforts. She noted that "the Indians seem to appreciate what we are doing for them. Several have shown this by sending us mutton on several occasions." The NMAIA appreciated her as well, providing funding for a second year in this location. A generous member of the EAIA went a step further and provided Reebel with a "splendid radio which in her isolated location is a joy and comfort to her."[61] Reebel continued at Navajo Mountain until mid-1935 when the BIA, better organized and more adequately funded, took over the field nursing program. When this change occurred, the BIA implemented the plans of Reebel and Forster into the federal health-care structure, arranging for traveling nurses and temporary clinics among the isolated sheep camps.

For more than a decade, the NMAIA had successfully demonstrated the value of field nursing among both the Pueblo people and the Navajos. When the program began in the early 1920s, the Indians' health needs were critical; the death rate exceeded the birth rate. Tuberculosis, trachoma, measles, whooping cough, venereal disease, and chronic malnutrition were common problems. The Indian groups needed immediate and appropriate health care, and clearly, the BIA was not providing those services. The cooperation of the Santa Fe-based volunteer group, the NMAIA, with the BIA, provided a significant service to the Southwest's Native Americans at a crucial time.

More important, cooperation between public and private organizations allowed female health-care reformers to effect change that was later incorporated into BIA policy. By the mid-1930s, nurses who had formerly worked for private agencies such as the NMAIA, or for the Red Cross or other public health agencies, held influential positions with the BIA nursing administration and were able to implement some of the more successful field experiments. In 1936, Albuquerque author Erna Fergusson exclaimed with pride:

> The tales those nurses told! And the things they did! Laundries and bathhouses appeared. Goats were supplied, and babies and mothers taught the uses of a bottle. Windmills came to groan in places where the water was particularly bad. Certain stiffnecked employees were advised to seek other zones of influence.[62]

More specifically, the changes the BIA found constructive included: the mobile dispensaries Reebel and Forster established among the Navajo sheep camps; the introduction of new and healthy foods into Indian diets; Duggan's success at convincing the BIA to build a sanatorium for tubercular children at Zuni and also to provide safe drinking water by digging new and deeper wells; and Stoll's pioneer efforts in introducing laundry and bathing facilities in the pueblos as well as devising a program for training young Indian women as nurse assistants. These improvements reaffirmed the importance of women's efforts in providing much-needed health-care services. Although the nurses who took part in the field nursing experiment fulfilled a traditional female role, they did so under unusual and difficult circumstances, crossing boundaries between cultures as well as between public and private agencies. Concurrently, as we will see in the next chapter, their urban sisters in Albuquerque and Santa Fe were crossing new boundaries in their work as clubwomen.

4

"AND THE DESERT SHALL BLOOM AS A ROSE"

WOMEN AND VOLUNTARISM

In 1911, a group of New Mexico women organized the New Mexico Federation of Women's Clubs, taking the above phrase as their motto. "As the men of the great Southwest have brought smiling orchards and fields of waving grain from the seemingly barren sands of the desert," the women pledged to do their part by cultivating "the flowers of the intellectual, artistic and social life."[1] Actually, they did far more. Given the state's frequent financial shortages, their efforts often made the difference between having or not having a particular service or project. More important, voluntarism met the needs of both the reformers and the dominant political structure, because the female reformers provided services the state needed. In the process, women became political, and politics became "domesticated."[2] This chapter will examine voluntarism as an activity of both black and white middle-class women and explore the roles these women played in the network of social services provided by state and local governments.

Voluntarism among New Mexico women echoed the national pattern, with the added consideration of the state's ethnic groups —blacks, Hispanics, and Native Americans. Yet in New Mexico as well, Anglo women were the providers of services and ethnic minorities the recipients. As agents of change, social reformers helped move women's traditional roles of support, healing, and nurturance into the public sphere.[3] Drawing on their domestic skills, they practiced social housekeeping by setting up libraries, creating institutions for blind, handicapped, and delinquent children, supplying milk for undernourished families and school children, and carrying out myriad other social programs. The needs soon outstripped the limits of voluntarism, however. In historian Mary Beard's words, women learned that to swat effectively "the fly, they must swat its nest" and "that to swat disease, they

The
NEW MEXICO
CLUB WOMAN

New Mexico Federation of
Women's Clubs

YEAR BOOK
1930·1931

18. Cover of the 1930 yearbook of the New Mexico Federation of Women's Clubs.

must swat poor housing, evil labor conditions, ignorance, and vicious interest."[4] Departing from nineteenth-century practice, the municipal housekeepers discovered that they could no longer carry out social programs through voluntary action but had to integrate their efforts with those of governments.[5] New Mexico women experienced this phenomenon firsthand in the 1920s and 1930s.

Clubwomen across the nation were in the vanguard of Progressive reform, one aspect of which was the increased role of government in American lives. In response to their demands, government began to assume some of the functions of the home. That women had much to do with this development stemmed from their roles in determining social policy through voluntary work. They labored to improve the physical environment, to establish trade schools for girls, and to introduce home economics courses. They sponsored sanitary reforms, helped elect women to school boards, and built playgrounds and parks. Although they continued to carry out traditional charity work, the municipal housekeepers found they needed help beyond the local level, causing an increased reliance on government intervention. This was as true in New Mexico as it was in larger and more heavily populated states. And once they reached out beyond volunteer work, they became political.[6]

Like women's clubs elsewhere, those in New Mexico proved to be fertile ground for developing female political skills. As historian Estelle Freedman has pointed out, women's clubs reflected women's emerging political consciousness as well as the limitations of gender-segregated politics.[7] The club movement had dual origins: the negative push of discrimination in the public (male) sphere and the positive attraction of the female world of close, personal relationships. Although women's clubs initially focused on literary and social activities, civic reform programs were common by the turn of the century. As Freedman notes, "These activities served to politicize traditional women by forcing them to define themselves as citizens, not simply as wives and mothers." Female institutions, such as women's clubs, therefore, were often the only places where women could pursue professional or political activities while men's institutions retained power over most of society.[8]

From the beginning, a base of cooperation existed between New Mexico clubwomen and local governments in which the Woman's Club of Santa Fe served as a model for clubs in other counties.[9] Organized in 1892 as a benevolent organization, then called the Woman's Board of Trade, the club initially focused on charity work. Raising money through social events proved to be successful, so the women moved on to other projects. Next came

Year Book

1929

Santa Fe
Woman's Club

Organized October Thirtieth
Nineteen Hundred
Twelve

19. Cover of the 1929 yearbook of the Santa Fe Woman's Club. Courtesy of the Santa Fe Woman's Club.

improvement of the city plaza—planting grass and trees, replacing the forlorn picket fence, and adding graveled paths and benches. The City Council, impressed with the women's efforts, helped defray the cost of plaza improvements and later made an annual appropriation to help pay for its upkeep. The spirit and determination of the Santa Fe club were evidenced in an exchange between one clubwoman and her husband: " 'Why the next thing you [women] will want to do is build a railroad.' 'Yes, if necessary,' " came the reply, with the assurance that women could carry out such a project if required.[10]

Within six years, the club undertook two more major projects, establishing a public library and taking over the care and maintenance of the city cemetery. Once again, funds were raised through teas, suppers, balls, concerts, and other entertainments. It was said that the number of cakes baked and sold in fundraising efforts would more than reach from Santa Fe to Albuquerque, placed side by side.[11]

The library was an especially successful project, one of the few in the country operated by a private organization for public benefit. Starting with 400 books when it opened in 1896, the Santa Fe Public Library had acquired 10,000 books and 2,000 patrons by 1926. In addition, the club established branch libraries in thirty-nine rural districts. The club made a special effort to reach the Hispanic audience, collecting books in Spanish as well as English, though the majority of books were in English. Eventually, the nature of the project made cooperation with city and county governments a must; charity had limits. In time, city and county school boards made regular contributions to the library as a service to school children.[12]

Similarly, clubwomen were instrumental in health and welfare work. In Santa Fe County, they persuaded county commissioners to employ a school nurse to cooperate with the club in holding health clinics. In fact, their work marked one of the earliest health and welfare projects in the state and later contributed to the establishment of the Department of Public Health. From this beginning, club work expanded into other counties, and when the state federation organized in 1911, seventeen clubs became charter members. Four years later, thirty-five clubs flew the federated banner with a total state membership of 1,500.[13]

The records of two women's clubs, in Santa Fe and Albuquerque, demonstrate how the process worked for New Mexico clubwomen. Both clubs provided a wide range of activities, divided into departments, the major ones being child welfare, civic affairs, philanthropy, music, art, and literature. Black women's clubs were similar in organization although they tended to emphasize public welfare issues as part of their felt obligation to help lower-class blacks. Despite a club policy that members would not take a political stand, white women actively wrote and passed resolutions, lobbied at the state legislature, and supported national bills on a variety of social issues.[14] The following examples illustrate the broad range of their activism, of which public welfare issues took precedence. For example, in November 1920, the Albuquerque club agreed to wire Congress urging passage of the Sheppard-Towner Bill; in 1923, President Emily LaBelle sponsored a resolution to restore cuts to the budget for the state Bureau of Public Health; and in February 1925, clubmember Mrs. George Valliant advised members on procedures for addressing the state legislature and urged their presence to endorse a bill to create a House for the Feeble-Minded.

On an issue of importance to women, the equalization of property laws, a delegation of clubwomen attended the 1927 legislature to show their support. In the interest of human welfare, the same group voted in 1924 to write to President Coolidge on behalf of a California convict, Roy Gardner, opposing his punishment of "solitary confinement in a dungeon for 75 years." The club was also asked to use its influence in presenting a petition to the Albuquerque City Commission asking for a restriction on a ten-story building. From federal bills to state and local issues, Albuquerque and Santa Fe women made their views known politically. In adopting such a political stance, they set the stage for future involvement that took them into the male political arena.[15]

Particularly significant was the clubwoman's role in helping to establish institutions for handicapped and delinquent children, which became part of the state social welfare structure. Along with other civic-minded groups, women's clubs lobbied for the Girls' Welfare Home, the Boys' Industrial School, the School for the Blind, the School for the Deaf, and the School for the Feeble-Minded. Clubwomen saw firsthand the need for such services and, taking the initiative, created an atmosphere for legislative action. In 1934, the Santa Fe club passed a resolution requesting that the governor name at least one member of the Woman's Club to the board of directors for each of the above institutions.[16] Carrie Tingley was one clubwoman who, with the support of her husband Clyde—mayor of Albuquerque and later governor of New Mexico—was able to see her dream realized; an orthopedic hospital bearing her name opened in Hot Springs (now Truth or Consequences) in 1937. Likewise, Bertha Nordhaus of Albuquerque spearheaded a drive to create the Girls' Welfare Home, a resource for girls who needed shelter. Clearly, New Mexico women were active politi-

The Woman's Club
of Albuquerque

1934-1935

20. Cover of the 1934 yearbook of the Woman's Club of Albuquerque. Courtesy of the Woman's Club of Albuquerque.

cally on social issues and were determined to be represented in the decision-making process.

Club records indicate that members looked optimistically to the future. Meeting in January 1929, the Woman's Club of Santa Fe featured the topic, "Ultra Modernism in the Home." Several women took part in the program that day, one speaking on women's attainments in industry, business, and professional life. Another contrasted the "self-confident woman of the day with the woman of a generation earlier." And in a thought-provoking presentation, Mrs. Francis C. Wilson predicted "some amazing revelations" for future generations, "when the last vestige of domestic drudgery on farms and homes of moderate means shall be removed by labor saving devices, [and] all women will be free to add their unhampered and best efforts to the world's achievements in the home and outside the home." Despite her optimism, Wilson's words implied a dependency on technology that came with its own drawbacks.[17] Nor did she foresee that, in the decades ahead, middle-class women would join the ranks of working women on a scale far greater than imagined, leaving few women "free" to contribute to world achievements.

This rosy view clearly portended a glowing future for those of "moderate means"—primarily middle-class Anglo women. This class view, however, included an ethnic component in New Mexico. Here, membership rosters overwhelmingly list Anglo surnames; there were few Hispanic members. Clearly, Anglo women initiated and directed many social welfare programs that targeted women and their families of other ethnic groups, particularly Hispanic and Indian. In other words, Anglo women were the "actors" and Hispanic and Indian women primarily the "acted upon," although lower-class Anglo women were also among the recipients.

Class and ethnicity were two important factors in forming the structure and programs of social welfare activities. Generally, middle-class Anglo women were in a position to do things for others outside their homes because they were educated, had access to resources, and had leisure time. This pattern began to take shape in the earliest days of voluntarism and became more apparent throughout the nineteenth and twentieth centuries, culminating in the settlement house movement. These establishments provided an opportunity for middle- to upper-class women and men to provide services to the lower classes, particularly in immigrant neighborhoods in large Eastern and Midwestern cities. Despite the lack of settlement houses in New Mexico, the pattern held, with Anglo women as the "doers."

Hispanic and Indian women differed from Anglo women

when it came to community involvement. Voluntarism in these populations was less formal because it was built into family, community, and even religious structures. Most Hispanic women, for example, tended to focus on their families and the Catholic church rather than community affairs. Anita Gonzales Thomas, descendant of early Spanish settlers in Santa Fe, described a typical situation among Hispanic families there. When queried about voluntarism, Thomas replied, "Most of us are so involved with our own family and cousins and aunts and uncles and grandparents, etc., so [we] don't have much time. And these Anglo women, they come, fall in love with Santa Fe, move here and one way to get to know people is to volunteer to do all these things." Thomas clearly saw Hispanics taking care of one another within the family setting, remarking that families also provided for widows and women who never married.[18]

Many writers examining Hispanic cultural patterns in the United States have commented that Spanish-speaking people as a group are not joiners of voluntary associations. Upon closer inspection, however, the historical record shows that the earliest Hispanics to New Mexico had "joining" habits similar to their contemporaries in Mexico and Europe. The earliest associations were the *cofradías* or *confraternidades* (lay brotherhoods) sponsored by the Catholic church. Women took an active role in these organizations, helping to maintain the church, caring for the statues of saints, and providing aid for church members during times of crisis.[19]

As with any group, Hispanics joined organizations that benefited them most, but patterns of affiliation are apparent based on social class, place of residence, and degree of acculturation. In northern New Mexico villages, voluntarism centered around the church, the nucleus of rural village life, and helped maintain community solidarity. In southern New Mexico, where the major component of the population was from Mexico, religious and community organizations seemed less important than longstanding mutual aid societies; joining organizations there was less common than in the north.[20]

In the church-centered communities, many Hispanic women found an outlet for their energies in the societies and sodalities of the local church. Sodalities, lay organizations within the Catholic church, were of a devotional or charitable nature that provided women and men an opportunity to develop organizational skills. Much as Anglo clubwomen learned parliamentary procedures and organizational techniques in women's clubs, Hispanic women developed similar abilities within church organizations such as the Young Ladies Sodality or the Altar Society. For instance, Thomas served as president of the Young Ladies Sodality in 1936, where she learned parliamentary skills and attended national conventions. These organizations also carried out charity work—providing clothing for the needy and milk for school children—and, in Santa Fe, established a health clinic still in operation. Through church and family, Hispanic women duplicated some of what Anglo women were doing in women's clubs.[21]

Indian women did not engage in volunteer work as their Anglo sisters did because tribal and kinship structures were not conducive to the type of organization this study focuses on. Central to their daily lives was the close connection to the federal government. Primarily, their needs were met through programs the Bureau of Indian Affairs conducted, although such programs were often short-sighted or misdirected. As it was among Hispanic families, immediate needs were usually taken care of within clan and tribal networks, although health care was the exception. Because the Indian Health Service was poorly managed and understaffed, Anglo organizations stepped in to provide doctors, nurses, and supplies to Pueblo and Navajo people on a regular basis.[22]

Voluntarism among middle-class black women in New Mexico more closely followed the pattern of Anglo women. As it did with white women, much of their early work began in the churches and gradually evolved to clubwork. After the Civil War, several factors combined to give rise to a national black women's club movement. First of all, migration from the South swelled urban centers in the North with large numbers of poor who depended on private relief. Eventually, a small number of educated women with leisure time began to form local clubs to meet these urgent social needs. In time, these local clubs, like white women's clubs, began to exchange information and form large federations. In 1896, the first national conference of black women resulted in the formation of the National Association of Colored Women (NACW), which became a unifying force in defense of black womanhood and spurred local and regional organization. By 1914, the NACW represented more than 50,000 black women in twenty-eight state federations and more than 1,000 clubs.[23]

Despite some similarities, however, it does not appear that black women simply imitated white organizations. According to historian Lynda F. Dickson, two important ideas formed the basis of the black club movement: (1) the overwhelming acceptance of the idea of self-help and racial solidarity among black women and (2) the desire to refute the prevailing opinion (held by whites) of black women as sexually promiscuous and lacking the virtues of noble womanhood. The spectacular growth of the black woman's club movement between 1890 and 1925 is linked to these two factors.[24] Black women saw as one of their objectives the opportunity to promote the elevation and advancement of the entire race, while uniting women of different backgrounds and religious persuasions. Unlike white clubwomen, these middle-class, educated black women felt duty-bound to guide "through precept and example" their less fortunate sisters. Where white women sought to uplift "the best women in the interest of the best womanhood," the black movement represented the "effort of the few competent in behalf of the many incompetent."[25] The motto of the NACW, "Lifting As We Climb," illustrates black women's commitment to the elevation of the race as a whole. By directing their energies toward the home, family, and educational activities, clubwomen contributed to the moral uplifting of the race while affirming the virtues of black womanhood.[26] In this way, black clubwomen were like their white counterparts. As Marilyn Dell Brady notes of Kansas clubwomen, they "glorified the home and viewed their role as nurturers as the source of their own importance and power."[27]

Although blacks made up only 1.6 percent of New Mexico's population in the 1920s and 1930s, Albuquerque had a close-knit, caring black community.[28] In one woman's words, "If someone came to town—a stranger—by noon everybody would know where he was from, what his intentions were, and how long he would be here."[29] Like their white counterparts, black women belonged to clubs that founded day nurseries, provided scholarships for black youths, collected clothing for needy families, and carried out other civic and social projects. Three women—Laura Webb, Zenobia McMurry, and Florence Napoleon—were instrumental in organizing clubwork in Albuquerque's black community. Each of these women and their clubs fit Dickson's model of the educated, middle-class woman contributing to the moral uplift of the race and improving home and family life.

Laura Webb was a member of the earliest black women's club in New Mexico, the Home Circle Club. Lula Black, a schoolteacher from Kentucky, organized the Home Circle Club in 1914; Webb joined in 1924, shortly after her marriage. In Webb's words, Black was a "very dignified and proper lady" who sought an outlet for young black married women of the middle class, who, in those days, did not work out of the home. Recalling the club's beginnings, Webb said, "Black felt [that] . . . after you did your housework and all your chores in the morning, then what did you do in the afternoon? She felt you should be occupied in improving your

21. Zenobia McMurry, 1938, one of the founders of the Eureka Matron's Club. Courtesy of Zenobia McMurry.

mind or in some sort of special [activity]."[30] So she brought several young black married women together and formed the Home Circle Club.

From the beginning, the club had an air of exclusivity about it, initially accepting only New Mexico-born young women as members, and never more than twenty (which is still true today). Nor were there chapters in any other New Mexico communities. Webb described the club as a "social binder" with special emphasis on the importance of family, particularly the mother-daughter relationship. Often, she remarked, there were more children present at meetings than members, and one ninety-year-old member still attends with her daughter. This intergenerational dimension was important to black women's clubs, for the older members acted as role models for the younger generation and ensured the survival of women's clubs.[31]

Not content to hold only social events, the members contributed to the community in several ways. They purchased books about blacks for the public library, created a scholarship fund for college students, and generally tried to impress a sense of social responsibility on their members. As fundraisers, they held baby contests, fashion shows, raffles, and craft displays at the state fair, activities much like those of Anglo clubwomen. In many ways, the Home Circle Club provided an outlet for middle-class black women much as the Woman's Club of Albuquerque did for Anglo women.[32]

Two other clubs, the Eureka Matrons and the Winona Art and Study Club, were born in the 1930s when the black community was suffering the effects of the Depression much like the rest of the state. Xenobia McMurry, "just a housewife," and several friends, organized the Eureka Matron's Club in 1934, primarily to carry out social welfare work.[33] Born in Texas in 1909, McMurry eventually married a man from Albuquerque and moved to that city in 1931. Prior to adopting two daughters in 1937 and 1939, she became active in the African Methodist Episcopal Church (AME). Although the church sponsored social welfare work, McMurry and her friends had the time and inclination to do more. The Eureka Matrons provided the outlet.

From their early beginning in Albuquerque, the Eureka Matrons expanded into other New Mexico cities, numbering as many as eight clubs at one time. In its first year, the club became a member of the state Federation of Colored Women's Clubs and in 1936 joined the national organization. McMurry has remained active through the years and served as president of the Southwest Regional District from 1983 to 1987.

Meeting in members' homes twice monthly, the Eureka Matrons planned the requisite social functions—teas, raffles, fashion and talent shows—to raise money for their projects. Since the beginning, the club has contributed to a scholarship fund, sponsoring two students in 1934. The fund now supports as many as ten students a year who receive 250 dollars each. The Eureka Matrons believe in the importance of education for each generation of young black people because, in McMurry's words, "We were urged to go in and take courses in schools where we wouldn't have to be cooks and such in homes. And when our children came on—they didn't want to do those jobs anyway."[34]

Like the Eureka Matrons, the Winona Art and Study Club

22. Unidentified members of the Eureka Matron's Club, Albuquerque, ca. 1940. Courtesy of Zenobia McMurry.

placed high value on education. Florence Napoleon, founding member in 1936, recalled seeking out good students in high school and presenting them and their achievements at a community program. The presentations made the parents aware of the importance of sending their children to school "because we [the clubwomen] felt like whatever they did was a reflection on us as a race, so we wanted them to do the best they could at all times."[35] Since awarding its first sixty-dollar scholarship in 1936, the club has contributed yearly to the state Federation of Colored Women's Clubs to maintain the award program for deserving students.

The Winona Art and Study Club undertook a variety of activities, all directed toward civic and educational goals. In addition to their scholarship program, the early members, numbering twelve, studied black history at evening meetings. They also encouraged artwork and taught one another different forms of arts and crafts.

Selling the results provided funds for their projects and for community welfare drives. As a result, the club was able to establish a day nursery in Albuquerque at 1609 Edith SE, which proved to be a great benefit to working mothers and provided jobs for other women as well.

Florence Napoleon's involvement in clubwork came as a result of leisure time. Napoleon, born in Oklahoma in 1908, came to Albuquerque with her husband and three small children in 1935. She had taught elementary school in Oklahoma but was unable to secure a position in Albuquerque. Lacking a paid job, she turned to volunteer work, which she found to be a unifying factor between Anglo and black women. Despite racial differences, white and black clubwomen found they shared many of the same ideas and desires, including motherhood. As Napoleon described it, "We can all relate to some things in our lives, if nothing [else], as mothers—we can all relate to that."[36]

The club motto, "Let love and goodwill prevail; together we stand, divided we fail," reflects the club attitude not just toward its own race but toward the larger community as well. Occasionally, the Winona Art and Study Club had joint meetings with the Woman's Club of Albuquerque. Overall, the two clubs, and their activities, were more alike than different.

During the Depression years, black and white communities struggled to meet everyday needs. Among blacks, the Depression did not make a drastic change in their lives because, in Zenobia McMurry's words, "We've always lived in a depression, jobwise, so it didn't hurt us as much as the other races."[37] Florence Napoleon echoed her sentiments. "We didn't have so much, so the Depression wasn't such a jolt as it would be to a person who was used to lots of things. . . . We didn't naturally get deprived of something all at once; we didn't have anything to start with. We just survived. . . . It seemed like it was just common in those days."[38] Laura Webb, who lived in California in the 1930s, remarked that the effects of the Depression were felt more keenly there than in New Mexico, an already depressed state prior to the Crash of 1929.

Given depressed conditions, voluntarism was heavily counted on at the local level. Clubwomen of both races responded generously. For example, the Eureka Matrons and the Winona clubwomen frequently held charity drives to collect food and clothing for needy families. The Santa Fe and Albuquerque Woman's Clubs held similar functions. In 1934, Bertha Nordhaus of Albuquerque directed a highly successful clothing drive and distribution project. As part of the project, Nordhaus induced local laundries to donate cleaning services as well. On Mondays, Albuquerque club members met to sew garments for the Red Cross. Gradually, women's clubs throughout the state began to take up and sponsor similar work.[39]

During the early 1930s, when unemployment was at a peak, the Woman's Club of Albuquerque served as the center of women's club social work for the entire state. Under the direction of President Mrs. George Heuser, a depot was established to dispense supplies sent in from districts throughout the state. Club members donated fruit and sugar and prepared hundreds of cans of food and jelly, along with holiday baskets at Christmas and Thanksgiving. Late in 1931, Mayor Clyde Tingley addressed the club, praising the women for their efforts and noting that "the charity organizations of the city were functioning mighty well." Clearly, volunteer organizers played a central role in easing the ache of hunger and want for many.[40]

Club efforts went beyond food and clothing drives, however, sometimes extending to job placement. Although the women's clubs did not run employment bureaus, they frequently helped locate work for individuals. For example, Heuser announced at a meeting in October 1931 that work had been found at the gas company for the father of a family the club had been sponsoring. Sometimes the club was able to place young women as domestic workers. On other occasions, a needy person was briefly allowed the use of a room in the basement of the clubhouse. When people needed help, clubwomen responded.[41]

In Santa Fe, similar events occurred. In 1934, the club reported they had "secured work for a great number of men and girls." (Just what those positions were is not clear, however.) In another instance, the club contributed twelve dollars a month for five months to care for a baby while the mother worked to support herself and five children. Clubwomen touched many people's lives during the Depression, but given the extent of the hardship, voluntarism fell short of solving the state's most severe Depression-era problems.

Clubwomen did not limit their efforts to local people but helped meet the problem of transients as well. In Santa Fe, city officials and local clubwomen instituted a novel solution: They lodged the travelers overnight in the city jail. The woman's club, through contributions, helped provide "clean and commodious quarters and wholesome food." In addition, laundry and bathing facilities allowed the transients, predominantly male, a comfortable place to freshen up before "moving on." In 1938, 400 transients availed themselves of the quarters, prompting the city to laud the women's club for their efforts and support.[42] In truth, the women provided a tidy solution to what could have become a bothersome problem for city officials.

In 1934, yet another group of women came together and formed a woman's club. Open to women under the age of thirty, the Junior Club of Albuquerque affiliated with the New Mexico Federation of Women's Clubs but remained a separate unit. Modeled after the national Junior League for the Promotion of Settlement Houses, created in 1901, the Albuquerque club focused on women, children, and the needy. A minimum of eight hours of volunteer work a month was required of members, with a penalty assessed if the requirement was not met. This provision suggested a determined effort to maintain the image and intent of a volunteer organization, not merely a social club.[43]

During the Depression, the club created a Bureau of Charities with a range of activities not unlike the Woman's Club. They distributed clothing to the needy, bought eyeglasses for those who could not afford them, provided medical treatment for Hispanic women, and helped maintain cabins for Albuquerque's poor by providing furniture, curtains, and paint. Junior Club members also volunteered time at prenatal and well-baby clinics, school health clinics, and the Francis Lynn Home for Unwed Mothers, and supported a venereal disease clinic. In 1936, the efforts of these young women earned them a certificate of honor from the General Federation of Woman's Clubs for their outstanding public welfare work in New Mexico.[44]

Another important example of voluntarism was the effort of several women in establishing the Maternal Health Center in Santa Fe in 1937. Concern over Santa Fe County's high infant mortality rate—fifth highest in the nation—prompted Faith Meem, Peach Mayer, Mary Schmidt, Florence Davenport, and Mary Goodwin to open a free clinic for underprivileged women and children in October of that year. The health center risked controversy, however, when it opened its doors in a predominantly Catholic community with funds obtained from a national birth control foundation. Through Mary Goodwin's friendship with Margaret Sanger, the clinic had obtained a grant from the Clinical Research Bureau of New York (the Sanger Foundation) to open the center. The founders' intent was to provide general health services for women and children, of which contraceptive information would be only one of the services offered. Well aware of the political/religious attitudes of the community toward birth control, they avoided singling out contraception as a primary service of the center. Nonetheless, the Catholic Church waged a vociferous campaign against the clinic in its first year.[45]

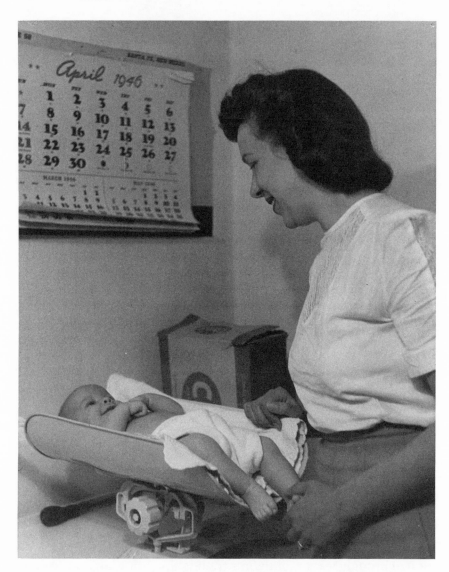

23. A nurse weighing in a happy baby at the Santa Fe Maternal Health Center. Courtesy Special Collections, Zimmerman General Library, University of New Mexico.

Speaking from the pulpit, Archbishop Rudolph A. Gerken denounced the center, calling it "in reality a birth control clinic," and urged Catholics to refrain from attending a charity event, the Gold Rush Ball, for the benefit of the center.[46] Gerken's condemnation "had the opposite result of awakening many good church people to the need for some birth control if the ghastly situation was to be remedied." Noted the center's historian, "Now many among his flock have become ardent contributors and some patients." Once community leaders realized the value of the center, recognizing that "this was an urgent case of charity beginning at home," the controversy subsided and the clinic became an indispensable part of the network of social services available in Santa Fe.[47]

Although the founders' initial intent was to offer birth control information for those who desired it, providing general health-care services took priority. Soon the clinic expanded to include prenatal, postnatal, and infant care classes, a unique home visitation and follow-up service, temporary and emergency medical care, nursing consultation at all times, and a variety of social services not readily available elsewhere in the city or county. With the exception of the salary of nursing director Marjorie Stoll, R.N., the clinic depended on, and received, volunteer help and contributions. For example, Santa Fe obstetrician/gynecologist Nancy Campbell frequently offered to deliver babies free if the center would cover hospital costs.[48] Board members, physicians, nurses, and local citizens donated time and services to create a valuable community asset that continues in operation today.[49]

Faith Meem, active in the center from its inception until 1975, described those early days of the clinic's operation. "We started in a tiny little room—12 feet by 12 feet—on West de Vargas Street and held clinic one day a week. In the beginning stages, the poor women were terrified and some of them didn't hardly dare come to the clinic; I don't know why not. But Mrs. Stoll spoke Spanish and that helped. Word of mouth helped also."[50] Another participant, Anita Thomas, recalled the need for the clinic:

> In those days, in the summer, there were so many babies that died
> [of diarrhea] and I think it was mostly because we didn't have indoor
> plumbing and there were so many flies and everything like that. And
> so many of the Spanish women couldn't afford to take the baby to the
> doctor. There was no way to get any kind of help. So they used all the
> [home] remedies they knew of.[51]

Attendance at the clinic during the first month was no more than four or five, since the center had opened without public announcement. But as the word spread among the underprivileged, attendance gradually increased, reaching thirty or more on Sunday afternoons. At first, Santa Fe physicians were reluctant to volunteer at the clinic for fear of losing their medical privileges at the only local hospital, which was Catholic. The board found a willing and dedicated doctor in the person of Evelyn Fisher Frisbie of Albuquerque to come to the tiny clinic on her one free day a week, Sunday.[52]

Frisbie, a Midwesterner who came to New Mexico in 1908, was one of New Mexico's pioneer women physicians. Trained in Chicago, she, like other women of the time and the profession, decided to specialize in the care of women and children. Setting up practice in Wagon Mound, southwest of Las Vegas, she became a horse-and-buggy doctor, administering to the needs of ranching communities within a twenty-five-mile radius. In 1911, Frisbie moved to Albuquerque and soon became active in the New Mexico Medical Society, serving as president in 1915, the first and, to date, only woman to do so.[53]

In addition to her thriving obstetric/gynecology practice (she delivered thousands of babies), Frisbie established and maintained her own small maternity hospital in downtown Albuquerque and was active in public health work. In the 1920s and 1930s, she worked with the medical missionaries of the Congregational Church of Albuquerque in western New Mexico. Twice a month, she held clinic (without running water) in Cubero, then in Grants, to provide medical service to the people in this isolated area. Frisbie's interest and commitment to social problems made her a likely choice when the Maternal Health Center needed a physician in 1937.

Former nursing director Marjorie Stoll warmly extolled Frisbie's value to the center in a message to the Maternal Health Center on the occasion of its twenty-fifth anniversary in 1962. Stoll appreciatively recalled those Sunday afternoon sessions when Frisbie drove up from Albuquerque on her free day, "holding clinic until the last patient had been seen, sometimes after eight at night."[54] Frisbie's enthusiasm and dedication to the task was especially valuable in the early months of the clinic's existence.

Six months after the clinic's inception, however, the Sanger Foundation withdrew its support on the grounds that not enough birth control work was being done, threatening the existence of the new institution. Not totally unexpected, the action prompted the founders to seek funds from other sources. Consequently, a finance committee composed of nine well-known Santa Fe women instituted a pledge card drive and successfully solicited enough pledges to keep the clinic going another year. To ensure the center's existence, the women held various fundraisers as well, to which local citizens responded enthusiastically. Artists within the Santa Fe community vied with each other to volunteer their services; there were dances, costume balls, concerts, luncheons, and teas. Moreover, an annual rummage sale became so successful it evolved into a permanent thrift shop by 1947. All in all, voluntary contributions supported the center. Peach Mayer, founding member, noted years later, "We never asked for nor received any public funds—federal, state, or county—but paid our bills from generous contributions and the rummage sales!" It helped that local publicity kept the center's purpose before the public. "A dollar a month," read one editorial, "from 300 Santa Fe people will keep the work going and will support the Maternal Health Center, upon which hundreds of poverty-stricken people are now dependent." Santa Feans answered the plea generously.[55]

From the beginning, the Maternal Health Center sought to cooperate with other state and local organizations and to avoid, as much as possible, duplication of services. If the center could not handle a particular case, it was referred to another source. Among clinic reports are frequent references to other agencies the center drew upon, such as the Catholic Maternity Institute, the Red Cross, and state welfare agencies. For example, in one month in 1939, nine patients were referred to the Proctor Eye Clinic, five to the Catholic Clinic, seven to the Public Health nurse; two were given help through the Household Aid Service; two were referred to dentists and four to physicians.[56] This cooperative spirit was a key ingredient in the center's success.

One of the center's most valuable services was the practice of home visits, including follow-up calls. Home visits were especially important in the early months when women sought birth control information but feared attending the center because of the church's stand against contraception.[57] When a pregnant woman visited the clinic for the first time, she was given a complete physical examination, including a Wasserman test for venereal disease. Shortly thereafter, the nurse made a home call, and where conditions were poor, as they often were, steps were taken to improve the situation. For example, the clinic supplied milk, juice, eggs, and fresh vegetables for proper nourishment, as well as linens and baby clothes. At the end of the first year, October 1938, the center listed 577 patients enrolled as prenatal cases. In addition, Wasserman tests were given to 450 adult patients and treatment was arranged for the 78 positive cases. Contraceptive advice was given

24. Mary Lennard, Red Cross nurse, making a home call for the Taos County Cooperative Health Association, 1943. Photo by John Collier, Library of Congress, USW3-18065.

to 105 women and free medicine to 320 patients. The staff and board members were hopeful that this positive beginning would encourage others to support the center.[58]

Most important were the postnatal visits the clinic nurse made to the new mother. At this visit, the nurse taught the mother how to care for the new baby and provided some stability until the mother was able to manage by herself. The nurses provided other services as well, such as dispensing numerous bolts of mosquito netting; teaching mothers how to make formula when nursing would not suffice; distributing hundreds of cans of milk; and helping young mothers-to-be prepare for midwife home deliveries. If they would bake newspapers and a potato in the oven until the potato was soft, explained Stoll, the papers would be sterile and could then be placed in covers made from old sheets, producing a tidy, sterile pad. Stoll and her volunteer help at the clinic also made tiny bassinettes from cardboard cartons—once filled with cans of tomatoes—neatly lined and covered with quilted pads, "so the new baby would have a private, clean little bed of his own, in homes where many slept on the floor and nobody had privacy." [59]

The early home visits quickly pointed up the need for services other than health care. Many families lacked proper food and decent clothing and usually could not afford needed medicines, so the Social Services committee was formed to help meet some of these urgencies. The proceeds from the second annual Gold Rush Ball, in 1938, went to this committee to help improve health and living conditions of the needy persons who came to the clinic.

Stoll and members of the committee tried to give assistance along every line possible, "from procuring jobs through relief agencies for penniless fathers out of work, to providing milk, cereal, fruit, cod liver oil, layettes, and preventable disease innoculations for babies." [60] In some cases, children were kept at home because they had no clothes to wear to school, so the committee supplied secondhand shoes and clothing, allowing children to return to the classroom. In 1939, the Social Service Committee provided relief of some kind to forty-four families, ranging from supplies of diapers and milk to recommending unemployed men for WPA employment. [61]

Florence Davenport, president of the center in 1939, reported that in addition to medical problems, hardly any of the center's clients had enough food or clothing or "the wherewithal to preserve the decencies of living." As Davenport noted, "overcrowding, poor sanitation, too many, and too frequent children combined to make the mothers and the children vulnerable to all the ills that flesh is heir to." [62] By combining social welfare work with medical care, the Maternal Health Center provided a major service to Santa Fe's needy poor.

Board members and nursing director Marjorie Stoll applied steady pressure to keep the center and its services before the public. Stoll urged informed and active participation through city and state legislative channels. In a speech on the future of the center, Stoll noted that too many bills important to the city's health and welfare were defeated or vetoed in 1938. Noting the prevalence of diarrhea among children in the summer, Stoll urged city officials to secure a proper sewage disposal system that would benefit the entire city. She also spoke of improving housing conditions and of the necessity for educating parents in such subjects as hygiene and child care.[63]

The reform issues Stoll spoke to increased in urgency in the 1930s along with Santa Fe's population. Over the decade, Santa Fe grew from 11,176 to 20,325. In the same period, an editorial in the *New Mexican* pointed out that the number of impoverished families increased in far greater proportion because the changing economy removed many traditional sources of livelihood. While New Deal work projects helped many on relief rolls, the WPA reduced allotments for Santa Fe County by the end of the decade. In the spring of 1940, requests for help at the center, which usually declined after the winter months, had not diminished but increased. Files at the center listed names of hundreds of people, "hungry, ragged and a prey to disease." Social welfare issues were a never-ending problem, and while clubwomen were unable to eradicate need and want, their efforts bolstered the existing welfare system in ways not previously available.[64]

Looking back on the first twenty-five years of the center's existence, Peach Mayer lauded the determination and hard work of the women who had first conceived the idea for the clinic. She might have included Bertha Nordhaus, Laura Webb, Florence Napoleon, Zenobia McMurry, Marjorie Stoll, Evelyn Frisbie, and all the other women volunteers active in those two decades. The organizations that these women created or joined provided a training ground for developing professional and political talents that took women beyond the circumference of the private sphere and contributed to their politicization as well as to the "domestication of politics." Applying social housekeeping skills on a wider scale, New Mexico women did more than make the desert bloom—they altered the social landscape itself.

5

"I DO NOT KNOW WHAT WE WOULD DO WITHOUT IT"

RURAL WOMEN AND THE AGRICULTURAL EXTENSION SERVICE

While their sisters were busy in the urban areas of New Mexico, women in the countryside were carrying out projects best suited to rural needs. In 1925, Edna H. Durand, Curry County extension agent, set forth in her annual report the major obstacle facing home extension agents in depression- and drought-plagued New Mexico:

> The big problem in the frontier home is not one that can be solved by education—there are plenty of college-trained women in these prairie shacks, but she must pay the price of pioneering and do much on very little. The mission of the extension worker is helping her make that little do as much as possible—perhaps just a little more than either of them thought possible—that is achievement.[1]

For rural women, the presence of a county home demonstration agent to help them stretch their resources meant better homes and farms, healthier families, and a reduction in the isolation attached to farm life. For the extension agents, however, conditions of poverty, extreme isolation, and ethnic diversity provided a challenge that forced them to discard rigid ethnic and gender guidelines and adapt their work, as well as their attitudes, to local situations. Both points of view—that of the extension agents and of those receiving their services—were a function of the formal structure of the Agricultural Extension Service (AES): male-dominated and divided administratively between federal, state, and county governments. At times, these separate points of view meshed and at times they diverged. Demographic conditions particular to New Mexico as well as outside forces played a role in how extension service goals were met.

Grim economic conditions affected New Mexico farm women, as they did rural women elsewhere in the 1920s and 1930s. Flanked

25. A daily chore for women and children: filling buckets and tubs from the village water source. Courtesy of State Records Center and Archives, Health and Social Services Division, no. 9951.

on each end by a world war, these decades were ones of economic depression and change for American families. The adjustment to changing world and domestic markets after World War I, combined with a postwar depression and one of the worst droughts in the history of the Southwest, left New Mexico farm families hardpressed to stay on the farm. As noted earlier, despite the 1920 Census Bureau report that, for the first time, more people nationwide lived in urban than rural areas, New Mexico remained heavily rural at 82 percent. These rural families became the targets of numerous federal and state agencies, expanded or established to deal with the depression and drought. Especially significant were benefits derived from the AES, particularly when female extension agents—the home demonstration agents—were present to initiate programs.[2]

In 1920, the rural population of the state numbered 295,390. Farm women (females over twenty-one) accounted for 75,237 of this total, the majority of whom were Hispanic women concentrated at opposite ends of the state—in the mountainous northern counties and in the southernmost counties. A few black women, less than 1 percent of the female population, lived either in Albuquerque or in southern and southeastern counties. Native American women, 7 percent of the farm women population, were concentrated in the northwest area of the state and in the pueblos along the northern Rio Grande. Rural Anglo women lived on farms and ranches in the eastern and central plains and the southwestern region, where homesteading reached a peak between 1916 and 1923. Overall, the typical rural woman in 1920 was Hispanic and lived on a farm of fifty acres or less, but this picture changed as more Anglo homesteaders arrived in the 1920s and 1930s.[3]

Anglo homesteaders arrived in three waves, gradually taking over traditional grazing lands Hispanics and Native Americans had occupied for generations.[4] Arid conditions, however, worsened by drought, forced many homesteaders to sell to large ranchers who continued to buy old Mexican land grants as well as new land in the state. This process altered the economic pattern of many Hispanic families, forcing men to look for day labor while leaving the subsistence farms in care of the women.[5] As their mothers and grandmothers had done before them, women cared for the livestock, irrigated the holdings, planted vegetable gardens, and cared for the children. When the AES began in New Mexico in 1914, agents found families practicing agriculture in simple, and often crude, ways. To many minds, conditions were ripe for change.

The Agricultural Extension System, created in 1914 under the provisions of the Smith-Lever Act, was a Progressive reform movement designed to improve and enhance the lives of America's three million farmers and farm homes.[6] Fueling this "Country Life" movement was the idea that rural depopulation was unhealthy and that better living conditions for farmers could stem the flow of population from farms to cities.[7] Typical of Progressive thought, the Smith-Lever Act hoped to raise the standard of living of rural dwellers, improve the image of rural life, and promote the educational and spiritual lives of rural people. By making the country more like the city, reformers—primarily white Protestant professional groups dedicated to an orderly transition to industrial capitalism—hoped to stem the migration to the cities while endowing farm families with the fruits of technology that made urban areas appear so desirable.[8]

Reacting to a backlash that pictured rural farm life as one of hard work and drudgery, and especially so for farm women, the U.S. Department of Agriculture surveyed "key" farm women in every section of the country in 1921 attempting to counter this harsh assessment. Couched in the women's own words and

26. Hanging clothes on the line in the northern New Mexico village of El Cerrito, 1940. Photo by Irving Rusinow, Library of Congress, neg. no. 37837.

backed by a "hundred echoes," the survey revealed "a chorus of praise, an anthem of joy, set to optimistic strains, telling anew the true and glorious meaning of life upon the soil." By connecting the role of farm women to the Pilgrim mothers and later pioneer women, the author of the final report declared that the rural woman had been the stabilizer in rural community life—courageous social pioneer as well as resourceful agricultural frontierswoman—who "delighted in finding ways and means by which to make her surroundings yield up to her and her family the best things of life." Shouldering the burden of responsibility for keeping America strong, the women declared, "As goes the rural home in these United States, so goes the nation, and not otherwise." To the USDA's gratification, the survey was able to confirm the belief that "farm women on the whole are more contented than the people at large think they are."[9]

The Country Life movement failed, however, to keep people "down on the farm," not because farm life could not be made more appealing through modernization, but because the movement's supporters failed to recognize the strong pull of the industrialization process. Embedded in this early twentieth-century reform movement were two goals that ultimately proved contradictory— "to preserve traditional agrarian ideals in the face of industrialism and to adapt agriculture to the modern age." While agents sought to make the farm wife more self-sufficient, the husband was encouraged to become more dependent on commercial agriculture. In time, many women left the farm to take jobs in town in order to contribute economically to the family farm.[10]

White middle-class standards and concepts formed the basic structure for extension work for both men and women. The assumption was that every rural home would come up to the standards AES deemed appropriate. Economic difficulties, however, slowed extension work in many New Mexico counties, especially in heavily Hispanic areas. Measuring by white middle-class standards, some agents saw little progress, but their expectations reflected their own values as well as economic problems. The work moved more quickly among Anglo communities, but standards were still unreachable or impractical for some. At the heart of the problem was the fact that the AES was "selling" middle-class capitalism. Could the New Mexico recipients afford it, Anglo or otherwise? In many cases, the answer was no.

Generally, the AES attempted to set standards within reach of most Americans. When extension home economist Mary Rohakr of Washington, D.C., came to a planning conference at New Mexico State College in 1930, she brought with her a clear program for Western homes. She wrote:

> Standards should be determined from an economic viewpoint—location, type of farm, and income of the farm home. Standards should be set by families themselves. In some communities, it may mean screens for the windows and doors to protect the family from flies and other insects, while in other communities, it may mean a modern home with all up-to-date conveniences.[11]

27. Washing wool in the irrigation ditch, or *acequia*, prior to dying it. Chamisal, New Mexico, 1940. Photo by Russell Lee, Library of Congress, USF33-12815-M3.

This prescription, while reasonable, remained a challenge for New Mexico extension workers throughout the 1920s and 1930s while the AES continued to model its programs on standards of home-making for middle America. Generally, these standards were relative to the expectations of those setting them and to the laborsaving devices available at the time.[12] More precisely, they reflected the goal of Progressive reformers who saw scientific housekeeping as a way to raise the status of homemaking.[13]

As the name suggests, extension work was an extension of the expertise of the United States Department of Agriculture through the land grant colleges and universities to county agents, then through these agents to local leaders who disseminated the information to all local farm families. At the core of the AES structure was the county agricultural agent (male) and the home demonstration agent (female). Men far outnumbered women nationwide from the beginning (3,879 agricultural agents and 1,960 home demonstration agents in 1939). In addition, a separate corps of agents worked with blacks in the South.[14] Programs were carried out strictly along gender lines; men were to develop programs for men while women created programs for women. There was no doubt that the programs were to promote traditional kinds of work for both sexes: farming and outdoor tasks for men, housekeeping and childcare for women. Despite the reality that women performed whatever tasks necessary, the structure of extension work did not reflect the true division of labor on most farms. From its inception in 1914, AES work was divided in a manner that reflected an urban middle-class ideal. Regarding the importance of learning home canning skills, for example, one agent remarked: "So many young wives who have been teachers, stenographers, etc., must learn to can after they are married to ranchers, farmers . . . so they turn to the Extension Service home demonstration agent to teach them the gentle art of homemaking." [15]

Adherence to such strict gender prescriptions frequently hampered extension work. For example, many counties lacked home demonstration agents, so unless the agricultural agents took over some of the functions of female agents, such as assisting with canning programs and helping women plan home gardens, the work went undone. When extension work began on Indian reservations in the early 1930s, male workers "fit themselves into the picture" and conducted canning and drying demonstrations and generally tried to encourage food preservation. [16] Agents soon learned that they could be more effective when they moved away from rigid "gender rules" and adapted their programs to local conditions. In these cases, when the agents diverged from the formal structure, they were able to increase the effectiveness of their work among farm families though the programs themselves remained gender biased. Poultry-raising, for example, was promoted explicitly as a male activity, although on most farms women were in charge of flocks. [17]

Headquarters for state extension work was the Agricultural College at Las Cruces. When the program was established, the home demonstration staff consisted of only one woman, Dora Ross. During World War I, however, twelve women were trained in food preparation and assigned around the state to help families conserve food as part of the war effort. [18] This number quickly dropped to four at the close of the war and fluctuated between two and four during the 1920s. Between 1929 and 1937, eight to sixteen women served; it peaked at twenty agents between 1938 and 1940. Clearly, AES work for women was inconsistent in the 1920s and 1930s, so when providers were unavailable, recipients went without services. [19]

Once a home demonstration agent was assigned to a county, she assembled a group of farm women in a community and discussed their needs and wishes for extension work. She also secured the assistance of a key woman in each community willing to serve as a local leader. To receive instruction, several interested women might attend a day-long meeting with the home demonstration agent, returning to their communities to pass on the information they learned to other groups of women. In this way, extension work was spread among rural women, and women's extension clubs were established throughout the county. Eventually, a county advisory council was formed that assumed the responsibility of planning county-wide programs. This method of organization seemed to be especially effective in New Mexico, where many counties did not have home demonstration agents. In these cases, the state director from Las Cruces, as well as other agents, could travel to various counties setting up programs and then return control of the programs to local leaders.[20]

Crossing the gender line sometimes occurred in counties or on the reservations where there were no home demonstration agents. In these areas, the agricultural extension agent took over the functions of female agents. Men often assisted with the canning program and helped farm women plan home gardens. Santa Fe county agent Juan Ramirez, for instance, handled canning demonstrations but did not feel competent to carry out clothing instruction. In these cases, men made arrangements for the meetings and handled the publicity, while home demonstration agents from the state college were brought in to make presentations. In areas where women's extension clubs were already organized, men continued to plan the yearly programs. When the home demonstration agent was unable to be present, male agents in Colfax, Eddy, Luna, and Sierra counties gave instruction on how to cure meat and prepare it for canning. As a whole, the agricultural extension agents had a favorable attitude toward home economics work, which made cooperation smoother between male and female leaders.[21] Crossing the gender line proved to be a one-way avenue, however, since no women were employed to teach farming methods or soil conservation. Still, the ability to be flexible within gender-prescribed AES guidelines was important, because it increased the success rate of extension work among women.

Emphasis on scientific methods, including domestic science (home economics), was a major feature of Progressive-era reform. Extension work was based on the premise that educated, middle-class men and women could achieve acceptance and cooperation from rural people by virtue of their knowledge and expertise, which they provided through demonstration—learning by doing—rather than lectures and books. The agents, both male and female, were college-trained in agriculture and home economics, and if they had grown up on a farm, that was considered an advantage. It was generally accepted that an extension worker should not be a resident of his or her home county, for the AES feared the agent might give too much attention to friends and relatives.[22] Instead, an "outsider" could command greater respect and cooperation.

This policy had its drawbacks in New Mexico, especially in areas where Hispanics predominated. If the agent did not speak Spanish, extension work could flounder. For example, in a study of two counties, Doña Ana and Santa Fe, historian Joan Jensen found that when Anglo agents carried out extension work strictly along ethnic and gender lines, they were generally unsuccessful (Doña Ana County), yet when Hispanic agents deemphasized or ignored ethnic and gender differences, they garnered support and approval (Santa Fe County).[23] The work of Fabiola Cabeza de Baca Gilbert, home demonstration agent in Santa Fe and Rio Arriba Counties from 1929 to 1940, is a clear example of such success. From the beginning, Gilbert recognized a potential field for the extension worker who understood the language, social customs, and food habits of the Hispanic culture. Within five years, she noted great success in diet and food preparation among Hispanic farm families.[24] But Gilbert was also able to work successfully with Anglo groups and in organizing children's clubs. Ignoring gender segregation that was common within extension work, she encouraged girls to expand beyond the traditional food and clothing projects and join boys in agricultural clubs. Her success as a Hispanic agent working with Hispanic and Anglo people demonstrated what could be done when rules were made more flexible. Yet Hispanic agents working with Hispanic people was only one small part of New Mexico extension work.

At best, extension work among ethnic groups was uneven between 1920 and 1940. When the AES first began in the 1910s, agents attempted to reach Hispanic women, especially during 1917–18. After the war, however, the program was drastically curtailed and confined primarily to Anglo women, until the 1930s when agriculture became a major focus of New Deal policy.[25] Annual reports during the 1920s made little mention of reaching Hispanic or Mexican and "native" women unless it was to say they were "difficult" to reach. Just how they were difficult to reach is unclear, although geography and language frequently restricted AES work. By the 1930s, when New Deal funding was more readily available, the

28. Mrs. Faro Caudill of Pie Town in west central New Mexico, admiring the canned goods in her storage cellar. Photo by Russell Lee. Library of Congress, USF36-36551.

annual reports reflected more positive results. One county agent
submitted the following response to an agency questionaire regarding the success of extension work in 1935.

> In this town, the majority of the people are Mexican with families of
> six to even ten children. The mothers are awkward in the caring for
> babies, the right foods for the older ones, the cleanliness of the homes,
> etc. This is where the Extension agent has done us so much good. She
> has barely been with us six months and in spite of this short time,
> I have noticed quite a change, especially with the young women and
> girls, but I do think that if our home agent continues her work among
> us, our people will show great improvement.[26]

Despite the agent's praise for extension work in this community, assumptions of cultural superiority are clear in her remarks.
Mexican mothers were seen as "awkward" (unsure of themselves?)
in caring for their babies; their housekeeping methods were suspect; and they clearly did not know how to provide proper nutrition for their growing families. But when the agents targeted
the younger generation, they generally found a ready acceptance
of their ideas that, no doubt, were transmitted to the mothers
and perhaps some grandmothers. Crossing the cultural boundary
proved to be one of the greatest challenges facing the extension
agents in New Mexico.

Language was part of that challenge. In 1920, nearly one-half
the state's population, 48.5 percent, was unable to speak English.
Women accounted for 56.3 percent of this figure, meaning that
the majority of rural women spoke only Spanish. Officials quickly
realized the necessity of procuring bilingual female agents in New
Mexico, but finding properly trained women proved difficult. Few
rural people had the education or the economic and social support to achieve the necessary training. After World War I, numerous agricultural agents (males) who could speak Spanish were
hired in predominantly Hispanic counties. Only three Spanish-
speaking women, however, were hired as home demonstration
agents: Gertrude Espinosa in Santa Fe County, Adelina Jaramillo
in San Miguel County, and Sarah Van Vleck in Doña Ana County.[27]
Espinosa promptly began translating extension bulletins on cooking, sewing, and poultry-raising into Spanish and organizing informal canning demonstrations in Hispanic homes. But the efforts
of these women fell short as postwar funds declined, and the
agents left AES work and were not regularly replaced. During the
1920s, then, Anglo reformers failed to reach the female Hispanic
majority.[28]

Language—although not Spanish—also proved to be a problem for the agent in McKinley County. There, many families in the Zuni Mountain area around Ramah were German, Russian, and Polish. Even though many women did not speak English well, if at all, the agent managed to make those that did aware of the projects. The language barrier apparently did not dampen their enthusiasm for extension work and the companionship it provided, for one woman walked five miles carrying a two-year-old child in order to attend a meeting.[29]

Other cultural differences also posed special problems. Hispanic families were often suspicious of Anglo agents with new ideas because of past historical experiences; in general, they did not trust outsiders. They also were cautious about purchasing new tools or equipment the agents promoted, waiting until an idea proved successful before making an investment.[30] Likewise, Hispanics were wary of extension activities for children. Where Anglo children learned about home and farm projects (4-H) at school or in community settings and took the ideas home to their parents, Hispanic youth had to have parental approval in the beginning. Espinosa, Jaramillo, and Gilbert were successful in organizing children because they made a point to first explain the work to parents. Despite the efforts of these three agents, cultural differences tended to slow AES work among rural Hispanic families.

For other cultural groups, the record is unclear. Little extension work appears to have been done among the few blacks in New Mexico, for example. AES records mention clubs for "colored girls" infrequently, noting a club for Negro girls at Vado in Doña Ana County and a sewing club at Lewis Flats in neighboring Luna County.[31] "Mixed" clubs were not organized. In the American South, however, AES met with success when black women with home economics training were hired to assist white home demonstration agents. In forty-two counties in North Carolina, the assistants traveled about the county to show the black housewife how to garden, can, and preserve food. In addition, the extension service enlisted the cooperation of black preachers to influence their congregations in the conservation and production of food. One county agent reported an enthusiastic minister who canned surplus produce from his home garden and became a member of the local canning club. In addition to organized canning and cooking clubs, these agents and their assistants organized laundry clubs, a reflection of one of the traditional forms of paid labor for black women. Given the small number of blacks in New Mexico, however, hiring black assistants was apparently not considered economically feasible.[32]

Not until the 1930s did extension work regularly reach into

29. A 4-H club member in her garden, Zuni, New Mexico. Courtesy of the National Archives, Record Group 75.

the reservations or pueblos, although projects for Indian youth began in the early 1920s when Bernalillo County home demonstration agent, Maud Doty, organized a chile club for girls and a corn club for boys at San Felipe Pueblo. The girls' club was an experiment—to see if they could farm as well as the boys—and it caused the boys to "keep an eye on the girls' work" and "to have their corn clear of weeds and in as good a condition as the girls' plot." Clubs at Jemez and Isleta followed more traditional gender lines— a sewing club and a cooking club, both for girls.[33] At Paguate (near Laguna Pueblo), the field matron, Donna Gordon, wrote Valencia County agent R. S. Conroy requesting pamphlets and circulars on organizing boys' and girls' clubs. In response, Conroy advised it was too late in the season to plant a garden but suggested she begin a girls' millinery club for fall and a crops club the following spring. Conroy's proposal for hatmaking by Indian women and girls demonstrated the cultural blinders of some AES officials.[34]

In 1929, the Indian Extension Service, headed by A. C. Cooley, was established in an attempt to reach Indian families across the nation. It was slow to develop in New Mexico. A survey of needs at the Northern Pueblos Agency showed "wonderful opportunities"

30. Indian girls preparing vegetables for canning, Cochiti Pueblo. Courtesy of the National Archives, Record Group 75.

for both a full-time agricultural agent and a home demonstration agent. When Henrietta Burton, supervisor of Home Demonstration Work, toured the nine northern pueblos in 1931, she came away convinced that the Indians could benefit greatly from extension projects that taught "thrift in the use of time and money," poultry-raising, furniture-making, and the promotion of 4-H club work. Yet by 1935, just 13 percent of Indian girls and 9 percent of the boys were enrolled in 4-H clubs.[35]

Reformers' goals often showed an insensitivity to cultural differences. For example, during her five-day tour, Burton saw possibilities for home extension work that ranged from doing child welfare work to teaching money management to improving home gardens and poultry flocks. She was most enthusiastic, however, about promoting opportunities for increasing the financial income of Indian homemakers. Impressed with the pottery-making abilities of many Indian women, especially Maria Martinez of San Ildefonso Pueblo, Burton went on to question their methods, asking, "Should these primitive methods be encouraged, or should modern methods be taught and modern equipment provided?" Burton was apparently unaware, or unappreciative, of the centuries-old method of pottery-making which requires many hand polishings

31. Navajo women and children outside their hogan, deemed "good" in the Agricultural Extension Work Annual Report for December 1933. Note that the traditional structure, here made of logs rather than earth, has a snug-fitting door, a window with glass panes, and is tightly chinked against dust and drafts. Courtesy of the National Archives, Record Group 75.

and several firings over an outdoor fire to produce the beautiful pottery so much admired today. Convinced, too, that the pueblo could benefit from the presence of extension workers who could help Native American women become small capitalists, Burton's ethnocentrism devalued an important aspect of Indian culture.[36]

A reading of extension club goals for 1934 fails to reflect the realities of Indian women's lives. The language of the memorandum is white middle-class America; the goals are attempts "to bring out higher ideals of homelife." Among the plans for the production and preservation of food and ways to stimulate interest in gardening, dairying, and poultry-raising are suggestions for "Improving Treatment of Window Shades and Draperies," the "Exchange of Sandwich Recipes," and a demonstration on "Making Dish Towels and Pot Holders." For families living in the desert in hogans without windows, window shades are not likely to command much interest. And after centuries of cooking over open fires, no doubt they had figured out how not to burn their hands and fingers.[37]

Gradually, and on a limited basis, extension work was introduced to Pueblo and Navajo people. When trained workers were available to guide them, Indian women responded as enthusiastically as Hispanic and Anglo women to home extension projects. Sometimes, cooperating field nurses, teachers, missionaries, and other state and federal workers helped the work along. Although coverage was inadequate and individual attention suffered, group meetings increased from 1,234 in 1934 to 2,093 in 1935. Miss M. E. Keener, working on the farflung Navajo reservation, organized women's clubs and presented lectures on sewing, cooking, childcare, health, bathing, and sanitation.[38]

At meetings among Anglos and Hispanics, only women attended. Here, however, Indian men took part in the all-day, three-week courses. For example, at the meeting in Red Rock, in northeastern Arizona, attendance averaged thirty: fifteen women and fifteen men. There, the men sewed along with the women, showing "as keen an interest in the work" as the women. To the agent's remark that "Indian women like to work with their hands," one might add, "so did the men!"[39]

While ethnic differences were one factor that disrupted extension work, poverty was a bond that united groups. The majority of Hispanic and Anglo farm women were desperately poor by middle-class standards. In families that could not afford agricultural equipment or even good tools, women usually lacked the small change necessary to buy materials to complete sewing projects. For this reason, extension agents focused on food preservation projects, labor intensive work that provided large amounts of food and required equipment that could be purchased collectively and used cooperatively.[40] Sharing canning equipment, including pressure cookers, tin can sealers, and glass jars, provided an inexpensive and thrifty way to provide food for impoverished families. Among the poor, poverty fostered cooperation regardless of race.

As Jensen points out, canning was an especially important skill, for it allowed rural women to provide nutritious food as well as to save money for the farm household.[41] For these reasons, home canning was introduced in the early years of AES work and remained a popular project throughout the 1920s and 1930s. In 1937 alone, families in twenty-one counties purchased 615 pressure cookers and 308 tin can sealers.[42] Among the Indians, canning and preserving food were priority projects, where Indian women learned new ways to preserve fruits and vegetables.

32. A canning club demonstration, Southern Pueblos. Courtesy of the National Archives, Record Group 75.

Because individual families could not afford canning equipment, portable equipment was made available or canning kitchens were set up in community centers.[43]

Not only did women can fruits and vegetables, they canned meats as well, including beef, pork, mutton, and chicken. In Grant, Hidalgo, and Luna Counties, where beef was readily available, meat canning was very popular with cattle ranchers. "Plan, Plant, and Can," the theme for this southwestern district in 1932, encouraged cooperative canning events that drew together those with equipment and those with food to be canned. For example, District Home Demonstration Agent Olive B. Cruse reported that "Mr. and Mrs. McCant had cans and equipment. Mr. and Mrs. Weatherby had meat and potatoes. They got together and had a 'canning bee' and divided the products."[44]

Canning provided an important link between town and country, one that the Country Life movement sought to encourage. In Luna County, for example, town women furnished equipment and cans; farmers provided the vegetables. As one agent noted, "Hundreds of cans were filled this way and many pantries filled when a great deal of food would otherwise have gone to waste." This food was especially valuable in the Depression years when many

33. Removing jars of canned fruit from a pressure cooker, Chamisal, New Mexico, 1940. Photo by Russell Lee, Library of Congress, USF34-37036.

families were struggling. Figures for 1936 and 1937 respectively show 928,274 and 1,260,397 quarts of fruits, vegetables, meat and fish, pickles, jellies and jams, and fruit juices canned.[45]

The community welfare canning plan for Eddy County provides a good example of Depression-era cooperation. Centered in Carlsbad, the program benefited people needing assistance. Frequently, large amounts of food could be canned in a few sessions. For example, 1,200 quarts of tomatoes, beets, and beans were canned in the summer of 1932. One citizen, Mrs. M. E. Lee, furnished the tomatoes; others donated the corn and beans. For her contribution, Mrs. Lee was allowed to keep one-fourth the total amount canned; the other workers received ten cans of vegetables for each day's work. This type of cooperation benefited both the growers with excess produce and needy families during difficult times. Similarly, in Luna County, 1,400 cans were filled and distributed among local citizens.[46]

Although food preparation and related projects were the most important work home demonstration agents carried out, agents also worked on other projects they considered appropriate for women. For example, the program in Union County in 1931 included "something of each of the three great subjects in which women are interested—food, clothing, and housing—with the emphasis on foods." Besides canning, agents taught nutrition and diet, cheese-making, poultry-raising, kitchen improvements, and how to plant vegetable gardens.

In neighboring Colfax County, Mela Vuicich remembers the work of agent Ruby Harris in the 1930s. Vuicich, who grew up in a Yugoslavian family in the coal camp of Van Houten, recalled how Harris visited numerous camps and company towns, showing women how to use patterns and flour sacks, how to renovate their mattresses, and how to can—when they had something to can. Since many men were hunters, she taught their wives how to preserve the meat.[47] Because food preparation was so important to farm homes, such projects and demonstrations remained a consistent priority of AES.

Home improvement projects, especially for kitchens, were also popular and urgently needed among farm families. Clearly, a woman's place was in the kitchen, according to the AES: "As the housewife spends the greatest part of her time in the kitchen, it is important that she have a cheerful and convenient place in which to do her work." Agents devised plans for "step saving kitchens" that emphasized several goals: running water with a drain for disposal of waste water, windows with screens on two sides of

34. Two women in their kitchen in Él Cerrito, New Mexico, 1940. Photo by Irving Rusinow, Library of Congress, neg. no. 37829.

the room, a floor that was easy to clean, work surfaces built to a comfortable height, and good lighting.

Home improvements were a good starting place for club work because, in the words of one club member:

> We were all living pretty primitively. We had no lights, no REA [Rural Electrification Administration], and we needed a buildup for our homes and our home living and we got it through the club. . . . We rebuilt kitchens and put in cupboards that were better than most women had.[48]

Water systems, however, were the technological system farm women most desired, and lacked. In a survey of San Miguel County in 1930, 89 percent of women in five communities listed the lack of running water as the most inconvenient thing in their kitchens. Water systems were costly, and apparently a low priority for policy planners, so installation of such systems was slow. When wells were installed, frequently it was at the convenience of farm livestock rather than the farm wife. Annual reports show just sixteen homes installed running water in 1928, seventeen in 1929, forty-seven in 1930, and twenty-eight in 1932. As late as 1945, 72 percent of farm women still carried their own water in this depressed county.[49]

Since modifications of the farm kitchen could be expensive, cost-saving measures were suggested as well. For example, high-quality roofing could provide an inexpensive floor covering by cutting it to room size, coating it with black shellac, then painting it with house paint. For maximum efficiency in the kitchen, agents recommended owning a sharp knife, keeping measuring cups grouped for ready use, placing cooking equipment and supplies conveniently arranged near the stove, having adequate towels and potholders, and hanging kitchen curtains and window shades. How many followed extension guidelines is difficult to gauge, but in these small and inexpensive ways, a farm wife could make her kitchen more efficient and cheerful.[50]

Enthusiasm and resourcefulness often made up for a lack of household conveniences. San Miguel County demonstrator and local leader Adelina Jaramillo reported how one group of women in tiny Trementina used their ingenuity when they were ready to paint food storage cans and discovered they had forgotten to order paint brushes. Since the nearest town, Las Vegas, was sixty miles away, they improvised with materials on hand. One woman had just cut her hair, so, using thread, they tied tiny bunches to sticks and matches. "It worked surprisingly well," reported Jaramillo, and sixty-nine cans were painted and labeled that day.[51]

35. Many rural women, such as this one, continued to draw water from the local well into the 1940s. Taos County, 1939. Photo by Russell Lee, Library of Congress, USF33-12427-M1.

36. Mrs. Whinery of Pie Town, making family clothing on her rotary (treadle) sewing machine. Photo by Russell Lee, Library of Congress, USF34-36744.

A major focus of the Country Life movement was to provide rural women with access to the new technology available to their city counterparts. If at all possible, agents recommended that families purchase at least one laborsaving device such as a washing machine, a refrigerator, electric or gasoline iron, a pressure cooker, a sewing machine, or a vacuum cleaner. Contingent upon these purchases, of course, was an electrical source. Nationwide, electric service was available in most cities by the turn of the century but reached rural areas very slowly. Only 422 New Mexico farms, or 1.4 percent, boasted electricity in 1920. At the beginning of the Depression, 85 percent of nonfarm dwellings had electric service but only about 10 percent of farm homes had electricity; for New Mexico, the figure had increased to 5.4 percent. After 1935, the New Deal's Rural Electrification Administration (REA) brought the new technology to rural areas through long-term loans made available to farmer's cooperatives and state and local governments, allowing farmers to electrify at minimum cost. Still, the service was heavily regionalized, with much of the Great Plains and West between the ninety-eighth meridian and the Rocky Mountains devoid of electrical wires. Although the percentage of New Mexico farm homes reached by electricity increased greatly between 1920 and 1940—from 1.4 percent to 19.2 percent—New Mexico farms still lagged behind other American farms, 35 percent of which had electricity.[52]

New Mexico women desired electrification, and extension agents wasted no time in encouraging farm women to invest in laborsaving devices. To interest them in better food storage, wrote Maud Doty, one group of clubwomen in Bernalillo County visited the home of Mrs. Dan Miller "to study" a new Frigidaire that had been installed in a remodeled kitchen. The home was newly built (1930) and boasted a modern kitchen, well-supplied with necessary cupboards, sink, and lights. Still, many homes could not afford even one of these appliances, while the slow pace of electrification kept farm homes from modernizing rapidly.[53]

By 1930, San Miguel County home demonstration agent Ivie Jones (who followed Jaramillo) expressed the frustration agents felt regarding home improvements. Unless the people requested help, said Jones, it was very hard to reach them. Most of the rural people had "scanty equipment, primitive conveniences, and very little income." She particularly noted the great need for bedding among the people, citing "poor beds, saggy springs, and scanty bed clothes" in many communities. Dust was often a problem, too, and excessive sunlight caused curtains to fade.[54] Yet the people were receptive to the agent's suggestions and attempted to implement her ideas where possible.

Agent Jones was especially pleased at the willingness of county women to serve their communities as local leaders or club officers. Of the twenty-two clubs meeting regularly in 1930, most were so well-planned and organized that work could continue with or without the presence of an agent. Organization and self-sufficiency were important AES goals—another lingering facet of Progressivism, which valued order and efficiency.[55]

One aspect of extension work that was very valuable to rural women and enjoyed a high success rate was social activity. "It is comparatively easy to perfect an organization among women. They seem to like the name CLUB; they like to meet together occasionally and forget the tiresome daily routine of housework," one agent reported. For women living in scattered and remote areas with few neighbors nearby, a day or an evening spent with the home demonstration agent was an important addition to their lives. Nona Berry remembers clearly the excitement such an event triggered. Often they were family affairs—"if the farmer could get away"—with a demonstration, covered-dish meal, and a business meeting. It was a big day and important to the women because "we lived far apart and that was worth a lot to a woman." [56]

Club meetings also gave farm wives a brief respite from their farm tasks. One club member stated, "I am glad for club meeting day because if it were not for that, I would not get a rest from the daily routine of house and outdoor work." [57] Another woman remarked that she "just picked up . . . [her] baby and went" and had no regrets at leaving her work for a day of fellowship and sharing. Another homesteader wife on the New Mexico/Arizona border west of Datil, Ruby Ruyle, recalled the monthly covered-dish suppers with pleasure; she did not remember the programs clearly, just the eating and socializing. [58] The women looked forward to the meetings, and "every hostess gave her house a thorough cleaning." [59] They also organized other kinds of social activities, often involving surrounding communities, such as putting on plays, holding quilting bees and box socials, and serving chicken dinners and pie suppers. [60] Generally, farm husbands supported their wives' participation in rural clubs. The demonstration meetings justified a day or evening away from home because the women were learning how to improve their domestic skills, thereby reinforcing their place on the family farm and in the American family.

The extension clubs were likewise valuable to women in ways beyond demonstrations in cooking or sewing. Like women's clubs in urban areas, they provided a place for women to learn leadership skills, develop public-speaking abilities, and direct meetings and organizations. For women who needed help with English, the clubs were a good place to improve language skills. A young French mother, Marie Rose Cauhape, who joined the Roswell extension club in 1924, discovered this advantage firsthand. Because she was an immigrant, she felt left out of community events until she joined the club and members helped her with her English. The club also provided a social outlet when her ranching husband was traveling. Cauhape listed club activities as an important source of support, especially regarding child-raising, when she wrote: "They gave me self-confidence. More abilities. I was learning through the Extension Club ways to get by in times of problems." [61]

Another farm wife, Ruth L. James, echoed Cauhape's sentiments. James's mother had been a member of an extension club in Oklahoma, so it was natural for Ruth to join the club in Colfax County when she moved to New Mexico in 1933. She, too, recalled how the club helped one young bride from Mexico improve her

English and reading skills and aided her in leading meetings and building confidence. James noted also that the club encouraged women to improve their appearances through clothing instruction, such as choosing flattering colors and styles.[62]

The skills women learned through extension work stayed with them all their lives. Mary Moore recalled life on a ranch southeast of Raton where she did all her own butchering, made lard, cured bacon and ham, canned meat, and made cheese—skills learned through extension work. Many times she called on those skills when she found herself cooking for fifteen to twenty cowboys. After her husband died in 1955, Moore and her daughter continued to run the ranch; she carried on the business or inside work and her daughter the outside chores. Moore also credits the extension club with developing her public-speaking abilities, enabling her to hold office at state and county levels many times over the years. She became active at the international level as well, attending Associated Country Women of the World meetings, an experience she found highly enjoyable and very educational.[63]

In addition to regular extension club work, the AES began to hold Farm Women's Camps in the 1920s. These camps provided an opportunity for rural women to gather in a relaxed and pleasant setting for five or six days, free from their domestic and farm duties. Each day was carefully organized to include training for community leadership in nutrition, clothing, home management, recreation, and boys' and girls' club work. Topics outside traditional gender lines were featured as well, such as "New Mexico Laws of Particular Interest to Women" and "Community Organization and Its Value." At week's end, the women returned home, prepared to give talks and demonstrations to their local communities. In this way, farm camps served as a training mechanism, using local women to interest others in extension work. They also served as social conduits through which middle-class values and standards were transmitted.[64]

In New Mexico, farm camps were held in four locations: San Miguel, Lincoln, Bernalillo, and Grant Counties. In 1930, 114 women from nineteen counties attended one of the camps. Although distance and transportation were often problems, the cost was nominal. Sometimes the delegate and her community divided the five dollar per person fee, making it easier for more women to attend. Although farm camps were educational, they were also designed to provide rural women a respite from their usual routines. Recreational activities were planned, in addition to speeches and demonstrations, and, importantly, cooks were provided at all

37. Mrs. Hutton of Pie Town, operating her newly-installed electric washing machine. Photo by Russell Lee, Library of Congress, USF33-12727.

camps, "thus rendering the farm woman free from the drudgery of the kitchen for a brief time, at least." [65] Fortunate was the rural woman who could happily wave goodbye to her family for a few days of relaxation among her farm sisters in a pleasant setting.

One such location was in Cienega Canyon, in the Sandia Mountains east of Albuquerque. The Business and Professional Women's Club owned a clubhouse at that site and allowed the AES to hold annual farm camps there. Here was a good example of community cooperation, a feature the AES promoted. Both the agricultural agents and the home demonstration agents were urged to take part in city affairs in order to keep business women and men in touch with rural problems and needs, as well as to help dispel the notion that rural people were backward and isolated. Among their city contacts were Chambers of Commerce, county schools, county health departments, and local civic clubs; local churches were another source. Business people could also be lucrative sources, as Ivie Jones discovered in San Miguel County. By using discretion, she was successful in getting what she needed for women's work from the business people and was not refused any request, even though at times a contribution was a hardship to the business.[66] Rural-urban cooperation helped reduce the isolation of many rural women.

There were other examples of urban-rural cooperation. In Chaves County, home demonstration agent Velma Borschell was active in the Woman's Club of Roswell and helped the club develop a cooperative market through which rural people could sell their farm products. In New Mexico's largest city, the Woman's Club of Albuquerque was especially supportive of extension work, electing home demonstration agent Maud Doty chair of their Home Economics section. Oftentimes, local newspapers were willing supporters, offering advertising space to extension news; Bernalillo County newspapers alone printed eighty articles in 1925. Cooperation between public and private agencies, urban and rural, strengthened extension work and provided a network of sources for farm women.[67]

Bernalillo County provides a good example of cooperation between rural and urban women's organizations. In 1933, 210 women were enrolled in eleven extension clubs, with a balance between Spanish and Anglo women. Included in this total were the Merrymakers of Mountainair, the Housekeepers Club in Ranchos de Atrisco, the Alameda Women's Club, the Miercoles Club in Los Griegos, the Spanish Women's Club, and the Old Town Albuquerque Club. Prior to 1925, organized work had not been attempted among the county's Hispanic women; Doty was instrumental in changing that. In a talk made at a district meeting, she reported on "What a Handful of Women Can Do," using the Atrisco club as an example. The women in that small rural community owned their own clubhouse on two acres of ground, electrically lighted and paid for. In addition, they installed a cannery with a capacity of five hundred quarts daily, definitely proving them a community asset. This club chose to join the New Mexico Federation of Women's Clubs, the first strictly rural club to become federated.[68]

To further encourage cooperation between rural and urban women, Doty was a frequent speaker at the Woman's Club meetings in Albuquerque. In 1925, she presented three special programs on food and nutrition that allowed city women to see and appreciate what their rural sisters were doing. That same year, the Woman's Club took an active role in the extension's Better Homes Campaign, working with a contractor to plan, design, and furnish a model home. The successful demonstration project drew 3,000 visitors in the week it was on display in the city.[69] The Woman's Club as a group often visited the extension clubs in the area, and the experience strengthened the relationship between rural and urban women and their interests.

Clubs in other counties shared similar relationships. For example, the cooperative market established in Roswell in 1932 was the outgrowth of an address Phoebe K. Warner gave at the state convention of the Federation of Women's Clubs in 1931. She also spoke to the United Rural Club in Chaves County on "The Value and Privilege of Being a Rural Woman." In Santa Fe County, the Woman's Club cooperated with local farmers by providing their clubhouse lot as a marketplace where farmers could sell their produce. The Woman's Club in Carlsbad (Eddy County) helped construct and equip a model home and served as guides for visitors. In these ways, the work of the AES was not confined strictly to the countryside but was enhanced and enlarged through cooperation with civic and county organizations.[70]

Overall, the AES provided an important network of information and self-help to rural women and their families. Always short of home demonstration agents, the AES, nevertheless, attempted to reach as many farm women as possible. Until the 1930s, these attempts were directed primarily toward Anglo women; in fact, a lack of Hispanic-speaking agents slowed the work among Mexican and Spanish families. Agents were most successful, however, when they moved away from rigidly prescribed gender and ethnic guidelines and demonstrated some responsiveness to local conditions. In addition, cooperation between private organizations and public agencies greatly facilitated the agents' efforts and strengthened extension work generally.

By the end of the 1930s, rural women were relatively well organized, perhaps more so than their urban sisters. Extension work coupled with federal and state projects eventually provided a rural infrastructure not available to earlier generations of New Mexicans.[71] The peculiarities of New Mexico—its cultural diversity, geographical isolation, and financial and drought-induced depression—did not prevent women reformers from doing their work, though they were often forced to adapt middle-class, middle-American expectations to those conditions. Home extension work became a valued and valuable component of rural life, prompting one farm woman to remark, "I do not know what we would do without it."[72]

6

"THE WOMEN ARE NOT GETTING A SQUARE DEAL"

WOMEN AND THE NEW DEAL

In 1934, Irene Polos of Farmington, New Mexico, wrote to President and Mrs. Roosevelt, pleading for assistance:

> *I was hoping it would never be necessary to intrude on your kindness again but I just do not know which way to turn. . . . I have been selling my empty fruit jars and other articles from our home, but now have nothing more to sell, nor do I know where I can get a loan of any more money. . . .*[1]

Polos was not alone; scores of other women pleaded similar cases to the first family, particularly to Eleanor Roosevelt, in the belief that relief and welfare could be personal rather than bureaucratic in its approach. Letters alone, however, were not enough to secure the relief that many women needed. Overall, New Deal programs provided some respite for women, but in New Mexico, as elsewhere in the nation, fell short of meeting long-term needs. Two reasons for the shortage stand out. First of all, prevailing notions of gender roles limited both the extent and nature of the programs established. And second, New Mexico's isolation, small population, and cultural diversity meant comparatively less funding and, hence, fewer relief opportunities for women, whether caregivers or recipients.

For those women in positions to provide services—as administrators, social workers, and office personnel—New Deal programs offered opportunities for better jobs and, in many cases, a great deal of authority. These women were part of a large female network nationwide who formed the bone and sinew of federal relief work. They managed vast sums of money, supervised thousands of employees, and helped promulgate programs and policies from the national to the local level. Many remained in the work force until reaching retirement age. More important, this influx of women into an initially male-biased welfare program forced a modification of the welfare structure. Contradictions remained, however, that reflected gender stereotypes and ethnic discrimination. In addition, political machinations often thwarted opportunities for women, especially in such a politically diverse state as New Mexico. At best, then, New Deal programs produced mixed results for New Mexico women, prompting Mrs. Douglas Wright of Raton and Mamie Mayes of Tucumcari to inform Eleanor Roosevelt that "the women are not getting a square deal in this WPA in New Mexico."[2] This chapter will examine the situation during the Great Depression and show how conditions in New Mexico, including ethnic and cultural attitudes and gender expectations, shaped women's lives under the New Deal.

Between the time of the stock market crash on October 29, 1929, and President Roosevelt's inauguration in March 1933, New Mexico, like the rest of the nation, experienced an economic decline that tested the limits of the state's already strapped financial coffers. Among the lowest ranking of the states in per capita income, New Mexico witnessed drastic declines in agriculture and in mining production. The agricultural industry, already depressed because of drought in the 1920s, continued to suffer further losses and by 1931, production had fallen to one-half the 1929 figure. Making matters worse, one of the state's largest corporate taxpayers—the Atchison, Topeka and Santa Fe Railway Company— registered a 33 percent decline in income between 1930 and 1931, resulting in employee layoffs of almost 40 percent. Despite the reassurances of Governor Arthur Seligman and Albuquerque Mayor Clyde Tingley in 1931 that New Mexico was not yet experiencing the serious consequences of the Depression felt elsewhere, indications to the contrary began to surface. Margaret Reeves, director of the state Bureau of Child Welfare, provided evidence in a series of county reports in mid-1932 that the Depression was indeed having an impact on the New Mexico economy.[3]

The Bureau of Child Welfare, established in 1919 and placed under the Department of Public Welfare in 1921, was the state agency empowered to direct all welfare activities, but it was never quite able to provide more than minimal aid to those in need. Instead, it fell to county governments to raise what funds they could to carry out relief work through the work of county-wide welfare offices and voluntary committees. In each of New Mexico's thirty-one counties, a levy of up to one-half mill was assessed taxpayers to provide funds for relief or public welfare. With the approval of the Bureau of Child Welfare, these funds were then distributed among the county's unemployed—read male—citizens.

Since 1924, Margaret Reeves, nationally recognized social

worker and welfare executive, had served as director of this key state agency. With limited state funding, the bureau could provide only small amounts of aid for the neediest of the state's deserving children and their families. This situation changed in the summer of 1932 when Congress authorized the Reconstruction Finance Corporation (RFC) to provide emergency loans to corporations, banks, and government agencies. From a modest budget of less than $30,000 a year in the late 1920s, Reeves's agency was suddenly responsible for administering $465,000 in 1932–33.[4]

Furthermore, when Congress approved the Federal Emergency Relief Administration (FERA) in the "first one hundred days," even larger sums passed through Reeves's agency. Harry Hopkins, director of the FERA, had decreed that funds would be distributed through existing state welfare structures and appointed Reeves director of the New Mexico FERA. In 1933–34, nearly six million dollars in FERA money crossed Reeves's desk. With the increase in funds came an increase in political pressure, and Reeves's consistent professional and nonpartisan stance would cause serious political repercussions for her and for some of the women and their families whom her agency sought to help.[5]

Early in 1932, the RFC began to dispense emergency loans to the states. To qualify for an RFC loan required a statement of financial need and an estimate of the funds New Mexico would require to carry its people through a twelve-month period. In August 1932, Margaret Reeves submitted a report to the RFC documenting conditions county by county and requesting $224,000, a conservative estimate considering the range of problems besetting the various counties.[6] These problems included crop losses due to both grasshoppers and hail in Rio Arriba County; a 50 percent reduction in the labor force employed on the Santa Fe Railway in Bernalillo County; a 35 percent bankruptcy rate among cotton farmers in Doña Ana County; and a disproportionately high rate of transients in Colfax County, which served as a gateway to the sunbelt states of New Mexico and Arizona. The problems were larger than the resources available in many county budgets. In truth, most counties were managing (barely) on contributions from local women's clubs, the Red Cross, and county welfare committees. Reeves's conservative figure of $224,000 was the minimum the state needed to get through the next year and when granted, marked New Mexico as one of only two states to receive relief for all of its counties.[7]

Despite the increase in federal funding, conditions did not improve in 1933, so volunteer efforts were crucial. The Bureau of Child Welfare, not normally a relief agency, carried a tremendous burden trying to organize the relief programs of thirty-one coun-

38. A tubercular patient from Iowa and part of his family of nine stranded and penniless in New Mexico, August 1936. Photo by Dorothea Lange, Library of Congress, USF34-9750.

ties. It was Reeves's belief that few people in New Mexico really understood the widespread needs of families throughout the state. "If it were not for federal aid right now," she observed, "there would literally be thousands of families where old people and children, as well as others, would be hungry."[8] In Las Vegas, for example, twenty-four Hispanic men petitioned for relief for their families "as we are on the point of starvation, and [for] clothes as we are without any." The men also asked for "work at any wages we can get, being not particular as to what kind and what pay we can get."[9] The best Reeves could do was advise the petitioners to seek help from the San Miguel County Welfare Committee and to watch for federal employment announcements in the local newspapers. Burdened with a mushrooming administrative task, the bureau counted on the help of more than 1,000 volunteers for assistance in matters like this. In fact, the proportion of federal funds required for administrative tasks was much smaller in New Mexico than in most other states, a fact Reeves credited to the high degree of voluntarism in New Mexico.[10]

In Colfax County, relief was well organized through a local social service association. Marjorie Butts, a social worker from St. Louis, Missouri, organized the county into thirteen welfare committees that were responsible for contacting all needy families and dispensing relief. Volunteers (men and women) then went to work on all manner of tasks, from providing clerical assistance to operating a soup kitchen to distributing flour and shoes. This northeastern county, one of the state's largest and one severely hampered by unemployment, organized effectively and early and was able to meet most of its needs in the early 1930s.[11] Over the years, conditions worsened, however, and Colfax County, once self-sufficient based on cattle and coal, became one of the many counties desperate for federal aid under FERA-WPA programs.

Initially, providing relief for women was not a primary goal of early New Deal projects. Putting men, whom the government recognized as "head of household," to work was, hence the large numbers of projects such as roadbuilding, dam construction, and forestry programs for men. It was not long, however, before women in government positions began to insist that something be done to help needy women, particularly those heading households themselves. By March 1933, millions of women in America were out of work, and an "army" of homeless girls, many under twenty-one years of age, was "wandering the streets."[12] Mary Anderson, director of the Woman's Bureau, urged that government officials consider women's problems more carefully, especially those of married women. By late 1933, Harry Hopkins admitted that "women as a group have had less attention than any other unemployed group" and promised to earmark FERA funds for women's projects. Yet of 1,600,000 Americans receiving work relief in 1934, only 142,000 were women.[13] Clearly, something needed to be done to reach more women, especially those in financially strapped New Mexico.

In truth, the New Deal was committed to supporting families but not married women, who suffered when the government required personnel reductions. The federal government set the tone, dismissing 1,600 married women from federal jobs, and state and local governments followed suit: three out of four cities excluded married women from teaching; eight states passed laws excluding them from state jobs. In the cultural climate of the Depression, women were seen as selfish if they were employed and men were not. Furthermore, when government—federal, state, or local—did provide employment for women, it was not well-paying jobs, day-care, or anything else that "might help alleviate women's economic dependence on women." Nor did the government promote the possibility of a new family structure based on gender equality. By ignoring the plight of working women, women's economic status deteriorated further.[14]

At this point, First Lady Eleanor Roosevelt insisted to Hopkins that activities for women must be made part of federal relief projects. Hopkins agreed and in August 1933 created a Women's Division within FERA and appointed Ellen S. Woodward, an outstanding social worker and welfare administrator in Mississippi, director of the new division. He also ordered each state relief director to appoint a qualified woman to work with Woodward to coordinate and direct employment activities for women. It was to be a full-time position for a woman familiar with existing governmental, social, and civic agencies as well as with employment service and relief work. In addition, each newly appointed director was expected to support New Deal policies (meaning Democratic politics).[15] In New Mexico, Mildred Andrews became the first state director of the Women's and Professional Projects Division.

With the creation of the Women's Division, Woodward, with welcome assistance from Eleanor Roosevelt, went into action. In November 1933, the two women quickly organized the White House Conference on the Emergency Needs of Women and invited prominent leaders of women's organizations and social service agencies to cooperate in alleviating the plight of jobless women. At this conference, Hopkins reported an estimated 300,000 to 400,000 women in need of immediate attention. The task was to create employment opportunities at a time when such opportunities were seriously diminished—in factories, service industries, and domestic work. Social restraints also limited the nature of work relief for women. For example, women could not be put to work on mass projects such as construction, for that would put them in competition with men; nor could they work on projects that competed with the private sector. In addition, Roosevelt added another qualifier: women would not be expected to leave their homes and families (as men often did) to work on projects. Women were to be employed within their own communities, an important factor in rural New Mexico, with its many isolated towns and villages.[16]

In August 1934, Woodward announced the mattress workshop program, designed to meet those criteria. Investigations had revealed a lack of adequate mattresses not only in rural areas but in cities as well, and the mattress-making project was designed to remedy that deficiency. More directly, the program had three objectives: to provide work relief for more than 60,000 women then on direct relief; to reduce the cotton surplus by at least 250,000 bales; and to provide mattresses for needy families. This was the first nationwide work project available for women, and Woodward was especially eager to see it implemented quickly and efficiently, as were New Mexico officials.[17]

Instructions immediately went out to state directors detailing procedures and requirements and urging close (weekly) contact with Woodward's office. Specifications called for the workrooms to be set up in any available space, such as warehouses, churches, and schools. The minimum-size workroom, fifty-by-fifty feet, provided working space and equipment for ten persons to produce ten fifty-pound, double-sized mattresses a day. Workers were paid the prevailing rate for similar work in their immediate locality, but in no instance was the wage to be less than thirty cents an hour.[18]

New Mexico women enthusiastically embraced the mattress-making project. Eager to get under way, state relief agencies made local purchases in July of thirty bales of cotton and 3,000 yards of mattress ticking. In addition, New Mexico requested and received 200 bales and 17,100 yards of cloth from the Federal Surplus Relief Corporation. Compared to neighboring states, such as Oklahoma (1,350 bales of cotton; 131,100 yards of ticking) and Arizona (350 bales; 34,200 yards of cloth), New Mexico's requests were small, but it was a beginning. By August of 1934, mattress-making projects were in place in ten counties in New Mexico, employing 152 women and 26 men.[19]

Employment in the mattress workshops quickly increased when the shops began to produce clothing and bedding as well as mattresses. By November of 1934, more than 600 women were employed in 24 sewing rooms in 17 counties. Their numbers varied. In Curry County, just four to eight women were employed daily at Clovis, while in Silver City in Grant County, 75 women worked in the local sewing room. In San Miguel County, the federal sewing project provided employment for 50 women at the sewing room on the plaza in Las Vegas. Working a six-hour day, which left time to care for their families and homes, the workers produced 9,000 garments for men, women, and children, in addition to 2,000 comforters.[20]

An important benefit of WPA projects was the sense of pride and responsibility the work generated in the women, which carried over into their lives outside the sewing rooms. The women were proud of their work and the sense of financial independence steady work produced. State relief headquarters reported that the women were happy to be working in the sewing rooms, where they

39. Members of a WPA weaving project, part of the work carried out in sewing rooms. Costilla, New Mexico, 1939. Photo by Russell Lee. Library of Congress, USF-34-34232-D.

could help others as well as themselves, instead of being supported on direct relief. Engaged in productive work, the women experienced a sense of achievement and well-being that came from developing and applying new skills. In the process, the sewing rooms also helped ease stress. The McKinley County Welfare Association reported that "in a number of cases, we have put women to work who were undergoing quite a severe mental strain at home and, in these instances, the sewing project has proven to be of actual therapeutic value." Ena Walter Mitchell of Lordsburg reaffirmed the impact of the sewing project in Hidalgo County as a "wonderful thing." "That was the only work those people had. . . . Some of the women were alone and that was the only income they had." Learning a skill induced a sense of pride, but it was the ability to command even a modest wage that made WPA sewing projects so valuable.[21]

Problems did arise in some New Mexico sewing rooms, however. Lena Robbins, a seamstress at Clovis in Curry County, wrote

Eleanor Roosevelt in June 1936 to report "how [her] plan has been abused." Robbins was unhappy that work in the Clovis sewing room had been cut back from full-time work of 130 hours per month at a salary of $44, to ten days at $22 monthly. In support of the cutback, the state Department of Public Welfare reasoned that the women could work privately as seamstresses on the days they were not employed in the sewing room. As Robbins explained to Mrs. Roosevelt, Clovis could not support even ten seamstresses, and if there had been any possibility of earning money in that fashion, there would have been no reason for the sewing room in the first place.[22]

Underlying Robbins's complaint was a pattern of employment policies that favored the office workers administering relief activities at public welfare headquarters in Santa Fe. The policy appeared to give "all the office workers good jobs and good salaries and steady work, and the women whom the plan was originally intended to help . . . will continue to work [less than] half time and $22.00 is their limit."[23] Money intended for relief then, was going into salaries for administrative jobs, reducing the amount available to women so in need of wage labor. In this light, Robbins's complaint was justified. In effect, some white women benefited at the expense of poorer, nonwhite women.

Gender bias also affected women's relief work. Early in 1936, all women in the Albuquerque sewing rooms in Bernalillo County were reduced to half-time work on orders of the state WPA administrator, Roswell businessman Lee Rowland, "who did not believe women should earn as much as men." Rowland's directive reflected the prevailing attitude that men were the primary breadwinners even though that breadwinner was not always present. This meant that all women, including those who were the sole support of as many as seven children, were forced to get by on $24 a month, an unquestioned hardship. True, the federal government was forced to scale down public relief programs, but those cutbacks did not begin until 1937. Clearly, Rowland's action in January of 1936 was arbitrary and gender-biased.[24]

A second factor at work was a cultural bias that affected how jobs were distributed among Anglo and Hispanic families. Here, Margaret Reeves clearly discriminated between the relief needs of Anglo and Hispanic women. Basically, she believed that New Mexico did not require many work projects for women because she was convinced that such projects were best suited to Anglo-American communities and to industrial areas. New Mexico was predominately Hispanic with an average of five children per family; Reeves was more concerned with providing employment for the male, leaving the wife free to care for the children and the home. In her view, "the mother [was] badly needed in the home."[25] When funds permitted the employment of only one member of the family on a work project, Reeves assigned the job to the male. Such a situation did not take into account those Hispanic families in which women were the de facto heads of households, such as when the husband was unemployable, or in the case of deserted, divorced, and widowed women.

The case of Domecinda Vigil Tixier of Albuquerque is exemplary. Tixier's husband contracted tuberculosis while they were ranching in Union County. Because he could not work for long periods of time, Domecinda was forced to become the breadwinner. Nevertheless, technically as well as culturally, he still was considered "head of household." Her role in the social welfare system will be discussed later in this chapter.[26]

This line of reasoning was not unique to New Mexico, but was the customary pattern underlying relief projects across the nation. The prevailing cultural belief that men were the breadwinners, leaving women in charge of the household and the children, permeated all aspects of American life.[27] Mamie Martin voiced this traditional viewpoint in a letter to Federal Director Ellen Woodward, stating she would "still vote to have married women and women with means of support taken out of public industry." In words descriptive of her personal situation, Martin stated: "If I had a home I would certainly be willing to stay in it."[28] Because this belief was so ingrained, the needs of single, divorced, and widowed women were overlooked. When bias against a cultural group was also part of the equation, Hispanic, black, and Indian women in New Mexico experienced further discrimination.

Women were not alone, however, in perceiving discrimination in federal work relief. Hispanic males were unhappy that more Hispanic men were not employed in the better-paying jobs of foremen and office managers. In Harding County in northeastern New Mexico, where 40 percent of the population was Spanish-American, only three of thirty-six employees in the county welfare office in Roy were Hispanic. Nor did the office employ an interpreter to aid older people who could not speak English. Similarly, in Rio Arriba County, then 90 percent Hispanic, there were no Hispanic supervisors. Responding to President Roosevelt's request to notify him regarding problems, David M. Valdez of Roy pleaded for opportunities for Hispanics to be assigned more than the "pick and shovel jobs"—"allow us to be given a chance to show our worth." Valdez assured the President there were plenty of school teachers, bookkeepers, and other educated Hispanics across the country ready to do a good job in relief offices if the government would but "let [them] have a fair deal." Discrimination against Hispanics on New Deal projects continued to be an ongoing problem for the Roosevelt administration.[29]

Placing women in federal work relief projects was always a difficult problem for the administration, partially because, in general, women lacked skills in some cases and physical strength in others, but primarily because the belief that women should not work outside the home was so deeply ingrained. Another factor was the resistance of all thirty-one county commissions (composed of men), who failed to recognize the value of many projects geared toward women.[30] As a result, sewing rooms—traditionally "women's work"—became the chief means of employment of women in the American West. The sewing rooms were especially functional because so many kinds of sewing were carried out: dressmaking, rehabilitating old garments, making hospital supplies as well as household goods, spinning and weaving, and mattress- and rug-making. By 1936, when projects for women were in full swing, 56 percent of all women on WPA projects across the nation worked in sewing rooms. In New Mexico, the percentage was even greater; 84 percent of women employed on WPA projects were working at sewing machines.[31]

New Mexico women did other work as well. Unique to New Mexico was the woman-directed task of plastering the exteriors of adobe buildings, particularly rural schools and churches. Hispanic women, long known for their skill at this work, were hired in Torrance, Mora, and Rio Arriba counties at forty cents an hour to finish the job once the men had done the heavy labor.[32] Other work included cataloguing and rebinding books in public libraries and translating the Spanish Archives in the Historical Society of New Mexico. In Albuquerque, a soap-making project employed five women to render scraps and spoiled meat left from the slaughter of cattle under FERA drought relief. In two weeks, the women produced 1,500 one-pound bars of laundry soap, later distributed to needy families.[33] Although the numbers of women on work relief projects were disappointingly small, the benefits to those families were substantial when measured against the impoverishment of their lives prior to New Deal programs.

While it may be true that the economic progress of women in the 1930s was not translated into permanent gains, the community services of the [Women's and Professional Projects] Division were integrated into federal, state, and local governments in the form of school hot lunches, nursery schools for low income groups, library extension, historic preservation, and delivery systems for social

40. Indian women replastering a home in Paguate village near Laguna Pueblo, 1925. Photo by Edward S. Curtis. Courtesy of Museum of New Mexico, neg. no. 31961.

services.[34] Overall, the women who were recipients of federal largesse in the 1930s gained new skills, developed self-confidence, and broadened their knowledge, while providing financial relief for their families. New Deal programs, however, did little to alter gender attitudes regarding work; men did heavy jobs such as construction; women sewed.

A second dimension to social welfare work brings into focus those women who provided the services, both middle-class professional women and women who lacked formal training but were integral in implementing New Deal programs and policies. Margaret Reeves, K. Rose Wood, Mela Vuicich, Domecinda Vigil Tixier, and Ena Walter Mitchell are representative of those women nationwide who were active at state and local levels. Reeves, a nationally known professional social worker, and Wood, a younger social worker with experience in private and public welfare work, found employment opportunities that lasted well beyond the New Deal years. Wood served in a supervisory or administrative capacity for over forty years, from 1935 to 1976, under both Democratic and Republican governors. Wood managed to remain free of political accusations that eventually brought down her mentor. Caught up in political demands and gender stereotypes, Reeves became a victim of New Mexico's political struggles. Her management style frequently displayed gender and cultural biases that provoked complaints on more than one occasion.

For more than ten years, from 1924 to 1935, Margaret Reeves, as director of the Bureau of Child Welfare, had managed to keep her agency out of partisan politics. In a state as faction-ridden as New Mexico, remaining free of political obligations was no easy task. Throughout the decade, the state Democratic party committee and its chairman repeatedly pressured Reeves and members of her department to give a portion of their salaries as a "voluntary contribution" to the Democratic party, to which they owed their jobs, he claimed.[35] She persistently refused, and this fact ultimately led to her downfall in 1935, early in the administration of Governor Clyde Tingley (1935–39).

A Progressive Republican, Reeves maintained good working relationships with four different Democratic governors and one two-term Republican during her tenure.[36] As a good public servant, she found it "unthinkable" that partisan politics should have a place in the administration of public assistance or civil works, and she was emphatic in her insistence on bipartisan committees. She was proud of her record of impartiality and nonpartisanship and noted in 1932 that "there never [had] been the slightest political interference with the work of the Bureau of Child Welfare in New Mexico."[37]

Democratic Governor Tingley was to be the exception to that record. Tingley, a colorful and quixotic individual who took great pride in the numbers of people he could hire and fire, took office in January 1935. This Democratic demagogue was not happy that a Republican woman was responsible for administering and distributing large sums of federal monies as part of her job as state director of FERA. Despite federal law that imposed strict, nonpartisan rules on its agencies, New Mexico Democrats assumed they had a right to dominate and run the entire public works structure. Tingley's election in November 1934 reinforced this attitude, for with the infusion of federal dollars, Democrats envisioned a windfall in jobs for "party faithfuls."[38] Reeves's efforts to deny outright patronage, coupled with her support of Bernalillo County FERA project manager E. N. Boule in a dispute with Tingley, led the newly elected governor to force Reeves out of her jobs as both state FERA administrator and as the director of the Bureau of Child Welfare in January 1935.

Tingley's attempt to replace Reeves was revealed in a letter to President Roosevelt nine days before Tingley's inauguration. Despite the President's frequently repeated utterances not to "play politics with human misery," Tingley informed Roosevelt that he intended to fire Reeves and replace her with someone willing to work more closely with his administration.[39] Tingley could not fire Reeves outright, however, as she was not a political appointee; the Board of Public Welfare was responsible for appointing the director of the Bureau of Child Welfare. Nor did Tingley have the authority to remove Reeves from her FERA position, since that was a function of the federal relief administration. Also, New Mexico law mandated that the head of the Bureau of Child Welfare must be a woman of experience and special training in child welfare work, and Reeves clearly qualified.[40] Tingley's ploy was to ask for the resignations of the members of the state welfare board, paving the way for the appointment of others who would bend to his wishes. He did so on Friday, January 4, 1935.

The following week was filled with intrigue and speculation. When Tingley made his intentions known, FERA field director Major Ellis O. Braught was immediately dispatched to Santa Fe to confer with Tingley regarding the governor's proposed changes. The newly reconstituted Board of Public Welfare, which included three members of the previous board, began daily meetings in an attempt to resolve the issue. Persistent rumors circulated in

Santa Fe that Reeves's "head was to fall under the Tingley axe, along with several others." Throughout the week of January 7, requests for information were repeatedly denied as Tingley effectively "muzzled" the new board, preventing any leaks to the press regarding the board's discussions.[41]

In the meantime, relief distribution was thrown into chaos when Tingley withheld from J. C. McConvery, state FERA treasurer, a January federal relief check for $1,039,000. Tingley had removed McConvery from the Board of Public Welfare, an action that was legally fuzzy at best and one that caused undue suffering among relief recipients. McConvery, like Reeves, was a federally appointed FERA official, and as treasurer, under $100,000 bond. At the time of his unexpected removal from the board, more than 2,000 relief checks and vouchers had been prepared and awaited his signature. Not willing to jeopardize his bond, McConvery refused to sign and send out the checks. This development made apparent Tingley's haste to replace McConvery with his own man, Donovan N. Hoover, who was then forced to "mak[e] a mad scramble Tuesday [January 15] to get checks printed, signed, and issued" to the anxious recipients. The haste was made more acute when twenty unemployed people forced their way into offices of the Bernalillo County Charity Bureau and demanded immediate relief for their families.[42]

The Board of Public Welfare continued to meet during the week, unable to agree on how best to replace Reeves. Despite the support of board president R. O. Brown, who contended that Reeves was efficient, honest, and competent and should not be fired, the majority of the board voted "to oust Reeves unless she would agree to the political dictates of Tingley." In view of her refusal, the outcome was clear. On January 16, Reeves and her assistant, Lillian Franzen, resigned from the Bureau of Child Welfare.

Reeves's forced resignation drew an immediate outcry from women's club members and other voluntary social service organizations around the state. Supporters of Reeves's decade of welfare work resented Tingley's remarks that he had engineered the resignations because he wanted to have "an efficient child welfare and FERA administration in New Mexico." In most minds, in and outside New Mexico, Reeves had ably developed just that—an efficient child and family welfare system. "Where is the governor going to find as well-qualified a woman as Miss Reeves to carry on the work?" was the question most frequently asked in New Mexico, in regional headquarters in Dallas, and in federal

41. K. Rose Wood, newly arrived social worker in Santa Fe, 1935. Courtesy of K. Rose Wood.

offices in Washington.[43] More important was the loss of a high-ranking woman in state government and her ability to influence the male-dominated political structure.

Reeves's reaction to the sudden turn of events was one of shock and disbelief. K. Rose Wood of Santa Fe recalled the event clearly. Wood was a social worker from Minnesota, newly arrived in New Mexico in December 1934 and a temporary guest in the home of Reeves and her assistant, Franzen. Returning home the evening of that momentous day, Wood found Reeves and Franzen in front of a cheerful fire in their spacious Canyon Road apartment. "Miss Reeves looked just like someone out of a Greek tragedy," Wood recalled. "Tingley had marched into her office and said, 'Out! You're fired!' It was very, very hard on Miss Reeves [and] I will never forget her face—anger, disbelief, frustration, defiance."

Wood described Reeves as a handsome dark-haired woman, elegantly attired and poised and always in command, one who did not "put up with any kind of nonsense." But on this night in January of 1935, Reeves was "wild-eyed that this 'idiot' [Governor Tingley] had done such a stupid thing, after all she had done for the people of New Mexico."[44]

Wood's understanding of the situation portrayed two strong-minded individuals, a woman who had built up a creditable public welfare agency and personal reputation and a man who wished to shape things to his own personal vision. Explaining Tingley's actions, Wood observed that Reeves "was entirely too independent, dogmatic, and even tyrannical, if you choose to call it that. And she had run it [the Bureau of Child Welfare] all by herself for so long she wasn't going to let Tingley or anybody else tell her what to do. So, out." Wood was aware that certain other males in the administration and in the Democratic hierarchy, as well as Tingley, were unhappy that a woman was in control of large sums of federal money. She believes this knowledge was an important factor in Tingley's decision to replace Reeves.

Reeves recovered from her ignominious dismissal, however. She left New Mexico shortly thereafter for Wisconsin, where she secured a position with the Milwaukee Council of Social Agencies. Describing her new work, Reeves stated that it was a job similar to the one she held in New Mexico but "without politicos at my heels." Her national reputation remained intact and she was soon elected one of three vice-presidents to the National Conference of Social Workers. At that group's annual meeting, in the spring of 1935, Reeves read a paper on planning and organization in rural communities based on her experiences in New Mexico; she received a standing ovation, and subsequently, a publication.[45]

For Margaret Reeves, her "New Mexico experience" proved to be a challenging, exciting, and frustrating period that demonstrated both the demands and the rewards placed on women in positions of power. Reeves was not alone; more and more women were securing positions of leadership and responsibility in public welfare jobs across the nation as the New Deal expanded. Largely unrecognized in New Mexico today, Reeves's work is testimony to her skill and determination, and is a reflection of the uncontrollable and unforeseen forces that buffet women, as well as men, in positions of power.

K. Rose Wood, a 1934 graduate of the newly created School of Social Work at the University of Minnesota, was one of many women who benefited from the expansion of administrative and executive positions as state and local agencies became responsible for public welfare. As one of Reeves's last appointments, Wood was assigned to Colfax County in January 1935 as assistant to county welfare director Tom Nelson; in addition, she supervised social services in nearby Union County. As the FERA gradually wound down (it was terminated in 1938; by then the WPA and the Social Security system were in place), other women, like Wood, found themselves moving into newly created positions, some at the administrative level. For example, women eventually replaced men as county directors in all of New Mexico's thirty-one counties. In 1936, Wood was appointed field representative in charge of seven counties in the southwest corner of the state: Doña Ana, Luna, Grant, Hidalgo, Catron, Sierra, and Socorro. She was one of five field representatives at that time, all of whom were women.[46] Wood's initial assignment would lead to more than forty years of public service work in New Mexico. She retired in 1976 at the age of 71.

Wood had majored in sociology and had a certificate to practice social work when she came to New Mexico; but not all social welfare openings went to professionally trained people. Many caseworkers and office personnel were local women whose personal situations pushed them into the labor force. Lacking formal skills, most had to be trained on the job, a task that fell to Wood and other field representatives. Mela Vuicich of Santa Fe, Domecinda Vigil Tixier of Albuquerque, and Ena Walter Mitchell of Lordsburg, for example, were part of a large core of women nationwide who played important and largely unrecognized roles in ministering to human needs during the Depression.[47] For them, federal relief programs provided wage labor while they were helping others survive the hard times. Their stories demonstrate the opportunities New Deal programs created for women, while providing a portrait of the bleak conditions in rural New Mexico in the 1930s.

Daughter of Yugoslavian immigrants, Vuicich grew up in the coal-mining camp of Van Houten, fifteen miles north of Raton in Colfax County. Her coal miner father died when she was very young, leaving her mother with the care of a son and daughter. By the time she finished high school in 1935, work was "absolutely necessary." The timing was right, as federal funds were suddenly available to expand county welfare services. Wood, the newly appointed social services director for Colfax County, hired the seventeen-year-old Vuicich as a clerk—"she had such good handwriting, could do figures, and was so bright"—at seventeen dollars a week, though she was sometimes forced to pay her (as well as other personnel) in scrip when cash was in short supply. Vuicich held clerical positions until February 1937, when she became an administrator and county director. Serving as director of Colfax, then Santa Fe County, Vuicich stayed in public welfare work until she retired in 1975, after forty years of public service to New Mexico.[48]

In her early years with the welfare department, Vuicich performed a variety of tasks that opened her eyes to both the suffering of people in Colfax County and the response of the community to their unmet needs. Relief rules allowed three dollars a month per family for food; Vuicich was sent, on foot, to deliver budget grocery orders. Often it was not enough. On one occasion, for example, a man came to the relief office requesting twenty-five cents to buy three cans of Pet milk for his children. Kindly neighbors or women's club volunteers often contributed extra food, clothes, shoes, and bedding. One man who caught more fish than his family could use offered the surplus to the welfare office. "So the county welfare office became a central place—a clearinghouse," said Vuicich. "We told them [the community] what we needed, and they gave us what they had."[49]

As a founding member of the Raton Quota Club, an international organization for businesswomen, Vuicich was instrumental in the club's efforts to initiate a hot lunch program for Raton's needy children. The women "begged and borrowed dishes, pots, and pans" and provided volunteer services to make the program a success. "It was for needy children, yes, but they were all needy," remembers Vuicich, who also arranged for a bus to carry handicapped children to a clinic at Las Vegas, nearly seventy miles southwest of Raton. Her efforts, along with those of other women and men, helped ease the beleaguered little town through some hard times.[50]

Retired social worker Domecinda Vigil Tixier related a grim story of conditions in Union County in the early 1930s, when drought and depression together brought terrible hardship to the people, especially to the ranchers. Tixier was unusual in that she was a married Hispanic woman working at wage labor when most Hispanic women did not work outside the home. Tixier was forced to work, however, when her family lost their 4,000 acre ranch in 1932 due to dust bowl conditions. In addition, her husband suffered from tuberculosis and was unable to work for many years. Economic hardship forced this untrained but talented woman into the labor market to provide for her husband and family; she continued to work for the next three decades, retiring in 1959 to Albuquerque.[51]

With the ranch gone, the family moved into Clayton, where Tixier secured work as a home visitor in the county welfare department.[52] Wood was part-time supervisor of Union County in 1935 and recognized that Tixier would be a valuable asset to the department because of her sensitivity to the needs of her clients, particularly Hispanics.[53] Assigned to work among the ranchers, Tixier compiled case records of the families and their financial needs. "You have no idea what the drought did to those poor ranchers," recalled Tixier. "I used to sit down and cry with them. They lost their stock, they lost everything. For three years, not a drop of rain and no grass, no nothing." The government provided some money for feed and hay for the animals, but even that was inadequate in the face of nature's relentless attack on the land. Tixier described vividly the scorched ranches with "farming equipment piled up and getting rusty," owners forced off the land, some to other states. Those that survived did so by keeping chickens and a milk cow, while accepting the food orders Tixier delivered from the welfare office.[54]

Tixier served as translator for many families unable to speak English. She was especially effective with older people as well. After four years in Union County, she was transferred in 1938 to Albuquerque and assigned to Martineztown and San Jose, all-Hispanic neighborhoods. There, she continued her work in public welfare. For Tixier, New Deal programs were crucial because they empowered her to support her family in difficult times.

Ena Walter Mitchell's story parallels Tixier's account in several ways. Mitchell, from Lordsburg in southwestern New Mexico, was a struggling young wife of a mechanic and mother of two children during the Depression years. Because her husband was unable to provide for the family, Mitchell took the children and moved in with her parents on their ranch near Virden. There, her life was anything but easy. Rising early, she would pick vegetables at neighboring ranches, then can them "on halves" (one-half to the owner, one-half for her family), clean houses, and do anything else "to buy sugar, lard, staples for the home. When you live on a ranch, you do anything to be able to buy your flour. Mother had a cow and some chickens, and we fared pretty good."[55]

But that was not enough for Mitchell. She moved back to Lordsburg and lived with her in-laws while she worked as a waitress. Then, as the county welfare system began to take shape under FERA, the Hidalgo County Commission hired Mitchell at eighteen dollars a week as a home visitor. Like Tixier, Mitchell interviewed families to determine their eligibility for relief, then distributed cash and goods accordingly. Her relief rolls showed an equal mix of Anglo and Hispanic families, but no black families. Her training came through staff and district meetings, conventions, and the assistance of field representative and supervisor K. Rose Wood. Late in 1935, Mitchell was appointed Hidalgo County Welfare Director. Recalling those difficult days, Mitchell remarked, "I learned it the hard way, but I enjoyed every minute of it."[56]

Mitchell, Tixier, and Vuicich are three examples of the many talented women K. Rose Wood introduced to welfare work in New Mexico. They are representative of women nationwide who filled entry-level jobs during the New Deal years. Such women played crucial roles in implementing policies and programs for desperate families that led to individual empowerment. Not only were they helping others, they were providing income and security for their families as well. And, once in the labor force, these women remained in it, finding satisfaction as well as necessity in work outside the home.

Overall, in New Mexico and elsewhere, New Deal relief programs affected women at two levels—those who provided services and those who were recipients. All too often, programs and policies reflected gender and cultural biases that limited opportunities for many, especially Hispanic women. Yet some women, usually social workers, administered programs and directed projects on a scale never dreamed of in the past. They handled millions of dollars, supervised thousands of employees, and helped to formulate programs and policies from the national to the local level. The opportunities provided Margaret Reeves, for example, made her a major, though largely unrecognized, figure in New Mexico during the New Deal. K. Rose Wood, Mela Vuicich, Domecinda Vigil Tixier, and Ena Walter Mitchell obtained jobs under WPA and FERA that allowed them to remain in the labor market until retirement age. For women who were recipients of New Deal services, prevailing cultural beliefs determined the nature of their work relief. While men worked on construction and forestry projects, women were seamstresses and secretaries. In this way, New Mexico fit the national pattern.

In another important way, New Mexico differed from many states because of its predominately Hispanic population. Embedded in New Deal policies was a pattern of discrimination that limited opportunities for Hispanic people, both women and men.[57] Bias toward this group was occasionally evident among administrators, as well, such as Reeves and Rowland. Almost always that bias took the form of reinforcing strict gender roles for women. Hispanic women were expected to remain in the home caring for family needs; when they were forced to seek work, sewing rooms were nearly their only recourse. As a result, the "square deal" bypassed many women, not only Hispanics but Anglo, black, and Native American women as well. While New Deal programs helped them survive, they did not alter or offer opportunities for change in their overall status. That change would not begin to occur on a large scale until the civil rights movement exploded in the 1960s, prompting a renewal of the woman's movement that continues today.

CONCLUSION

In the two decades between World War I and World War II, New Mexico, like other Western states, experienced severe social and economic dislocations that forced the state to develop new methods of cooperation between public and private organizations. Women played significant roles in facilitating this interaction, thereby helping shape the nature and direction of social welfare policies in the young state for decades. Their influence depended on three factors: (1) the needs of the people; (2) the priorities of social reformers; and (3) what the existing political structures would allow. The outcome was a compromise among the three, affected additionally by characteristics unique to New Mexico: its highly rural nature and its small, multicultural population.

The most pressing need in New Mexico after statehood was to improve the health of its citizens by reducing the high levels of contagious disease and the maternal and infant mortality rates. Toward those ends, women were instrumental in the creation of the state Board of Public Welfare in 1921, and their activism ensured that their demands would shape ensuing health and welfare policies. Women activists convinced the legislature that the five-member Board of Public Welfare must include at least two women and that the director of the Bureau of Child Welfare be a woman. For the next fourteen years, two women, Janet Reid and then Margaret Reeves, directed this agency, determining policy and influencing the development of social welfare.

The needs of the state and the desires of female social reformers meshed well. Since women traditionally have been responsible for the welfare of family and children, it was natural that they would be concerned with issues that affected their health and welfare. Public health, in this sense, was not a new arena for women. They had always been among the caretakers for society's ill, needy, and poor. Women found meaning in public work because society sanctioned their role as municipal housekeepers, actions that brought approval and reward.[1] New Mexico women, then, were not unlike women elsewhere who moved easily across the blurring lines of private and public spheres.

Because they had established female-based organizations and goals, women were able to exercise power within the prevailing political structure. Reformers' desires complemented the state's needs, so male leaders were willing to grant women at least limited authority. In some cases, the need was in an area to which males were not welcomed, such as the training and regulation of midwives. In other cases, many women rose to administrative positions during the New Deal because they were professionally trained social workers, a field traditionally considered women's work. As county directors, they occupied key positions in the state welfare administration. In New Mexico, however, women did not always fare well at higher levels unless they were willing to bow to the dictates of male politicos, as the Reeves case demonstrated.

New Mexico's chronically weak financial condition also enhanced women's power through voluntarism. Because the state budget could never meet the population's needs, the welfare structure was forced to seek assistance from volunteer organizations. Women had established their place as volunteers "par excellence"; the state welcomed their help. In fact, a combination of public and private relief has always characterized American welfare.[2] Neither private support nor government assistance alone has met the needs of dependent people. Because women early on co-opted the volunteer arena, their ability to influence events and policy in these matters increased their social power.

Regarding female social power, historians have frequently disagreed on the relationship between women's separatist activities and their public activism.[3] This study shows that New Mexico women were most successful when they built their organizations from within and then went outside their group to cooperate with male-dominated institutions. The women's clubs of Santa Fe and Albuquerque are good examples of the process. Club members were able to create support for issues within the club setting and present those issues to city hall, the state legislature, the Department of Public Welfare, or other appropriate agency. The two women's clubs examined here demonstrated the process repeatedly, when they supported legislation to create institutions for the blind, deaf, and handicapped; when they raised money for parks, libraries, and milk for school children; and when they lobbied for the creation of the state Department of Public Welfare and the federal-level Children's Bureau.

The success of the Maternal Health Center in Santa Fe further demonstrates the power that women achieved by building their strength from within separate political organizations and then allying with the wider political structure. This female-staffed organization faced strong opposition from the Catholic church, yet was able to overcome the male leadership's resistance to health work because of the need for the services and the women's determination to carry them out. But most important, their strength as a female-based organization allowed them to reach out beyond the Maternal Health Center to the wider community. As a result, the cooperation and support of male-run agencies and institutions reinforced the women's work and endowed them with considerable social power.

The informal power that women wielded in private organizations such as women's clubs differed only by degree from that of women working for public agencies or state and local government. For the most part, New Mexico women who were in administrative positions possessed power and influence as long as they cooperated with the ruling male authorities. Margaret Reeves is a good example of a professional administrator who effectively headed a state agency for ten years, but who was forced to resign when she resisted male political power greater than her own. In this case, Reeves's attempt to remain bipartisan failed; she was forced to accede to the governor's demands or leave. Yet her dismissal in New Mexico did not diminish her ability nor her influence elsewhere, since she continued to be a leader in the field of social welfare.

For other women, such as those who found job opportunities during the New Deal years, especially at the county level, becoming political could be rewarding and effective. Many of the women in this study, for instance, who worked their way up through the state social welfare agency to become county welfare directors, continued in careers in state government through the 1960s and 1970s. They found, like K. Rose Wood, excitement and challenge in their increasing public power. Most important, as women and as public employees, they used their gender influence to promote policies that affected recipients of social welfare in a more balanced way.

Ethnicity as well as gender affected the direction of social welfare in New Mexico. The high numbers of Hispanics and small numbers of blacks and Native Americans forced welfare authorities to adjust programs and policies to fit the population's needs. The most obvious obstacle was the language barrier, but other problems included isolation and cultural differences, particularly regarding the birthing process. In most cases, women reformers were sensitive to cultural differences and attempted to adjust the welfare system to accommodate them.

Adjustment was most visible in the implementation of maternity and infancy work. First, health reformers recognized that, given the isolation of most New Mexicans, the reformers would have to take their programs to the families and small communities scattered across the state. And, to be most effective, health workers needed to be able to speak Spanish or have an interpreter. Second, female rather than male maternity and infancy workers proved to be more effective because Hispanic and Native American women expressed strong cultural preferences for women to assist with births. Similarly, nurses or nurse-midwives, not male physicians, were best equipped to train midwives. Equally important, among Native Americans, public health nurses (females) served as the bearers of health reform between the dominant Anglo political authority and a racial minority. In assessing their efforts, reformers recognized that they made their greatest impact when they adapted health reform to cultural differences.

Flexibility proved to be important regarding gender and race. Public or private, welfare organizations were most successful when they ignored rigid gender and racial segregation. For example, the Agricultural Extension Service, organized along distinct gender and racial lines, was more successful when extension agents moved away from prescribed behavior and showed flexibility. Hiring Hispanic women as demonstration agents, for example, greatly facilitated extension work among Spanish-speaking people. Likewise, the Maternal Health Center introduced home visits in which Spanish-speaking nurses visited Hispanic homes; the Anglo reformers understood that many Hispanic women were reluctant to come to the center. Clearly, the ability to be adaptable in a multicultural population was an important component in social welfare reform.

In addition to gender and ethnicity, class distinctions characterized social welfare reform. The most obvious manifestation of class was in the distribution of services: the providers were middle-class Anglo women; the recipients were lower- or working-class families. This pattern resembled social reform in other states where the conditions of education, access to resources, and leisure time allowed middle-class white women the opportunity to initiate social reform. Reform did not always flow from the providers, however. The recipients were active participants in shaping the welfare structure to meet their demands as well as those of the providers.[4]

Implicit in this study is a strong thread of Progressive reform. Historians once considered Progressivism moribund by the end of World War I, but now they have given the reform movement a second life. Indeed, although recent research has shown that political reform declined, social reform did not.[5] In matters of health, education, labor, and social justice, women kept the reform impulse alive between World War I and the New Deal and its abundance of welfare programs. At the national level, women lobbied determinedly for a child labor law, mother's pensions, and social security. In their local communities, women raised funds for parks and playgrounds, petitioned for sewage systems, looked after needy families, and helped establish institutions for the blind, deaf, and delinquent. New Mexico women were no exception; in fact, their efforts were especially valuable because of the state's difficulty in meeting social welfare needs. Women, then, were key figures in the crucial years of the 1920s and 1930s.

Progressive reform was based squarely on the values, attitudes, and expectations of America's white middle class. In this respect, New Mexico's female reformers fit the national pattern, from Eastern-born and educated demonstration agents and public health nurses to New Deal administrators and social workers. These reformers worked hard to instill their Progressive values in the New Mexico population. In 1924, the attempt to "Anglo-cize" New Mexico was made clear in a letter from Robert O. Brown, secretary of the state Board of Public Welfare, to Grace Abbott, director of the Children's Bureau. Because of the "peculiar condition of being more than half Hispanic," Brown wrote, "it will be many years before we have a homogeneous civilization in New Mexico, but that time is bound to come."[6] Reformers met with limited success in imposing Anglo values and standards on the population during these decades, but they were able to weave Progressive ideas into the cultural fabric in a way that benefited the multiethnic population.

This study also reveals the presence of the federal government in the twentieth-century West. Like other Western states, New Mexico profited from federal funding that built roads, dams, schools, and other public facilities during the New Deal era. Additional programs in these two decades contributed to the health, education, and welfare of New Mexicans. For example, the AES, created in 1914 under the provisions of the Smith-Lever Act, greatly benefited the rural population, especially farm women, through the work of home demonstration agents. Then, in the 1920s, the Sheppard-Towner Act was instrumental in providing funds for maternity and infancy work in a state that registered the highest infant mortality rate in the nation. And finally, in the 1930s, FERA/WPA money provided jobs for women in county and state offices, sewing rooms, schools, and libraries, and gave direct assistance to needy families.

These examples illustrate historian Patricia Limerick's thesis of the continuity of the federal presence in the nineteenth- and twentieth-century Wests.[7] From the Lewis and Clark expedition of the early nineteenth century to the post-World War II boom in government-sponsored projects in the mid-twentieth century, the West has welcomed federal assistance. The state of New Mexico, frequently tottering on its youthful financial legs, was especially gratified to accept government aid. Given the state's size, its low population, and its equally low tax base, meeting citizens' needs was always a challenge. When drought and depression brought further hardships, state and federal monies fell short. Although grants and loans from private organizations such as the Commonwealth Fund, the Rockefeller Foundation, and the Milbank Memorial Fund supplemented state and federal contributions, shortages remained. Consequently, women's volunteer efforts to provide services became an important link between federal aid, private contributions, and local donations.

Voluntarism continued to engage New Mexicans into the 1940s, as well as women nationwide, especially as it related to health.[8] During World War II, the shortage of physicians and nurses hampered public health care, requiring an increase in volunteer help in maternity and infancy work. The training of midwives was accelerated and a demonstration unit established at El Rito in Rio Arriba County in 1945.[9] Women's clubs continued their social reform efforts, holding "Baby Weeks" and clinics for school children as well as supporting the war effort in other ways. The Maternal Health Center added a summer dental clinic and a cardiac clinic to its expanding services in the 1940s and, by 1965, had come full circle when it opened a Planned Parenthood clinic.

New Mexico clubwomen maintained their political activism. Carrying on a struggle they began in the 1910s, they continued their efforts to reform state community property laws, taking the battle into the 1940s and finally securing favorable legislation in 1959.[10] Moreover, women became more visible in public office. Between 1923 and 1950, thirty-six women served in the state legislature, two of them in top-ranking positions—Concha Ortiz y Pino as minority whip in the state House of Representatives from

1936–44 and Georgia Lusk as the first woman representative from New Mexico in the United States Congress.[11] Historian Susan Ware found the 1930s to be especially productive years for women in government and politics, and the New Mexico case is similar.[12] The political skills and expertise that women learned in the 1920s and 1930s laid the groundwork for continued political power in later decades.

For example, K. Rose Wood maintained an influential role in the welfare system for more than thirty years. In 1959, she was instrumental in forming the state Commission on Aging. Important components of her political activism were the connections she made with other agencies and organizations, the necessary "bridges" she built and used.[13] The politicization of New Mexico women, then, was crucial to the formation of the state's welfare structure. In the process, government took over many of the functions of the home and social policy, contributing to the "domestication of politics."[14]

The approach and outbreak of World War II affected New Deal programs on the national level. Specifically, for women, it meant exclusion from decision-making bodies, as the emphasis turned to war-related activities rather than social housekeeping.[15] Nevertheless, the private and public assistance efforts of the 1920s and 1930s remained as the cornerstones of the modern "welfare state," thus establishing a continuity in the texture of twentieth-century life. Although New Mexico was less affected than other Western states by burgeoning defense industries as a result of the war, agencies and programs established in the 1920s and 1930s unquestionably continued in the postwar years.[16] Politically, the "domestication of politics" continued in New Mexico as it did nationwide. Less clear is whether, as a result of the increased legitimacy of social welfare programs and funding, men replaced women as heads of administering agencies, resulting in a loss of political power on that level.

In the world of public work between 1940 and 1960, New Mexico women lagged behind their national counterparts. In 1940, women in New Mexico were 18 percent of the work force, compared to 24.6 percent nationally; in 1950, these figures had risen to 22 percent compared to 27.8 percent. Similarly, in New Mexico, 19 percent of all females were employed in 1940, 23 percent in 1950, while comparative national figures were 25.4 percent and 29 percent. This discrepancy, no doubt, reflects job opportunities and the nature of economic development, since in New Mexico women were not employed in industrial work to the same degree as they were on the national level. By 1950, 26 percent of New Mexico's working women were in retail work, 45 percent in service industries, and 7 percent in white collar government work. It is noteworthy that on the local level, women were more often listed as holding managerial/administrative/technical positions than were women nationwide. Whether this development was the result of the federal government's role in the state, and a continuation of the patterns of the 1920s and 1930s, when women were an important component of the social welfare administration, is not clear and would require additional work in census and archival records.[17]

Overall, the two decades between winning the vote and the outbreak of war proved to be fertile ground for female social reformers in New Mexico. Although focused on a brief period in the social history of one Western state, this study illustrates continuities in patterns of social welfare reforms in the twentieth century. More important, this research shows how gender, ethnicity, and class affected social reform in a unique, multicultural state. Clearly, the private and public spheres of women and men were not separate, but overlapped at many points, creating a complex web of interrelationships that empowered women in ways they had not previously experienced.

NOTES

Introduction

[1] For overviews of women's history in this period, see William H. Chafe, *The American Woman: Her Changing Social, Economic, and Political Role, 1920–1970* (Oxford: Oxford University Press, 1972); Aileen Kraditor, *Ideas of the Women's Suffrage Movement, 1890–1920* (New York: Columbia University Press, 1965); Estelle B. Freedman, "The New Woman: Changing Views of Women in the 1920s," *Journal of American History* 61 (September 1974), 372–93; Winnifred Wandersee, *Women's Work and Family Values, 1920–1940* (Cambridge, MA: Harvard University Press, 1981); Dorothy Brown, *Setting a Course: American Women in the 1920s* (Boston: Twayne, 1987); Sheila Rothman, *Woman's Proper Place: A History of Changing Ideals and Practices, 1870 to the Present* (New York: Basic Books, 1978); Susan Ware, *Holding Their Own: American Women in the 1930s* (Boston: Twayne, 1982) and *Beyond Suffrage: Women in the New Deal* (Cambridge, MA: Harvard University Press, 1981); and Penina Glazer and Miriam Slater, *Unequal Colleagues: The Entrance of Women Into the Professions, 1890–1940* (New Brunswick, N.J.: Rutgers University Press, 1987).

[2] The demographic material in this paragraph is from the *Fourteenth Census of the United States, 1920*, vol. III, Population (Washington D.C.: Government Printing Office, 1923) and John L. Andriot, comp. and ed., *Population Abstract of the United States*, vol. I, Tables.

[3] Joan Jensen, "New Mexico Farm Women, 1900–1940," in Robert Kern, ed., *Labor in New Mexico: Strikes, Unions and Social History Since 1881* (Albuquerque: University of New Mexico Press, 1983); Sarah Deutsch, *No Separate Refuge: Culture, Class and Gender on an Anglo-Hispanic Frontier in the American Southwest, 1880–1940* (New York: Oxford University Press, 1987). It is difficult to determine precisely the number of people of Spanish and Mexican heritage because the census combined Anglo and Hispanic groups. In the 1930 census, "Mexican" was listed as a separate non-white category, an implied slight that offended many Spanish-speaking people. Numbers for New Mexico Hispanics seem to have been based on county school censuses. See Suzanne Forest, *The Preservation of the Village: New Mexico's Hispanics and the New Deal* (Albuquerque: University of New Mexico Press, 1989), 8, fn. 11.

[4] *Fourteenth Census of the United States, 1920*, vol. III, Population.

[5] A great deal has been written on female voluntarism. For example, see Barbara J. Berg, *The Remembered Gate: Origins of American Feminism, the Woman and the City, 1800–1860* (Oxford: Oxford University Press, 1978); Karen Blair, *The Clubwoman as Feminist: True Womanhood Redefined, 1868–1914* (New York: Holmes & Meier Publishers, 1980); Rothman, *Woman's Proper Place*; Mary P. Ryan, *Womanhood in America From Colonial Times to the Present* (New York: Franklin Watts, 1983); Theodora Martin, *The Sound of Our Own Voices: Women's Study Clubs, 1860–1910* (Boston: Beacon Press, 1987); and Arlene Kaplan Daniels, *Invisible Careers: Women Civic Leaders From the Volunteer World* (Chicago: University of Chicago Press, 1988).

[6] Michael Messner, "Review Essay: Women's Public Lives," *Social Science Journal* 25 (1988), 233–36.

[7] *Ibid.*, 234. Also see the remarks of five feminist historians on the significance of women's culture and politics: Ellen DuBois, Mari Jo Buhle, Temma Kaplan, Gerda Lerner, and Carroll Smith-Rosenberg, "Politics and Culture in Women's History: A Symposium," *Feminist Studies* 6 (Spring 1980), 26–64.

[8] Berg, *The Remembered Gate*, 151.

[9] Marilyn Gittell and Theresa Shtob, "Changing Women's Roles in Political Volunteerism and Reform of the City," *Signs* 5 (Spring 1980), 567–78.

[10] Daniel Scott Smith, "Family Limitation, Sexual Control and Domestic Feminism in Victorian America," in *Clio's Consciousness Raised*, Mary Hartman and Lois W. Banner, eds. (New York: Harper & Row, 1974), 119–36. Also see the introductory chapter in Mary P. Ryan, *The Empire of the Mother: American Writing About Domesticity, 1830–1860* (New York: Haworth Press, 1982), and Carroll Smith-Rosenberg, "Beauty, the Beast, and the Militant Woman," *American Quarterly* 23 (1971), 562–84.

[11] Blair, *Clubwoman as Feminist*, 10; also see Carl N. Degler, *At Odds: Women and the Family in America from the Revolution to the Present* (Oxford: Oxford University Press, 1980), 324–26.

[12] Blair, *Clubwoman as Feminist*, 70. Also see Margaret Gibbons Wilson, *The American Woman in Transition: The Urban Influence, 1870–1920* (Westport, CT: Greenwood Press, 1979). Wilson suggests that domestic feminism and municipal housekeeping represented a compromise between a traditional home-centered life and the pursuit of a career.

[13] Ryan, *Womanhood in America*, 202–210. Also see Kathryn Kish Sklar, "Hull House in the 1890s: A Community of Women Reformers," *Signs* 10 (Summer 1985), 658–77.

[14] See Mary Ritter Beard, *Women's Work in Municipalities* (New York: D. Appleton and Company, 1915), x.

[15] *Ibid.*, 93; Paula Baker, "The Domestication of Politics: Women and American Political Society, 1780–1920," *American Historical Review* 89 (June 1984), 620–47.

[16] Baker, "Domestication of Politics," 639–44; Rothman, *Woman's Proper Place*, 119–27. Also see Kathleen D. McCarthy, *Noblesse Oblige: Charity and Cultural Philanthropy in Chicago, 1849–1929* (Chicago: University of Chicago Press, 1982).

[17] Rina Swentzell and Tito Naranjo, "Nurturing the Gia at Santa Clara Pueblo," *El Palacio* 92 (Summer/Fall 1986), 35–39.

[18] Richard Griswold del Castillo, *La Familia: Chicano Families in the Urban Southwest, 1848 to the Present* (Notre Dame: University of Notre Dame Press, 1984).

[19] Deutsch, *No Separate Refuge*, 207.

[20] Griswold del Castillo, *La Familia*, 102–106; Martha Oehmke Loustaunau, "Hispanic Widows and Their Support Systems in the Mesilla Valley of Southern New Mexico, 1910–1940," in Arlene Scadron, ed., *On Their Own: Widows and Widowhood in the American Southwest, 1848–1939* (Urbana: University of Illinois Press, 1988). Also see Joan M. Jensen, "Crossing Ethnic Barriers in the Southwest: Women's Agricultural Extension Education, 1914–1940," *Agricultural History* 60 (Spring 1986), 169–81.

[21] Several scholars have published work on black women in their communities. See, for example, Lynda F. Dickson, "The Early Club Movement Among Black Women in Denver, 1890–1925" (Ph.D. dissertation, University of Colorado, 1982); Tullia Brown Hamilton, "The National Association of Colored Women, 1896–1920" (Ph.D. dissertation, Emory University, 1978); Marilyn Dell Brady, "Kansas Federation of Colored Women's Clubs, 1900–1930," *Kansas History* 9 (Spring 1986); Susan Armitage, Theresa Banfield, and Sarah Jacobus, "Black Women and Their Communities in Colorado," *Frontiers* 11 (1979). Also see Lawrence B. de Graaf, "Race, Sex, and Region: Black Women in the American West, 1850–1920," *Pacific Historical Review* 49 (May 1980), 285–313. To date, little has been published on black women in New Mexico, with the exception of Charlotte K. Mock, *Bridges: New Mexican Black Women, 1900–1950* (Albuquerque: New Mexico Commission on the Status of Women, 1985), and Barbara Richardson, comp., *Black Directory of New Mexico: Black Pioneers in New Mexico* (Rio Rancho: Panorama Press, 1976).

[22] Linda Gordon, "Family Violence, Feminism, and Social Control," *Feminist Studies* 12 (Fall 1986), 453–78; also see Gordon, *Heroes of Their Own Lives: The Politics and History of Family Violence, Boston 1890–1960* (New York: Penguin Books, 1988).

[23] Among the journals that have taken women in the West as a theme are *Pacific Historical Review* 49 (May 1980); *Journal of the West* 21 (April 1982); *Great Plains Quarterly* 5 (Spring 1985); *New Mexico Historical Review* 57 (October 1982) and 65 (April 1990); *Montana, Magazine of Western History* 32 (Summer 1982) and 41 (Spring 1991); and *Utah Historical Quarterly* 49 (Summer 1981). Also see Susan Armitage, "A Stereoptical View," *Western Historical Quarterly* 16 (October 1985), 381–95; and Paula Petrik, "The Gentle Tamers in Transition: Women in the Trans-Mississippi West," *Feminist Studies* 11 (Fall 1985), 677–94.

[24] Joan M. Jensen and Darlis A. Miller, "The Gentle Tamers Revisited: New Approaches to the History of Women in the American West," *Pacific Historical Review* 49 (May 1980), 173–213.

[25] Elizabeth Jameson, "Toward a Multicultural History of Women in the Western United States," *Signs* 13 (Summer 1988), 761–91. References to twentieth-century women appear in the discussion of work on Japanese-Americans.

[26] Karen Anderson addresses this topic in "Western Women: The Twentieth Century Experience," in Gerald D. Nash and Richard W. Etulain, eds., *The Twentieth-Century West: Historical Interpretations* (Albuquerque: University of New Mexico Press, 1989), 99–122.

[27] Richard Lowitt, *The New Deal and the West* (Bloomington: Indiana University Press, 1984); Gerald D. Nash, *The American West in the Twentieth Century: A Short History of an Urban Oasis* (Albuquerque: University of New Mexico Press, 1973); John Braeman, Robert H. Bremner, and David Brody, eds., *The New Deal: The State and Local Levels* (Columbus: Ohio State University Press, 1975); and

Charles D. Biebel, *Making the Most of It: Public Works in Albuquerque During the Great Depression, 1929–1942* (Albuquerque: Albuquerque Museum, 1986).

[28] Julia Kirk Blackwelder, *Women of the Depression: Caste and Culture in San Antonio, 1929–1939* (College Station: Texas A&M University Press, 1984); Deutsch, *No Separate Refuge*; Griswold del Castillo, *La Familia*; and Forest, *Preservation of the Village*.

Chapter 1

[1] Michael Miller, comp., *Chronology of the U.S. Constitution and New Mexico Statehood* (Santa Fe: Office of Cultural Affairs, New Mexico State Library, 1986).

[2] See Judith R. Johnson, "Health Seekers to Albuquerque, 1880–1940" (Master's thesis, University of New Mexico, 1983); Judith L. DeMark, "Chasing the Cure: A History of Health Seekers to Albuquerque, 1902–1940," *Journal of the West* 21 (July 1982), 49–58; Stephen D. Fox, "Healing, Imagination, and New Mexico," *New Mexico Historical Review* 58 (July 1983), 213–37; Karen D. Shane, "New Mexico: Salubrious El Dorado," *New Mexico Historical Review* 56 (October 1981), 387–99; and Billy M. Jones, *Health-Seekers in the Southwest, 1817–1900* (Norman: University of Oklahoma Press, 1967).

[3] "Public Health in New Mexico, 1919–1979," in *New Mexico: Fifty Years as a Vital Statistic Registration State, 1929–1979* (Santa Fe: New Mexico Health and Environment Department, 1979), 72. See also Jake W. Spidle, Jr., *Doctors of Medicine in New Mexico: A History of Health and Medical Practice, 1886–1986* (Albuquerque: University of New Mexico Press, 1986), 72; and Myrtle Greenfield, *A History of Public Health in New Mexico* (Albuquerque: University of New Mexico Press, 1962), 14–21.

[4] Quoted in Rothman, *Woman's Proper Place*, 126.

[5] Rose Ethel Hubbard, "Infant Mortality in New Mexico" (Master's thesis, Tulane University, 1924).

[6] "The Child Welfare Association of New Mexico," Central File, 1921–24, box 160, folder 0-1-3-3, RG 102, Children's Bureau, National Archives and Records Administration (NARA).

[7] *Ibid.*

[8] Greenfield, *A History of Public Health*, 14.

[9] *Fifty Years as a Vital Statistic State*, 68.

[10] *American Medical Association Bulletin* 11 (1916), 74.

[11] [Santa Fe] *New Mexican*, September 28, 1918. For an excellent article on the effects of the flu epidemic, see Richard Melzer, "A Dark and Terrible Moment: The Spanish Flu Epidemic of 1918 in New Mexico," *New Mexico Historical Review* 57 (July 1982), 213–36.

[12] Worldwide, 1.2 million died from influenza; 400,000 deaths occurred in the United States. In New Mexico, 13.2 persons in 1,000 died from the flu. This compares with 10.4 per 1,000 in New York City and 10 per 1,000 in Pittsburgh. Melzer, "A Dark and Terrible Moment," 223, 227.

[13] "The Influenza Epidemic in New Mexico," New Mexico Public Health Association Press Release, State Records Center and Archives (SRCA).

[14] *Ibid.*

[15] A. M. Bergere Family Papers, Nina Otero-Warren, Personal Papers, 1928–

1962, SRCA; M. C. Mechem to Adelina Otero-Warren, December 31, 1921, Mechem Papers, Letters Sent and Received, Department of Public Health, 1921–1922, SRCA.

[16] *Fifty Years as a Vital Statistic State*, 72.

[17] Greenfield, *A History of Public Health*, 223.

[18] Spidle, *Doctors of Medicine*, 239.

[19] These private agencies contributed thousands of dollars to various states in order to support health improvement at the state and local levels. In New Mexico, Clinton B. Anderson, later senator, played a key role in securing money from the Rockefeller Foundation to fund the newly created Board of Public Health in 1919. See Greenfield, *A History of Public Health*, for information on Anderson's activities.

[20] J. Stanley Lemons, *The Woman Citizen: Social Feminism in the 1920s* (Urbana: University of Illinois Press, 1973), 154–55.

[21] Clarke A. Chambers, *Seedtime of Reform: American Social Service and Social Action, 1918–1933* (Minneapolis: University of Minnesota Press, 1963), 49.

[22] *Ibid.*, 50.

[23] *Ibid.*

[24] *Ibid.*, 51. It was a great disappointment to reformers to lose Sheppard-Towner funding, but by the late 1920s the American medical profession had come to view the government's preventive health program as a threat to private practice. As early as 1922, the first year Sheppard-Towner operated, the AMA began its campaign to remove the government from the business of health care, insisting that all health care, including the reduction of infant and mortality rates, was the exclusive domain of private doctors. See Rothman, *Woman's Proper Place*, 142–53.

[25] Greenfield, *A History of Public Health*, 23.

[26] *Ibid.*, 23–24. The act creating a state Department of Public Welfare is reprinted in Appendix F.

[27] "Memorandum Governing the Division of Work Between the State Bureau of Public Health and the State Bureau of Child Welfare," December 27, 1921, Central File, box 250, folder 11-33-1, RG 102, NARA.

[28] "The Child Welfare Association of New Mexico," Central File, 1921–24, box 160, folder 0-1-3-3, RG 102, NARA.

[29] *Ibid.*

[30] Minutes, Woman's Club of Albuquerque, February 10, 1922; January 21, 1927; November 8, 1929.

[31] *Ibid.*, November 5, 1920; March 6, 1931; January 14, 1921.

[32] Rothman, *Woman's Proper Place*, 135–42.

[33] Organization of State Child Welfare Work, *Bulletin*, 1921, 5, Department of Public Welfare, SRCA.

[34] *Ibid.*, 8.

[35] *Ibid.*, 8–12.

[36] Quoted in Gordon, *Heroes of Their Own Lives*, 72.

[37] Chambers, *Seedtime of Reform*, 99.

[38] Monthly Report, November 1922, box 568, RG 200, Red Cross, NARA.

[39] Minutes, 1932–1940, Southwest Association on Indian Affairs, SRCA.

[40] New Mexico, State Board of Health, 1922, box 48, folder 0665, RG 90, Public

Health Service, NARA.

[41] *Ibid.*

[42] Joan M. Jensen, "Canning Comes to New Mexico: Women and the Agricultural Extension Service, 1914–1919," Jensen and Miller, *New Mexico Women.*

Chapter 2

[1] For a thoroughgoing discussion of the Sheppard-Towner Act, see Rothman, *Woman's Proper Place*, 136–53; Lemons, *The Woman Citizen*, 153–80; Michael B. Katz, *In the Shadow of the Poorhouse: A Social History of Welfare in America* (New York: Basic Books, 1986), 142–45; Walter I. Trattner, *From Poor Law to Welfare State: A History of Social Welfare in America* (New York: The Free Press, 1974), 206–208; Mimi Abramovitz, *Regulating the Lives of Women: Social Welfare Policy From Colonial Times to the Present* (Boston: South End Press, 1988); and Theda Scopol, et al., eds., *The Politics of Social Policy in the United States* (Princeton: Princeton University Press, 1988).

[2] James R. Scott, "Twenty-Five Years of Public Health in New Mexico, 1919–1944," *New Mexico Health Officer* 12 (December 1944), 13–14.

[3] Baker, "The Domestication of Politics," 620–47.

[4] The leading proponent of these new ideas was G. Stanley Hall, the most influential child psychologist in the country at that time. See Dorothy Ross, *G. Stanley Hall: The Psychologist as Prophet* (Chicago: University of Chicago Press, 1972), 279–308; Rothman, *Woman's Proper Place*, 98–100.

[5] Robert H. Wiebe, *The Search for Order, 1877–1920* (Westport, CT: Greenwood Press, 1967), 169.

[6] Nancy Schrom Dye and Daniel Blake Smith, "Mother Love and Infant Death, 1750–1920," *Journal of American History* 73 (September 1986), 329–53.

[7] Nancy Pottisham Weiss, "Save the Children: A History of the Children's Bureau, 1903–1918" (Ph.D. dissertation, University of California, Los Angeles, 1974), 64–65.

[8] Weiss, "Save the Children," 53.

[9] *Ibid.*, 190.

[10] Rothman, *Woman's Proper Place*, 126–27.

[11] *Fifty Years as a Vital Statistic State*, 69. To meet Bureau of the Census standards for a Birth and Death Registration state, a minimum registration of 90 percent of all vital events was required. Although the state began to keep records in 1919, it took a full decade to achieve 90 percent registration.

[12] Memorandum Governing the Division of Work Between the State Bureau of Public Health and the State Bureau of Child Welfare, 1921, Central File, box 250, folder 11-33-1, RG 102, Children's Bureau, NARA.

[13] Spidle, *Doctors of Medicine*, 256.

[14] Joseph B. Chepaitis, "The First Federal Social Welfare Measure: The Sheppard-Towner Maternity and Infancy Act, 1918–1932" (Ph.D. dissertation, Georgetown University, 1968), 25–26.

[15] New Mexico was 82 percent rural, compared to 48.6 percent for the United States. John L. Andriot, comp. and ed., *Population Abstract of the United States*, vol. I, Tables, and *Fourteenth Census of United States, 1920*, Population, vol. III.

[16] Amanda Metzger to Bertha Rowe, New Mexico State Nurses Association,

Correspondence, 1922, folder 12; and same collection, "History: New Mexico Early Hospitals and Nurses," folder 60, University of New Mexico Medical Center Library, Albuquerque.

[17] Report of Public Health Nursing and Child Hygiene, 1920, Central File, box 195, folder 4-11-1-3, RG 102, NARA.

[18] Ryan, *The Empire of the Mother*; Smith, "Family Limitation"; and Sklar, "Hull House in the 1890s," 659-77. Also see Joyce Antler, "Female Philanthropy and Progressivism in Chicago: Essay Review" *History of Education Quarterly* 21 (Winter 1981), 461-69.

[19] Weiss, "Save the Children," 156, n. 6.

[20] Rothman, *Woman's Proper Place*, 137-40.

[21] *Ibid.*, n. 12.

[22] Spidle, *Doctors of Medicine*, 197-98.

[23] Personal interview with Esther Van Pelt, May 18, 1987, Albuquerque.

[24] *Ibid.*

[25] Rothman, *Woman's Proper Place*, 139.

[26] Plan Proposed by the New Mexico State Bureau of Public Health for Activities to be Continued Under the Terms and Appropriations Provided in the Sheppard-Towner Act, Correspondence and Reports Relating to Programs and Surveys, 1917-54, box 21, folder New Mexico, RG 102, NARA.

[27] *Ibid.*

[28] Quoted in Scott, "Twenty-Five Years," 6.

[29] Plans of the Work of the New Mexico State Child Welfare Bureau, July 11, 1923, Correspondence, box 21, folder "New Mexico Plans of Work," RG 102, NARA.

[30] Grace L. Meigs, "Other Factors in Infant Mortality Than the Milk Supply and Their Control," *American Journal of Public Health* 6 (August 1916), 847-53.

[31] Woman's Club of Santa Fe Minutes, Civic and Child Welfare Department, 1919-30, Woman's Club Archives, Santa Fe.

[32] Plans of the Work, Correspondence, box 21, folder "New Mexico Plans of Work," RG 102, NARA.

[33] Weiss, "Save the Children," 206.

[34] Dorothy R. Anderson, "Why New Mexico Nurses Cooperate in Maternity and Infancy Work," *American Journal of Public Health* 16 (May 1926), 473-75.

[35] Activities Report, July 1926 to June 1927, Correspondence, box 21, folder 11-33-8, RG 102, NARA.

[36] Weiss, "Save the Children," 196.

[37] *Ibid.*, 209.

[38] *Ibid.*, 206, 198, 3.

[39] Report of the Work Done Under the Federal Maternity and Infancy Act in the State of New Mexico, Correspondence, 1917-54, RG 102, NARA.

[40] Semi-Annual Report of Maternity and Infancy Work, January 1, 1924 to June 30, 1924, Correspondence, box 21, folder 11-33-8, RG 102, NARA.

[41] Scott, "Twenty-Five Years," 4.

[42] Semi-Annual Report, January 1, 1924 to June 30, 1924, RG 102, NARA.

[43] *Ibid.*

[44] Cheryl J. Foote, " 'Let Her Works Praise Her': Women's Experiences in the Southwest, 1846-1912" (Ph.D. dissertation, University of New Mexico, 1985), ch.

6. Many women were active in the missionary field in New Mexico, both Protestant and Catholic, and health reform was part of their efforts, though I have chosen not to include them in this study.

[45] *Ibid.*

[46] Semi-Annual Report, January 1, 1924 to June 30, 1924, RG 102, NARA.

[47] Scott, "Twenty-Five Years," 10.

[48] Activities Report, July 1, 1927 to June 28, 1928, Correspondence, box 21, folder 11-33-8, RG 102, NARA.

[49] "History: New Mexico Early Hospitals and Nurses," n.d., folder 60, New Mexico State Nurses Association, Medical Center Library, University of New Mexico, Albuquerque.

[50] *Ibid.*

[51] *Ibid.*

[52] Anderson, "Why New Mexico Nurses Cooperate," 74–75.

[53] *Fifty Years as a Vital Statistic State*; Judith Barrett Litoff, *American Midwives: 1860 to the Present* (Westport, CT: Greenwood Press, 1978), 113.

[54] J. Whitridge Williams, "Medical Education and the Midwife Problem in the United States," *Journal of the American Medical Association* 58 (January 1912), 1–2; and Litoff, *American Midwives*, 72–73. Both infant and maternal mortality rates were lower in most European countries than in America, especially in England. Litoff attributes this in part to the passage of the English Midwives Act of 1902 which reduced the infant mortality rate of 151 deaths per 1,000 live births in 1901 to 106 deaths per 1,000 live births in 1910. Litoff, *American Midwives*, 92.

[55] Litoff, *American Midwives*, 82. This decline continued until the early 1970s when it reached an all-time low of 0.5 percent. Since then, midwife-attended births have increased to 2.1 percent, with New Mexico, especially the Santa Fe area, leading the nation. Litoff, *The American Midwife Debate: A Sourcebook on Its Modern Origins* (Westport, CT: Greenwood Press, 1986), xi.

[56] Charles Edward Ziegler, "How Can We Best Solve the Midwifery Problem?" *American Journal of Public Health* 12 (May 1922), 403–23.

[57] Litoff, *American Midwives*, 123–25, 128; Fran Leeper Buss, *La Partera: Story of a Midwife* (Ann Arbor: University of Michigan Press, 1980), 128–30; and Nancy Schrom Dye, "Mary Breckinridge, the Frontier Nursing Service and the Introduction of Nurse-Midwifery in the United States," in Judith Walzer Leavitt, ed., *Women and Health in America: Historical Readings* (Madison: University of Wisconsin Press, 1984), 327–43.

[58] Spidle, *Doctors of Medicine*, 257–59.

[59] *Fifty Years as a Vital Statistic State*, 69.

[60] Personal interview with Esther Van Pelt, May 18, 1987. Silver nitrate is used in the eyes of newborn infants to prevent blindness caused by gonorrhea.

[61] Litoff, *American Midwives*, 113.

[62] Greenfield, *A History of Public Health*, 211.

[63] Buss, *La Partera*, 2, 6–7. Deutsch, *No Separate Refuge*, 46–48.

[64] Richard Bolt to Grace Abbott, September 21, 1924, Correspondence, box 66, folder 20-83-5, RG 102, NARA.

[65] Monthly Report, November 3, 1928, Central File, 1925–28, box 266, folder 4-2-1-2-1, RG 102, NARA.

66 Yearly Report, February 1, 1925 to February 1, 1926, and Weekly Reports, April 25 to May 20, 1925, by Agnes Courtney, all in Correspondence, box 70, folder 20-95-5, RG 102, NARA.

67 *Ibid.*; Litoff, *American Midwife Debate*, 6.

68 Activities Report, July 1926 to June 1927.

69 Yearly Report, February 1, 1925 to February 1, 1926.

70 Monthly Report, November 3, 1928.

71 Matilda Narris to Grace Abbott, October 18, 1924, Correspondence, box 70, folder 20-95-6, RG 102, NARA.

72 Courtney to June M. Hull, June 15, 1925, Correspondence, box 70, folder 20-95-5, RG 102, NARA.

73 G. S. Luckett to Florence E. Kraker, July 13, 1925, Correspondence, box 70, folder 20-95-6, RG 102, NARA.

74 Monthly Report, November 3, 1928, Central File, 1925–28, box 266, folder 4-2-1-2-1, RG 102, NARA.

75 Courtney's records for a five-county area, 1925–26, show an illiteracy rate of 60.4 percent (116 of 192 midwives). Yearly Report, February 1, 1925 to February 1, 1926.

76 Activities Report, July 1, 1926 to June 30, 1927, Correspondence, box 21, folder 11-33-8, RG 102, NARA.

77 Louise Wills, "Instruction of Midwives in San Miguel County," *Southwestern Medicine* 6 (July 1922), 276–79.

78 Regulations Governing the Practice of Midwifery, 1922, Bureau of Public Health, box 70, folder 20-95-5, RG 102, NARA.

79 *Ibid.*; [Santa Fe] *New Mexican*, March 11, 1938. Much of this paragraph and the preceding one are paraphrased from the Midwife's Pledge found in the Regulations Governing the Practice of Midwifery.

80 Yearly Report, February 1, 1925 to February 1, 1926.

81 *Ibid.*

82 Courtney to Hull, May 17, 1925, Correspondence, box 70, folder 29-95-5, RG 102, NARA.

83 *Ibid.*

84 Eleventh Biennial Report, 1939–1940, 18, Bureau of Public Health, New Mexico; Greenfield, *A History of Public Health*, 122–23.

85 Buss, *La Partera*, 52–53.

86 Greenfield, *A History of Public Health*, 122–23.

87 Weekly Reports, June 11, 1925 to July 4, 1925.

88 Weekly Report, September 26, 1925.

89 Minutes, December 10, 1937, New Mexico Association on Indian Affairs, SRCA.

90 Weekly Report, September 26, 1925; Dr. Gertrude Light to Dr. Ethel M. Watters, January 5, 1924, Central File, box 250, folder 11-33-1, RG 102, NARA.

91 *Ibid.*

92 Progress Report on Maternal and Child-Health Services, June 30, 1937, Information File, box 182, folder 13-2-7, RG 102, NARA.

93 Scott, "Twenty-Five Years," 61.

Chapter 3

[1] Quoted in Elizabeth Forster and Laura Gilpin, *Denizens of the Desert: A Tale in Word and Picture of Life Among the Navajo Indians*, Martha A. Sandweiss, ed., (Albuquerque: University of New Mexico Press, 1988), 11.

[2] Minutes of the Initial Meeting, September 24, 1922, Southwestern Association on Indian Affairs, SRCA; [Santa Fe] *New Mexican*, September 22, 1922; Robert William Mayhew, "The New Mexico Association on Indian Affairs, 1922–1958" (Master's thesis, University of New Mexico, 1984).

[3] Deutsch, *No Separate Refuge*, 185–86.

[4] Prucha, Francis Paul. *The Great Father: The United States Government and the American Indians* (Lincoln: University of Nebraska Press, 1984), vol. II, 852–63; Lewis Meriam, *The Problem of Indian Administration*, reprint (New York: Johnson Reprint Corporation, 1971), 189–91. This comprehensive report, known informally as the Meriam Report, marked the first major report on the status of American Indians and the effectiveness of federal administration. The report produced some specific changes in policy, but, more important, it set the stage for the major reforms embodied in the Indian Reorganization Act of 1934.

[5] H. J. Hagerman, *The Indians of the Southwest: A Memorandum for the Secretary of the Interior and the Commissioner of Indian Affairs*, Santa Fe, July 1, 1931, Sophie D. Aberle Papers, box 18, Special Collections, Zimmerman General Library, University of New Mexico, Albuquerque.

[6] The Bursum Bill, introduced by Senator Holm O. Bursum on July 20, 1922, was an attempt to legislate a solution to an on-going land dispute between Pueblo Indians and their non-Indian neighbors who had settled on lands claimed by the Pueblos. The bill strongly favored the non-Indian claimants and placed the burden of proving title not on the claimants but on the Pueblos. Pueblo friends and supporters quickly raised a challenge to the discriminatory bill, led by former social worker John Collier. He was backed by two new white reform groups, the NMAIA and the Eastern Association on Indian Affairs, that came into being in response to the Pueblo crisis. See Prucha, *The Great Father*, 797–800.

[7] Marian F. Love, *The History of the Southwestern Association on Indian Affairs*, (Santa Fe: Southwestern Association on Indian Affairs, 1974), 2–3; *New Mexico Association on Indian Affairs: A History of Its Activities* (Santa Fe, n.p. 1953), 1; Margretta S. Dietrich, *New Mexico Recollections* (Santa Fe: Vergara Printing Company, 1959), Part I, 15. Reliable statistics on Indian birth and death rates were generally unavailable, but some generalities could be made. The Indian population in general showed a high birth rate, a high death rate, and an excessively high infant mortality rate. In 1925, BIA statistics showed 140 deaths of Indian children under three years of age, which comprised 40.2 percent of all reported Indian deaths (348) in New Mexico. The estimated infant mortality rate for non-Indians was 140 per 1,000 live births. See the Meriam Report, 196–201.

[8] *New Mexico Association on Indian Affairs*, 1; Love, *History of the Southwestern Association on Indian Affairs*, 4–5; Annual Report of the Chairman, 1922–1923, SWAIA, SRCA. Trachoma was prevalent among American Indians, especially Navajos. Until the discovery of sulpha drugs in 1937, those with the disease could expect to become blind or partly sightless by the time they reached adulthood. Though still fairly common (especially among Navajo schoolgirls who share eye

makeup), trachoma is a minor and curable disease today. See Donald L. Parman, *The Navajos and the New Deal* (New Haven: Yale University Press, 1976), 226–27.

[9] Elinor D. Gregg, *The Indians and the Nurse* (Norman: University of Oklahoma Press, 1965), 19. Also see Martha C. Knack, "Philene T. Hall, Bureau of Indian Affairs Field Matron: Planned Culture Change of Washaki Shoshone Women," *Prologue* 22 (Summer 1990), 151–67; and Lisa Elizabeth Emmerich, " 'To Respect and Love and Seek the Ways of White Women': Field Matrons, the Office of Indian Affairs, and Civilization Policy, 1890–1938" (Ph.D. dissertation, University of Maryland, College Park, 1987).

[10] Report of Board of Indian Commissioners on "The Problem of Indian Administration," box 17, folder 092, Northern Pueblos Agency, Record Group 75, Bureau of Indian Affairs, Denver Branch, NARA.

[11] Helen M. Bannan, " 'True Womanhood' on the Reservation: Field Matrons in the United States Indian Service," Working Paper no. 18 (Tucson: Southwest Institute for Research on Women, 1984).

[12] Report of Board of Indian Commissioners, 16, 23; Bannan, " 'True Womanhood' on the Reservation," 18–19.

[13] Mayhew, "The New Mexico Association on Indian Affairs," 41.

[14] Gregg, *The Indians and the Nurse*, 76.

[15] Report of Health Activities in the Southern Pueblos, May 1925, Indian Pueblo Cultural Center Archives, Albuquerque, New Mexico; Leo Crane to Charles Burke, January 17, 1922, Decimal File 1911–35, box 108, folder 710, Southern Pueblos Agency, RG 75, Denver Branch, NARA. For reasons of administrative efficiency, the Pueblo Lands Board Act of 1924 separated the pueblos of New Mexico into northern and southern agencies.

[16] Report on Health Conditions at the Northern Pueblos, August 7, 1925, Indian Pueblo Cultural Center Archives, Albuquerque.

[17] Erna Fergusson, "Crusade from Santa Fe," *North American Review* 243 (December 1936), 377–78; Love, *History of the Southwestern Association on Indian Affairs*, 3; Mayhew, "New Mexico Association on Indian Affairs," 12–14. Also see Arrell Morgan Gibson, *The Santa Fe and Taos Colonies: Age of the Muses, 1900–1942* (Norman: University of Oklahoma Press, 1983); Kay Aiken Reeve, *Santa Fe and Taos, 1898–1942: An American Cultural Center* (El Paso: Texas Western Press, 1982); and Jane M. Gaither, "A Return to the Village: A Study of Santa Fe and Taos, New Mexico, as Cultural Centers, 1900–1934" (Ph.D. dissertation, University of Minnesota, 1958).

[18] Mayhew, "New Mexico Association on Indian Affairs," 15–16; Fergusson, "Crusade From Santa Fe," 381; and Love, *History of the Southwestern Association on Indian Affairs*, 8.

[19] Margaret McKittrick to Secretary of the Interior, April 16, 1924, Central File, box 250, folder 11-33-1, RG 102, Children's Bureau, NARA. By 1928, the Meriam Report included in its recommendations the suggestion that the BIA cooperate with local and state health authorities by sharing the costs of public health nurses. Meriam Report, 259, 262–64.

[20] Fergusson, "Crusade From Santa Fe," 382–83.

[21] Gregg, *The Indians and the Nurse*, 95; Mayhew, "New Mexico Association on Indian Affairs," 42–43; Meeting Minutes, February 19, 1926, SWAIA, SRCA.

[22] Public Health Nursing Service Report 1926–27, Decimal File 1912–38, box

17, folder 096, Northern Pueblos Agency, RG 75, Denver Branch, NARA; Love, *History of the Southwestern Association on Indian Affairs*, 5. The primary reason for the difference in attitudes between Indians and Anglos regarding bathing centered around the availability of water. For the Native Americans, the irrigation ditches provided their only source of running water and they were not always accessible; family members frequently had to go several miles to obtain a few gallons of water. Doctors, nurses, and teachers all commented that bathing was not a problem once the issue of running water was solved. See Alexander H. Leighton and Dorothea C. Leighton, *The Navajo Door: An Introduction to Navajo Life* (Cambridge: Harvard University Press, 1945), 63, 73.

23 *Ibid.*

24 P. G. Eilers to C. E. Farris, September 24, 1924, Indian Pueblo Cultural Center Archives, Albuquerque.

25 Public Health Nursing Service Report, 1926–27.

26 Bannan, " 'True Womanhood' on the Reservation," 4.

27 Public Health Nursing Service Report, 1926–27.

28 Hagerman, *The Indians of the Southwest*, 34–35.

29 Dietrich, *New Mexico Recollections*, Part I, 15; Mayhew, "New Mexico Association on Indian Affairs," 44.

30 *Ibid.*

31 Eastern Association on Indian Affairs Bulletin 18, Indian Rights Association Papers, 1864–1973, microfilm edition, reel 129, item 318, November 1929, Zimmerman General Library, University of New Mexico; Mayhew, "New Mexico Association on Indian Affairs," 45.

32 *Ibid.*; Public Health Nursing Service Report, 1926–27; Janet Reid to Grace Abbott, September 28, 1923, Central File, box 250, folder 11-33-1, RG 102, NARA.

33 Elizabeth V. Duggan to Commissioner of Indian Affairs, September 26, 1931, Santa Fe Agency, file 55072-700, RG 75, NARA; Sophie D. Aberle Papers, box 18, folder 43.

34 *Ibid.* First and last names are used as they appear in the documents. Occasionally, a first name does not appear, as in the cases of Martin and Donovan.

35 Elizabeth V. Duggan to Commissioner of Indian Affairs, October 3, 1931, Field Matron Report 972, Decimal File 1911-35, box 151, Southern Pueblos Agency, RG 75, Denver Branch, NARA; interview with Robert W. Mayhew, October 15, 1986, Santa Fe, New Mexico.

36 Duggan to Commissioner of Indian Affairs, October 3, 1931; Louise Kuhrtz, Isleta Summary of Work, Field Matron Report 972, Decimal File 1911–35, box 151, Southern Pueblos Agency, RG 75, Denver Branch, NARA.

37 Monthly Narrative Report, July 1931, San Felipe, and Nurse Reports, Laguna, 1928–34, both in box 111, folder 722.3, Southern Pueblos Agency, RG 75, Denver Branch, NARA.

38 Elizabeth V. Duggan to Commissioner of Indian Affairs, March 29, 1934, Southern Pueblos Agency, Indian Pueblo Cultural Center Archives, Albuquerque.

39 Gregg, *The Indians and the Nurse*, 108–11.

40 *Ibid.* Also see Parman, *The Navajos and the New Deal*, chapter 9. In 1930, the Henry Phipps Institute in Philadelphia established guidelines for visiting nurses, suggesting one nurse per 5,000 people. This figure was subsequently

revised to one per 3,000, then one per 2,500 by the mid-1930s. By 1932, the BIA declared their nursing program among the Navajos "well within the range for Philadelphia, which may be considered practical"—nine to fifteen nurses—although many areas of the reservation were yet unreached. As in other situations, standards set by Easterners in densely populated urban settings did not accurately reflect conditions in the isolated West. Field Matron Work, 1926–32, box 151, folder 972, Southern Pueblos Agency, RG 75, Denver Branch, NARA. Also see the Meriam Report, 249.

⁴¹ Mayhew, "New Mexico Association on Indian Affairs," 45–46; Annual Report of Nursing committee, 1932, Meeting Minutes, 1932–1940, SWAIA, SRCA.

⁴² *New Mexico Association on Indian Affairs*, 2; Annual Report of Nursing Committee, 1932.

⁴³ *Ibid*.

⁴⁴ Martha A. Sandweiss, *Laura Gilpin: An Enduring Grace* (Fort Worth, TX: Amon Carter Museum, 1986), 51–53. Forster and Gilpin were lifelong friends and it was their close friendship that allowed Gilpin to make photographs of the Navajos, for which she later became well known.

⁴⁵ Annual Report of Nursing Committee, 1932; Sandweiss, *Laura Gilpin*, 53. See also Forster and Gilpin, *Denizens of the Desert*.

⁴⁶ Annual Report of Nursing Committee, 1932; Elizabeth Forster to Margaret McKittrick, January 10, 1932, Meeting Minutes, 1932–1940, SWAIA, SRCA; Sandweiss, *Laura Gilpin*, 54.

⁴⁷ Forster to McKittrick, January 1, 1933, Meeting Minutes, 1932–40, SWAIA, SRCA.

⁴⁸ Sandweiss, *Laura Gilpin*, 53.

⁴⁹ Laura Gilpin, *The Enduring Navaho* (Austin: University of Texas Press, 1968), 31–32.

⁵⁰ Meeting Minutes, October 30, 1933, SWAIA, SRCA; Sandweiss, *Laura Gilpin*, 56–57; Gilpin, *The Enduring Navaho*, 32. One physician, Dr. Lynwalter at Keams Canyon, displayed such a contemptuous and insensitive attitude toward Indian patients that the Navajo themselves petitioned the BIA to remove him. It is unclear if they were successful. Letter to Commissioner Rhoads, July 5, 1930, box 141, folder Rhoads, Commissioner, 1930, AAIA, Princeton University Library.

⁵¹ Margaret Burge to Oliver La Farge, April 28, 1933, Moris Burge-Oliver La Farge Correspondence, box 142, folder 1933, AAIA, Princeton University Library; and in the same box, National Association on Indian Affairs, May 31, 1933; and Margaret and Moris Burge to Oliver La Farge, n.d.

⁵² Meeting Minutes, October 30, 1933; Mayhew, "New Mexico Association on Indian Affairs," 48–49.

⁵³ Annual Report of Nursing Committee, March 1935, SWAIA, SRCA.

⁵⁴ *Ibid*. John Collier to C. E. Farris, May 9, 1934, Decimal File 740–741, box 64, folder 736, Northern Pueblos Agency, RG 75, Denver Branch, NARA.

⁵⁵ Sally Jean Lucas to L. A. Towers, May 17, 1935, Decimal File 740–741, box 64, folder 736, Northern Pueblos Agency, RG 75, Denver Branch, NARA. Molly Reebel attended the institute held in 1934, drawing on her experience in the BIA to serve as a nurse instructor. Margaret Burge to Oliver La Farge, July 20, 1934, Moris Burge-Oliver La Farge Correspondence, box 142, folder 1934, AAIA, Princeton University Library.

⁵⁶ *Ibid.*

⁵⁷ *Ibid.*; Meeting Minutes, July 27, 1935, SWAIA, SRCA.

⁵⁸ Annual Report of Nursing Committee, March 1935, SWAIA, SRCA.

⁵⁹ *Ibid.*; Meeting Minutes, July 27, 1935, SWAIA, SRCA.

⁶⁰ Annual Report of Nursing Committee, March 1935, SWAIA, SRCA.

⁶¹ *Ibid.* The generous member was Aimee Lamb of the Eastern Association on Indian Affairs, who donated $300 "for the express purpose of going toward Mrs. Reebel's salary." Jackson Percy to Oliver LaFarge, La Farge Correspondence, box 141, folder Jackson Percy, AAIA, Princeton University Library.

⁶² Fergusson, "Crusade From Santa Fe," 382–83.

Chapter 4

¹ New Mexico Board of Exposition Managers, *New Mexico, The Land of Opportunity: Official Data on the Resources and Industries of New Mexico, The Sunshine State* (Albuquerque: Press of Albuquerque Morning Journal, 1915), 56–57. Although my study does not examine women's political activity in detail (a study long overdue), one of the earliest acts of the state federation was to present a petition to the state constitutional convention in support of women's right to vote on issues relating to public schools. New Mexico clubwomen continued their fight for political rights through the winning of suffrage in 1920 to the successful community property reform legislation in 1959. See Jensen's articles on this topic, " 'Disenfranchisement Is a Disgrace': Women and Politics in New Mexico, 1900–1940" and "The Campaign for Women's Community Property Rights in New Mexico," both in Jensen and Miller, eds., *New Mexico Women*.

² An important article on this topic is Baker, "The Domestication of Politics." The many works on voluntarism include Berg, *The Remembered Gate*; Blair, *Clubwoman as Feminist*; Rothman, *Woman's Proper Place*; Ryan, *Womanhood in America*; Martin, *The Sound of Our Own Voices*; and Wilson, *The American Woman in Transition*.

³ Baker, "The Domestication of Politics," 624.

⁴ Beard, *Women's Work in Municipalities*, x.

⁵ Baker, "The Domestication of Politics," 647.

⁶ Baker, "The Domestication of Politics," 239–41; Blair, *Clubwoman as Feminist*, 119. Also see Daniels, *Invisible Careers*.

⁷ Estelle Freedman, "Separatism as Strategy: Female Institution Building and American Feminism, 1870–1930," *Feminist Studies* 5 (Fall 1979), 512–29.

⁸ *Ibid.*, 517; Carroll Smith-Rosenberg, "The Female World of Love and Ritual: Relations Between Women in Nineteenth-Century America," *Signs* 1 (Autumn 1975), 1–29. Also see Sklar, "Hull House in the 1890s," 659–77. Sklar expands Freedman's thesis to suggest that while female institutions provided a power base for women, they also allowed women to integrate with male institutions, thereby enhancing women's political influence.

⁹ Women in southern New Mexico organized in the decade as well. In 1894, women in Las Cruces formally organized the Women's Improvement Association (WIA) and like the Santa Fe club, were quickly involved in municipal projects such as installing drinking fountains in public areas, having the dusty streets watered in summer, establishing a park, and starting a library. Jensen, "The

Campaign for Women's Community Property Rights."

[10] Papers of the Woman's Club of Santa Fe, on file at the Santa Fe Public Library.

[11] *Ibid.*

[12] Scrapbook, Woman's Club of Santa Fe, Santa Fe Public Library.

[13] *New Mexico, The Land of Opportunity*, 56. National membership reached one million in 1910.

[14] Minutes, 1933–34, Woman's Club of Santa Fe; Minutes, 1920–24, April 4, 1924, Woman's Club of Albuquerque. The minutes of February 25, 1921, and September 25, 1933, show that club members read and passed resolutions on keeping club projects out of politics.

[15] It is interesting to note that unlike New Mexico women, Kansas club-women did not continue their social activism beyond 1920, instead retreating to less significant issues and activities they had once eschewed. See June Underwood, "Civilizing Kansas: Women's Organizations, 1880–1920," *Kansas History* 7 (Winter 1984/85), 291–304.

[16] Minutes, October 8, 1924, Woman's Club of Santa Fe.

[17] Minutes of the Art and Literature Department, 1926–29, Woman's Club of Santa Fe. Two excellent studies of the effects of technology on women's lives are Susan Stresser, *Never Done: A History of American Housework* (New York: Pantheon Books, 1982) and Ruth Schwartz Cowan, *More Work for Mother: The Ironies of Household Technology From the Open Hearth to the Microwave* (New York: Basic Books, 1984).

[18] Personal interview with Anita Gonzales Thomas, August 28, 1986, Santa Fe; Griswold del Castillo, *La Familia*; Lousteneau, "Hispanic Widows."

[19] Nancie L. Gonzalez, *The Spanish Americans of New Mexico: A Heritage of Pride* (Albuquerque: University of New Mexico Press, 1969), 86–115.

[20] Gonzalez, *The Spanish Americans of New Mexico*, 113–14.

[21] *Ibid.* As others have suggested, further research on Hispanic women's activities will expand these tentative beginnings. See Jameson, "Toward a Multicultural History of Women in the Western United States."

[22] Sources on Native American women's activities in the twentieth century are sparse, making generalizations difficult. For a discussion of New Deal efforts to provide health care to the Navajos, see Parman, *The Navajos and the New Deal*, ch. 9.

[23] Gerda Lerner, *Black Women in White America* (New York: Pantheon Books, 1972), 435–37.

[24] Dickson, "The Early Club Movement Among Black Women." Also helpful is Hamilton, "The National Association of Colored Women."

[25] Lynda F. Dickson, "Toward a Broader Angle of Vision in Uncovering Women's History: Black Women's Clubs Revisited," *Frontiers* 9 (1987), 67.

[26] Dickson, "The Early Club Movement Among Black Women," 21–71.

[27] Brady, "Kansas Federation of Colored Women's Clubs."

[28] In 1920, blacks numbered 5,733, or 1.6 percent, of the state population; 213 lived in Albuquerque, of whom 110 were women. The figure dropped statewide in 1930 to 2,850, or .07 percent of the total, but increased for Albuquerque to 441. *Fourteenth Census of the United States, 1920*, vol. III, Population, and *Fifteenth Census of the United States, 1930*, vol. III, part 2, Population. Two authors have made a

start on the much-needed study of the lives of black women in New Mexico. See Mock, *Bridges: New Mexican Black Women* and Richardson, comp., *Black Directory of New Mexico*.

[29] Personal interview with Laura Webb, October 6, 1986, Albuquerque.

[30] *Ibid.*

[31] Marilyn Dell Brady focuses on the importance of junior clubs within the black women's club movement in "Organizing Afro-American Girls' Clubs in Kansas in the 1920s," *Frontiers* 9 (1987), 69–72.

[32] Brady, "Kansas Federation of Colored Women's Clubs," 29; Dickson, "Toward a Broader Angle of Vision," 63–64.

[33] Personal interview with Zenobia McMurry, October 8, 1986.

[34] *Ibid.*

[35] Personal interview with Florence Napoleon, September 25, 1986, Albuquerque. Winona is an Indian word meaning "wide awake."

[36] *Ibid.*

[37] Interview with McMurry, October 8, 1986.

[38] Interview with Napoleon, September 25, 1986.

[39] Minutes, April 1, 1932, and November 4, 1932, Woman's Club of Albuquerque.

[40] *Albuquerque Tribune*, February 24, 1940; Minutes, November 20, 1931, Woman's Club of Albuquerque.

[41] Minutes, October 2, 1931, November 13, 1931, and December 1, 1933, Woman's Club of Albuquerque.

[42] Semi-Annual Report, 1938, Woman's Club of Santa Fe.

[43] Special thanks to Pamela F. James for sharing her seminar paper on this topic: "The Junior League of Albuquerque: Not Just a Social Club," University of New Mexico, 1986.

[44] *Ibid.* The following year the club changed its name to the Junior Service League and continued with a roster of similar community welfare projects into the 1940s.

[45] History of the Santa Fe Maternal Health Center, folder 2, Maternal Health Center Papers, Special Collections, Zimmerman Library, University of New Mexico.

[46] *New York Tribune*, December 27, 1937.

[47] History of the Santa Fe Maternal Health Center, n.d.

[48] Personal interview with Mela Vuicich, August 27, 1986.

[49] *Ibid.*

[50] Personal interview with Faith Meem, September 16, 1986, Santa Fe.

[51] Interview with Thomas, August 28, 1986.

[52] *Ibid.*

[53] Spidle, *Doctors of Medicine*, 175–84.

[54] Speech, April 30, 1962, Maternal Health Center Papers.

[55] History, n.d., Maternal Health Center Papers.

[56] *New Mexico Examiner*, November 19, 1939.

[57] Interview with Vuicich, August 27, 1986.

[58] *Ibid.*

[59] Speech, April 30, 1962, Maternal Health Center Papers.

[60] Scrapbook, November 1938, Maternal Health Center Papers.

[61] *New Mexico Examiner*, November 19, 1939.

[62] History, Maternal Health Center Papers.

[63] Scrapbook, n.d., October 1939, Maternal Health Center Papers.

[64] Andriot, comp. and ed., *Population Abstract of the United States*, vol. 1, Tables; [Santa Fe] *New Mexican*, June 30, 1940.

Chapter 5

[1] Edna Durand, Home Demonstration Agent, Annual Report, Curry County, 1925, reel 8, New Mexico College of Agriculture and Mechanical Arts, State College, Agricultural Extension Service (hereafter cited as NMCAAES), New Mexico State University, Las Cruces, New Mexico.

[2] Joan M. Jensen, "I've Worked; I'm Not Afraid of Work: Farm Women in New Mexico, 1920–1940" in Jensen and Miller, eds., *New Mexico Women*, 227–55.

[3] *Abstract of the 14th Census of the United States, 1920*; Jensen, "New Mexico Farm Women, 1900–1940" in Kern, ed., *Labor in New Mexico*, 61–81; and Jensen, "Crossing Ethnic Barriers in the Southwest," 169–81.

[4] D. W. Meining, *Southwest: Three Peoples in Geographical Change* (New York: Oxford University Press, 1971), 66–71.

[5] Jensen, "New Mexico Farm Women," 65; Deutsch, ch. 2. *No Separate Refuge.*

[6] Clarence Beaman Smith and Meredith Chester Wilson, *The Agricultural Extension System of the United States* (New York: John Wiley & Sons, 1930), 1.

[7] H. W. Beers and I. T. Sanders, "Effective Communication in Agricultural Extension" in *United States Papers Prepared for United Nations Conference on the Application of Science and Technology for the Benefit of the Less Developed Areas, 1963*, vol. III, Agriculture (Washington, D.C., 1962), 61–62; William L. Bowers, *The Country Life Movement in America, 1900–1920* (New York: Kennikat Press, 1974). Bowers argues that the Country Life Movement, a Progressive era attempt to stem the rapid move away from farms and into cities, failed because its supporters underestimated the power of industrialization that made city life attractive to so many.

[8] Cynthia Sturgis, " 'How're You Gonna Keep 'em Down on the Farm?' Rural Women and the Urban Model in Utah," *Agricultural History* 60 (Spring 1986), 182–99. Katherine Jellison argues that Great Plains farm women eagerly sought labor-saving household equipment, although most had to wait until after World War II, when postwar prosperity finally allowed women to improve their technological lives. See Jellison, "Women and Technology on the Great Plains, 1910–1940," *Great Plains Quarterly* 8 (Summer 1988), 145–57.

[9] "Farm Life Through the Eyes of Farm Women: The Work Side," also "The Social Side" and "The Home Side," box 2, entry 149, Manuscript File, 1917–1935, Records of the Division of Farm Population and Rural Life and Its Predecessors, Bureau of Agricultural Economics, RG 83, NARA; C. J. Galpin to Edwin C. Powell, December 28, 1920, General Correspondence 1919–1934, box 12, folder Farm Women, RG 83, NARA. In the same box, editor Bess M. Rowe reported to C. J. Galpin on March 15, 1922, on the responses her magazine, *The Farmer's Wife*, had received to the question, "Do you want your daughter to marry a farmer?" The evidence was "overwhelming" in favor of farm life. Nearly 90 percent of the 7,000 respondents cited the automobile, the telephone, rural mail delivery, and

modern conveniences that eliminated tiresome tasks as reasons to be happy on the farm. The growth of community spirit and community organizations also contributed to farmwomen's contentment.

[10] Bowers, *The Country Life Movement*, 134; Jensen, "Canning Comes to New Mexico," 221. Susan Armitage, in "Farmwomen and Technological Change in the Palouse, 1880–1980," unpublished paper, explores how technology has transformed the lives of farm women to the extent that mechanized farming and improved domestic technology have removed a traditional source of economic activity for farm women. As a result, women are leaving the family farm for jobs in town; men and machines remain.

[11] Annual Report, 1930, reel 12, NMCAAES.

[12] For further discussion of this idea, see Ruth Schwartz Cowan, "Two Washes in the Morning and a Bridge Party at Night: The American Housewife Between the Wars," *Women's Studies* 31 (1976), 147–71; and Maxine L. Margolis, *Mothers and Such: Views of American Women and Why They Changed* (Berkeley: University of California Press, 1984).

[13] Cowan, *More Work for Mother*; and Strasser, *Never Done*.

[14] Russell Lord, *The Agrarian Revival* (New York: George Grady Press, 1939), 4–5.

[15] "What Folks Say About Extension Work," Director's Annual Report, June 1935, reel 16, NMCAAES.

[16] Annual Report of the Director, 1938, 17, Agricultural Extension Division, RG 75, NARA.

[17] Deborah Fink, *Open Country, Iowa: Rural Women, Tradition and Change* (Albany: State University of New York Press, 1986), 98.

[18] The county home demonstration agent was a wartime measure designed to help housewives do their part for the war. About 800 home demonstration agents were employed in Northern and Western states; this number fell to 296 by June 30, 1920. Bulletin, New Mexico Federation of Women's Clubs, 1921–22, Special Collections, Zimmerman Library, University of New Mexico.

[19] Helen D. Crandall, "Twenty-Five Years of Home Demonstration Work in New Mexico," typescript, box 34, UA 78–43, Agricultural Extension Service, Rio Grande Collections, New Mexico State University; and Jensen, "Crossing Ethnic Barriers," 172.

[20] Annual Report, 1932, microfilm T876, reel 14, NMCAAES; Lord, *Agrarian Revolt*, 64–65.

[21] Annual Reports, 1925, 1929, 1930, and 1937, reels 7, 11, 12, 19, NMCAAES.

[22] Smith and Wilson, *The Agricultural Extension System*, 48.

[23] Jensen, "Crossing Ethnic Barriers," 170.

[24] Fabiola Cabeza de Baca Gilbert, "New Mexican Diets," *Journal of Home Economics* 34 (November 1942), 668–69; and Gilbert, *We Fed Them Cactus* (Albuquerque: University of New Mexico Press, 1979).

[25] Jensen, "Canning Comes to New Mexico," 361–86.

[26] Director's Annual Report, 1935, reel 16, NMCAAES.

[27] Jensen, "Canning Comes to New Mexico," 367.

[28] Jensen, *ibid.*, and "Crossing Ethnic Barriers," 172–73.

[29] Annual Report, McKinley County, 1930, reel 12, NMCAAES.

[30] Jensen, "Canning Comes to New Mexico," 371–72.

31 Annual Reports, 1927 and 1930, reels 9, 12, NMCAAES.

32 RG 83, Bureau of Agricultural Economics, General Correspondence, 1919–1934, Farm Women, box 12, folder Farm Women; Phyllis Palmer, *Domesticity and Dirt: Housewives and Domestic Servants in the United States, 1920–1945* (Philadelphia: Temple University Press, 1989), 97.

33 Maud Doty, Home Demonstration Agent, Bernalillo County, Annual Reports, 1925, 1929, reels 8, 11, NMCAAES.

34 Donna Gordon from R. S. Conroy, June 4, 1924, Southern Pueblos Agency, Field Matron Work, box 151, folder 971, RG 75, NARA.

35 Memorandum to A. C. Cooley from Henrietta K. Burton, March 7, 1931, Santa Fe, file 28429–910, RG 75, NARA; Annual Report of Director, 1935, RG 75, NARA.

36 Burton to Cooley, March 7, 1931.

37 Program for Women's Extension Clubs of Northern Pueblos, New Mexico, United Pueblos, 28429–910, RG 75, NARA.

38 Annual Report of the Director, 1935, Weekly Reports and Programs 1934–1943, Agricultural Extension Division, RG 75, NARA.

39 Monthly Report, Shiprock, August 1934, Reports and Related Correspondence, Extension Work Reports: Leupp, Northern Navajo, RG 83, NARA.

40 Jensen, "I've Worked; I'm Not Afraid of Work."

41 Jensen, "Canning Comes to New Mexico," 361.

42 Annual Report, Foods and Nutrition, 1937, reel 19, NMCAAES.

43 Annual Report, Santa Fe, 1934, Weekly Reports and Programs 1934–1943, Agricultural Extension Division, RG 83, NARA; [Annual Report of Director, 1938,] Agricultural Extension Division, RG 75, NARA.

44 Olive B. Cruse, Home Demonstration Agent, Grant, Hidalgo, and Luna Counties, Annual Report, 1932, reel 14, NMCAAES.

45 *Ibid.*; Annual Report, Foods and Nutrition, 1937, reel 19, NMCAAES.

46 *Ibid.*; Eddy County, Annual Report, 1932, reel 14, NMCAAES.

47 Personal interview with Mela Vuicich, August 27, 1986, Santa Fe.

48 Interview with Nona Berry, December 8, 1981, Raton, New Mexico, as part of the Voices of American Homemakers, National Extension Homemakers Council Oral History Project, Rio Grande Special Collections, New Mexico State University. Hereafter cited as Voices of American Homemakers, NMSU.

49 Home Demonstration Report, San Miguel County, 1930, reel 12, and Annual Reports, 1930 and 1932, reels 12 and 14, NMCAAES; Jensen, "I've Worked; I'm Not Afraid of Work," 245.

50 Home Demonstration Agent Annual Reports, 1930 and 1938, reels 12, 30, NMCAAES.

51 San Miguel County, Annual Report, 1924, reel 6, NMCAAES.

52 *Fifteenth Census of the United States, 1930*, vol. II Agriculture; *Sixteenth Census of the United States, 1940*, vol. I Agriculture; Strasser, *Never Done*, 81–82; Jellison, "Women and Technology," 148.

53 Maud Doty, Home Demonstration Agent, Annual Report, 1930, reel 12, NMCAAES.

54 Annual Report, San Miguel County, 1930, reel 12, NMCAAES.

55 *Ibid.*

56 Ivie H. Jones, Annual Report, San Miguel County, 1924, reel 6, NMCAAES;

Berry, Voices of American Homemakers, NMSU.

[57] *Ibid.*

[58] Personal interview with Ruby Ruyle, July 14, 1987, Albuquerque.

[59] Berry, Voices of American Homemakers, NMSU.

[60] Annual Report, 1930, reel 12, NMCAAES.

[61] Interview with Marie Rose Cauhape, April 15, 1982, Hope, New Mexico, Voices of American Homemakers, NMSU.

[62] Interview with Ruth L. James, January 7, 1982, Raton, New Mexico, Voices of American Homemakers, NMSU.

[63] Interview with Mary Moore, August 30, 1981, Raton, New Mexico, Voices of American Homemakers, NMSU.

[64] Annual Reports, 1929 and 1930, reels 11, 12, NMCAAES.

[65] *Ibid.*; Smith and Wilson, *The Agricultural Extension System*, 66–68.

[66] Ivie H. Jones, Annual Report, San Miguel County, 1924, reel 6, NMCAAES.

[67] Annual Reports, Bernalillo County, 1925, San Miguel County, 1925, and Chaves County, 1932, reels 7, 14, NMCAAES.

[68] Annual Reports, 1933, 1930, 1925, reels 15, 12, 7, NMCAAES.

[69] Maud Doty, Annual Report, Bernalillo County, 1925, reel 7, NMCAAES.

[70] Velma Borschell, Annual Report, Chaves County, 1932, reel 14, NMCAAES; Minutes, September 1929, Woman's Club of Santa Fe; Annual Report, 1930, reel 12, NMCAAES.

[71] Jensen, "I've Worked; I'm Not Afraid of Work," 230.

[72] "What Folks Say About Extension Work," Director's Annual Report, June 1936, reel 17, NMCAAES.

Chapter 6

[1] Irene Polos to President and Mrs. Franklin D. Roosevelt, June 14, 1936, box 661–90, folder 662, New Mexico, Record Group 69, Works Progress Administration, NARA. In addition to WPA records, Record Group 69 contains the records of the Federal Emergency Relief Administration and the Civil Works Administration. Subsequent citations will note specific collections within this record group.

[2] To Mrs. Franklin D. Roosevelt, January 22, 1936, RG 69, 661–90, folder 662, New Mexico, RG 69, WPA, NARA. This chapter focuses on Anglo and Hispanic women as part of the general population receiving New Deal benefits. Because black population figures are so small for New Mexico, black women as recipients are not singled out here. Similarly, the Indian New Deal, under the leadership of John Collier, provided services and programs to the Pueblos and reservations separate from the non-Indian population. A study of welfare issues and Indian women has yet to be done.

[3] Biebel, *Making the Most of It*, 21; Bureau of Child Welfare Relief, 1932, Reconstruction Finance Corporation, Governor Arthur Seligman Papers, SRCA; and Albert G. Simms to Walter S. Gifford, January 6, 1932, box 246, folder New Mexico, RG 73, President's Organization on Unemployment Relief, NARA. Also see Forrest, *The Preservation of the Village*, ch. 6.

[4] Biebel, *Making the Most of It*, 28.

[5] In addition to FERA, two other programs were part of the "alphabet soup" on the New Deal menu. In 1931, Franklin D. Roosevelt, then governor of New

York, organized the Temporary Emergency Relief Administration (TERA), the prototype of FERA and the first state agency of its type. The State Emergency Relief Administration (SERA), which began in 1933, handled the emergency loans authorized by the RFC. Maurine Beasley and Richard Lowitt, eds., *One Third of a Nation: Lorena Hickok Reports on the Great Depression* (Urbana: University of Illinois Press, 1983), xvii; K. Rose Wood to author, telephone conversation, April 4, 1988.

[6] Bureau of Child Welfare Relief, 1932, Reconstruction Finance Corporation, Seligman Papers, SRCA.

[7] Report on Federal Relief Administration in the State of New Mexico, January 14, 1933, Seligman Papers, SRCA.

[8] Margaret Reeves to Arthur Seligman, May 3, 1933, Relief: Administration of Federally Assisted Public Welfare in New Mexico, Seligman Papers, SRCA.

[9] Pedro Lucero, et al., to Arthur Seligman, June 23, 1933, Seligman Papers, SRCA.

[10] Comparisons with Arizona, comparable in population and nature of relief needs, showed that state caring for twice as many families as New Mexico at more than three times the cost. Reeves described the New Mexico figure of $4.50 to $5.00 per month per family as "exceedingly conservative" and very close to actual need. Reeves to Seligman, May 3, 1933, Relief: Administration of Federally Assisted Public Welfare in New Mexico, Seligman Papers, SRCA; Federal Relief in New Mexico, August 14, 1922, New Deal, 1931–33, Seligman Papers, SRCA.

[11] *Raton Daily Range*, April 17, 1933.

[12] Helena Hill Weed, "The New Deal That Women Want," *Current History* 41 (November 1934), 179–83; Susan Wladaver-Morgan, "Young Women and the New Deal: Camps and Resident Centers, 1933–1943" (Ph.D. dissertation, Indiana University, 1982), 48.

[13] Weed, "The New Deal," 183.

[14] Elaine Tyler May, *Homeward Bound: American Families in the Cold War Era* (New York: Basic Books, Inc., 1988), 47–57.

[15] Report of the Division of Women's and Professional Projects, February 17, 1937, RG 69, WPA, NARA; Joan Hoff-Wilson and Marjorie Lightman, eds., *Without Precedent: The Life and Career of Eleanor Roosevelt* (Bloomington: Indiana University Press, 1984), 137–39; Martha H. Swain, " 'The Forgotten Woman': Ellen S. Woodward and Women's Relief in the New Deal," *Prologue* (Winter 1983), 201–13.

[16] *Ibid.*; also see Deutsch, *No Separate Refuge*, 51–55.

[17] News Release, August 17, 1934, Mattress-Making, Old Subject File, RG 69, FERA, NARA.

[18] *Ibid.*; Ellen S. Woodward to State Directors of Women's Work, July 5, 1934.

[19] New Mexico Relief Bulletin, RG 69, 1933–1936, New Mexico folder 453.1, Director of Women's Work, NARA. Mattress Project, 1934–35, Work Division, Women's Section, RG 69, FERA, NARA.

[20] New Mexico Relief Bulletin, November 15, 1934, New Mexico folder 453.1, Director of Women's Work, RG 69, FERA, NARA; *Clovis Evening News-Journal*, November 22, 1934; *Silver City Independent*, December 27, 1934; *Las Vegas Daily Optic*, November 24, 1934.

[21] New Mexico Relief Bulletin, November 15, 1934, New Mexico folder 453.1, Director of Women's Work, 1933–36, RG 69, FERA, NARA; *Clovis Evening News-Journal*, November 22, 1934; Margaret Daniel to Helen Dail Thomas, September 7,

1934, box 542, New Mexico Director of Women's Work, 1933–36, RG 69, FERA, NARA; personal interview with Ena Walter Mitchell, November 8, 1986, Lordsburg, New Mexico.

²² Lena D. Robbins to Eleanor Roosevelt, June 29, 1936, box 661–690, folder 662, New Mexico, RG 69, WPA, NARA.

²³ Ibid.

²⁴ Report on New Mexico, Field Reports, Region V, box 132.5, RG 69, WPA, NARA; Mrs. Douglas Wright to Mary W. Dewson, January 10, 1936, box 661–690, folder 662, New Mexico, RG 69, WPA, NARA.

²⁵ Margaret Reeves to Ellen Woodward, September 21, 1934, and October 16, 1935, New Mexico 1933–1935, box 452, folder New Mexico Administrator, RG 69, WPA, NARA.

²⁶ Personal interview with Domecinda Vigil Tixier, September 14, 1986, Albuquerque.

²⁷ In 1936, a Fortune poll indicated that 48 percent of Americans disapproved of married women working outside the home, with 37 percent giving conditional approval. When asked if wives should work if their husbands had jobs, 82 percent of all the respondents said no. Valerie Kincaide Oppenheimer, *The Female Labor Force in the United States: Demographic and Economic Factors Governing Its Growth and Changing Composition* (Westport, CT: Greenwood Press, 1976), 44–45, 53.

²⁸ Mamie Martin to Ellen S. Woodward, July 22, 1935, New Subject File 375, Women's Work, RG 69, FERA, NARA.

²⁹ David M. Valdez to Franklin D. Roosevelt, May 3, 1935, box New Mexico, folder 452, RG 69, FERA, NARA; Report of Mass Meeting, El Rito, New Mexico, FERA Correspondence, September 1933–34, Seligman Papers, SRCA. Two recent studies have clearly documented the discrimination Hispanics and blacks experienced under federal relief programs. See Deutsch, *No Separate Refuge*; and Blackwelder, *Women of the Depression*. Also see Lorena Hickok's comments on this topic in Beasley and Lowitt, eds., *One Third of a Nation*.

³⁰ *Salt Lake Tribune*, October 28, 1935.

³¹ Ware, *Holding Their Own*, 40; Summary of WPA Program in New Mexico, April 1936, State Series, Central Files, box 230, AAAA, Women's Work Program, 1933–36, folder State Reports Sent to Conference, RG 69, WPA, NARA. Women worked on a variety of other projects as well, including clerical work in city, county, and state institutions; in canning and preserving centers; service in public schools, traveling libraries, and in museums and art galleries; in recreation and on playgrounds; in nursing, both in hospitals and clinics and in private care; and in laundries, nursery schools, and the arts. Professional as well as unskilled workers filled these positions. Still, of more than four million persons certified for WPA work in January 1936, only 15 percent (677,869) were women; in New Mexico, the figure was 14.3 percent (3,140).

³² While men made the adobes and built the basic structure, women were responsible for plastering the buildings, both individual homes and public structures. This was a yearly communal event that provided women an important role in shaping their communities. See Deutsch, *No Separate Refuge*, 54, 56.

³³ Biebel, *Making the Most of It*, 34.

³⁴ Swain, "The Forgotten Woman," 213.

³⁵ In November 1933, the state Democratic committee passed a resolution

requesting a "voluntary contribution" of 2 percent of one's monthly wage. [Santa Fe] *New Mexican*, July 10, 1934; E. B. Swope to Corrine Madden, July 31, 1934 and Margaret Reeves to Aubrey Williams, January 19, 1934, Administrative Correspondence, New Mexico Official Civil Works Administration, January 1934, RG 69, CWA, NARA.

36 The Democratic governors were James F. Hinkle, Arthur T. Hannett, Arthur Seligman, and A. W. Hockenhull. Richard C. Dillon was the lone Republican governor in this ten-year period.

37 Reeves to Fred C. Croxton, August 26, 1932, Bureau of Child Welfare Relief, 1932, Seligman Papers, SRCA. Partisan politics, however, did color the distribution of jobs and monies in many states. Perhaps the most shocking example was the case of the governor of North Dakota, who was removed from office and convicted for tampering with the relief organization in that state. [Santa Fe] *New Mexican*, January 7, 1935. California was also the scene of improprieties when state Republican party officials attempted to manuever New Deal political appointments. See Bonnie Fox Schwartz, "Social Workers and New Deal Politicians in Conflict: California's Branion-Williams Case, 1933–1934." *Pacific Historical Review* 15 (September 1987), 53–73.

38 William Hickman Pickens, "The New Deal in New Mexico: Changes in State Government and Politics, 1926–1938" (Master's thesis, University of New Mexico, 1971). See also Pickens, "New Deal in New Mexico," in John Braeman, Robert H. Bremner, and David Brody, eds., *The New Deal: The State and Local Levels* (Columbus: Ohio State University Press, 1975). In a similar case in California, Reba Crawford Spivalo was also forced out of her job in that state's relief administration. See Schwartz, "Social Workers and New Deal Politicians," 56–57.

39 Biebel, *Making the Most of It*, 35; [Santa Fe] *New Mexican*, January 5, 1935.

40 *Albuquerque Journal*, January 16, 1935.

41 [Santa Fe] *New Mexican*, January 7, 8, 1935.

42 *Albuquerque Journal*, January 16, 1935; [Santa Fe] *New Mexican*, January 9, 10, 1935.

43 *Albuquerque Journal*, January 16, 1935. It is not clear if women were among the protesters.

44 Personal interviews with K. Rose Wood, October 3, 1985 and August 6, 1987, Santa Fe.

45 [Santa Fe] *New Mexican*, June 26, 1935. K. Rose Wood attended that conference and acknowledged the recognition of Reeves, "a remarkable woman who deserved all of it and accepted it graciously." Wood to author, telephone conversation, April 4, 1988.

46 Interview with Wood, August 6, 1987. Wood retired as Director of the State Commission on Aging in 1975 but has continued to be a "government- and legislator-watcher ever since." She was 85 in 1990.

47 Beasley and Lowitt, eds., *One Third of a Nation*, xix.

48 Personal interview with Mela Vuicich, August 27, 1986, Santa Fe.

49 *Ibid.*

50 *Ibid.*

51 Personal interview with Domecinda Vigil Tixier, September 4, 1986, Albuquerque.

52 Home visitor was the term used for those who had no formal training in

social work although they did, in effect, carry out casework. Wood to author, telephone conversation, April 4, 1988.

[53] *Ibid.*

[54] *Ibid.*

[55] Personal interview with Ena Walter Mitchell, November 8, 1986, Lordsburg.

[56] *Ibid.* Wood conducted many of the district meetings while she served as field representative for the Southwest District as it was organized under the Department of Public Welfare in 1936. Mitchell was instrumental in getting a senior citizens program started in Lordsburg in 1984. When I interviewed her in 1986, she told me, "I'm eighty and taking care of others younger than me."

[57] Beasley and Lowitt, eds., *One Third of a Nation*, 235–36.

Conclusion

[1] Smith, "Family Limitation, Sexual Control and Domestic Feminism in Victorian America"; Ryan, *The Empire of the Mother*; and Rothman, *Woman's Proper Place.*

[2] Katz, *In the Shadow of the Poorhouse*, 280, 291.

[3] Freedman, "Separatism as Strategy," 512–29; Sklar, "Hull House in the 1890s," 659–77; DuBois, et al., "Politics and Culture in Women's History," 26–64.

[4] Gordon, *Heroes of Their Own Lives.*

[5] Chambers, *Seedtime of Reform*; Trattner, *From Poor Law to Welfare State*; Arthur S. Link, "What Happened to the Progressive Movement in the 1920s?" *American Historical Review* 64 (July 1959), 833–51; and Jacob Fisher, *The Response of Social Work to the Depression* (Boston: G. K. Hall, 1980).

[6] Robert O. Brown to Grace Abbott, June 4, 1924, Correspondence, box 66, folder 20-84-6, RG 102, NARA.

[7] Patricia Nelson Limerick, *Legacy of Conquest: The Unbroken Past of the American West* (New York: W. W. Norton & Company, 1987).

[8] Chafe, *The American Woman*; Susan Hartmann, *The Home Front and Beyond: American Women in the 1940s* (Boston: Twayne, 1982).

[9] Greenfield, *A History of Public Health in New Mexico*, 216.

[10] Jensen, "The Campaign for Women's Community Property Rights in New Mexico, 1940–1960."

[11] Jensen, "Pioneers in Politics," *El Palacio* 92 (Summer/Fall 1986), 12–19.

[12] Although Ware says the gains for women did not become a permanent part of the American political system, I see them as a modest beginning for New Mexico women at the county and state levels, gains that did not disappear once the New Deal ended. Ware, *Beyond Suffrage.*

[13] Personal interview with K. Rose Wood, October 3, 1985.

[14] Baker, "The Domestication of Politics," 620–47.

[15] Ware, *Beyond Suffrage*, ch. 6; and Trattner, *From Poor Law to Welfare State*, ch. 13.

[16] While no planes or ships were built in New Mexico, the war years did bring a rush of scientific research development to the state, centering on the science research facility at Los Alamos that produced the atomic bomb; a nuclear research and rocket experiment facility in Albuquerque (that evolved into the present-day Sandia Corporation); and the Lovelace Clinic, also in Albuquerque,

that specialized in aviation medicine. See Nash, *The American West Transformed*.

[17] Employment Security Commission, Research and Statistics Section, *Women Workers in New Mexico* (Albuquerque, 1977). For more general patterns, see Hartmann, *The Home Front and Beyond*; Alice Kessler-Harris, *Out to Work: A History of Wage-Earning Women in the U.S.* (New York: Oxford, 1982); Lynn Weiner, *From Working Girl to Working Mother: The Female Labor Force in the U.S., 1820–1980* (Chapel Hill: University of North Carolina Press, 1985); and Claudia Goldin, "The Changing Economic Role of Women: A Quantitative Approach," *Journal of Interdisciplinary History* 13 (Spring 1983), 707–33.

SELECTED BIBLIOGRAPHY

Manuscripts and Archival Materials

National Archives and Records Administration (NARA), Washington, D.C.
Record Group 69: Works Progress Administration (WPA)
              Federal Emergency Relief
              Administration (FERA)
              Civil Works Administration (CWA)
      73: President's Organization for Unemployment Relief (POUR)
      75: Bureau of Indian Affairs (BIA)
      83: Bureau of Agricultural Economics
      86: Women's Bureau
      90: Public Health Service
    102: Children's Bureau
    200: Red Cross
State Records Center and Archives (SRCA), Santa Fe
    Arthur Seligman Papers
    Clyde Tingley Papers
    New Mexico Association on Indian Affairs (NMAIA) Papers
American Association on Indian Affairs, Seeley G. Mudd Manuscript Library, Princeton University Archives, Princeton, New Jersey
Archives of the Indian Pueblo Cultural Center, Albuquerque
Agricultural Extension Service Records (NMCAAES) New Mexico State University, Las Cruces.
National Extension Homemakers Council Oral History Project, Rio Grande Special Collections, New Mexico State University, Las Cruces.
Santa Fe Maternal Health Center Papers, Special Collections, Zimmerman General Library, University of New Mexico, Albuquerque
Sophie D. Aberle Papers, Special Collections, Zimmerman General Library, University of New Mexico, Albuquerque
New Mexico State Nurses Association, Medical Center Library, University of New Mexico, Albuquerque
Papers of the Woman's Club of Albuquerque, Woman's Club Archives, Albuquerque
Papers of the Woman's Club of Santa Fe, Woman's Club Archives, Santa Fe

Documents

Abstract of the 14th Census of the United States, 1920. Department of Commerce, Bureau of the Census. Washington, D.C.: 1923.

Andriott, John L., comp. and ed., *Population Abstract of the U.S.* vol. 1, Tables. McLean, Virginia: Andriott Associates, 1983.

Crandall, Helen D. "Twenty-five Years of Home Demonstration Work in New Mexico." Typescript, box 34, UA 78–43, Agricultural Extension Service, Rio Grande Collections, New Mexico State University, Las Cruces, 1939.

Fourteenth Census of the United States, 1920. Vol. III, Population. Washington, D.C.: Government Printing Office, 1923.

Fifteenth Census of the United States, 1930, Vol. II, Agriculture. Washington, D.C.: Government Printing Office, 1932.

Sixteenth Census of the United States, 1940, Vol. I, Agriculture. Washington, D.C.: Government Printing Office, 1942.

Hagerman, H. J., *The Indians of the Southwest: A Memorandum for the Secretary of the Interior and the Commissioner of Indian Affairs.* Santa Fe, July 1, 1931. Sophie D. Aberle Papers, box 18, Special Collections, Zimmerman General Library, University of New Mexico, Albuquerque.

New Mexico Board of Exposition Managers. *New Mexico, The Land of Opportunity: Official Data on the Resources and Industries of New Mexico, The Sunshine State.* Albuquerque: Press of Albuquerque Morning Journal, 1915.

"Public Health in New Mexico, 1919–1979." In *New Mexico: Fifty Years as a Vital Statistic Registration State, 1929–1979.* Santa Fe: New Mexico Health and Environment Department, 1979.

Books

Abramovitz, Mimi. *Regulating the Lives of Women: Social Welfare Policy From Colonial Times to the Present.* Boston: South End Press, 1988.

Allen, Frederick Lewis. *Only Yesterday: An Informal History of the Nineteen-Twenties.* New York: Harper & Row, 1964.

Banner, Lois W. and Mary Hartman, eds. *Clio's Consciousness Raised.* New York: Harper & Row, 1974.

Beard, Mary Ritter. *Women's Work in Municipalities.* New York: D. Appleton & Company, 1915.

Beasley, Maurine, and Richard Lowitt, eds. *One Third of a Nation: Lorena Hickok Reports on the Great Depression.* Urbana: University of Illinois Press, 1983.

Berg, Barbara J. *The Remembered Gate: Origins of American Feminism, The Woman and the City, 1800–1860.* Oxford: Oxford University Press, 1978.

Biebel, Charles D. *Making the Most of It: Public Works in Albuquerque During the Great Depression, 1929–1942.* Albuquerque: Albuquerque Museum, 1986.

Blackwelder, Julia Kirk. *Women of the Depression: Caste and Culture in San Antonio, 1929–1939.* College Station: Texas A&M University Press, 1984.

Blair, Karen. *The Clubwoman as Feminist: True Womanhood Redefined, 1868–1914.* New York: Holmes & Meier Publishers, 1980.

Bowers, William L. *The Country Life Movement in America, 1900–1920.* New York: Kennikat Press, 1974.

Braeman, John, Robert H. Bremner, and David Brody, eds. *The New Deal: The State and Local Levels*. Columbus: Ohio State University Press, 1975.

Brown, Dorothy M. *Setting a Course: American Women in the 1920s*. Boston: Twayne, 1987.

Buss, Fran Leeper. *La Partera: Story of a Midwife*. Ann Arbor: University of Michigan Press, 1980.

Chafe, William H. *The American Woman: Her Changing Social, Economic, and Political Role, 1920–1970*. Oxford: Oxford University Press, 1972.

Chambers, Clarke A. *Seedtime of Reform: American Social Service and Social Action, 1918–1933*. Minneapolis: University of Minnesota Press, 1963.

Cowan, Ruth Schwartz. *More Work for Mother: The Ironies of Household Technology From the Open Hearth to the Microwave*. New York: Basic Books, 1984.

Daniels, Arlene Kaplan. *Invisible Careers: Women Civic Leaders From the Volunteer World*. Chicago: University of Chicago Press, 1988.

Degler, Carl N. *At Odds: Women and the Family in America From the Revolution to the Present*. Oxford: Oxford University Press, 1980.

———. *Out of Our Past: The Forces That Shaped Modern America*. New York: Harper Colophon Books, 1957.

Deutsch, Sarah. *No Separate Refuge: Culture, Class and Gender on an Anglo-Hispanic Frontier in the American Southwest, 1880–1940*. New York: Oxford University Press, 1987.

Dietrich, Margretta S. *New Mexico Recollections*. Part One. Santa Fe: Vergara Printing Company, 1959.

Fink, Deborah. *Open Country, Iowa: Rural Women, Tradition and Change*. Albany: State University of New York Press, 1986.

Fisher, Jacob. *The Response of Social Work to the Depression*. Boston: G. K. Hall, 1980.

Forrest, Suzanne. *The Preservation of the Village: New Mexico's Hispanics and the New Deal*. Albuquerque: University of New Mexico Press, 1989.

Forster, Elizabeth and Laura Gilpin. *Denizens of the Desert: A Tale in Word and Picture of Life Among the Navajo Indians*. Martha A. Sandweiss, ed. Albuquerque: University of New Mexico Press, 1988.

Gibson, Arrell Morgan. *The Santa Fe and Taos Colonies: Age of the Muses, 1900–1942*. Norman: University of Oklahoma Press, 1983.

Gilbert, Fabiola Cabeza de Baca. *We Fed Them Cactus*. Albuquerque: University of New Mexico Press, 1979.

Gilpin, Laura. *The Enduring Navaho*. Austin: University of Texas Press, 1968.

Glazer, Penina and Miriam Slater. *Unequal Colleagues: The Entrance of Women Into the Professions, 1890–1940*. New Brunswick, N.J.: Rutgers University Press, 1987.

Gonzalez, Nancie L. *The Spanish Americans of New Mexico: A Heritage of Pride*. Albuquerque: University of New Mexico Press, 1969.

Gordon, Linda. *Heroes of Their Own Lives: The Politics and History of Family Violence, Boston 1890–1960*. New York: Penquin Books, 1988.

Greenfield, Myrtle. *A History of Public Health in New Mexico*. Albuquerque: University of New Mexico Press, 1962.

Gregg, Elinor D. *The Indians and the Nurse*. Norman: University of Oklahoma Press, 1965.

Griswold del Castillo, Richard. *La Familia: Chicano Families in the Urban Southwest,*

1848 to the Present. Notre Dame: University of Notre Dame Press, 1984.

Hartmann, Susan. *The Home Front and Beyond: American Women in the 1940s*. Boston: Twayne, 1982.

Hoff-Wilson, Joan and Marjorie Lightman, eds. *Without Precedent: The Life and Career of Eleanor Roosevelt*. Bloomington: Indiana University Press, 1984.

Hofstadter, Richard. *The Age of Reform: From Bryan to FDR*. New York: Vintage Books, 1955.

Jensen, Joan M. and Darlis A. Miller, eds. *New Mexico Women: Intercultural Perspectives*. Albuquerque: University of New Mexico Press, 1986.

Jones, Billy M. *Health-Seekers in the Southwest, 1817–1900*. Norman: University of Oklahoma Press, 1967.

Katz, Michael B. *In the Shadow of the Poorhouse: A Social History of Welfare in America*. New York: Basic Books, 1986.

Katz, William L. *The Black West*. Garden City, NJ: Doubleday, 1971.

Kelly, Lawrence G. *The Assault on Assimilation: John Collier and the Origins of Indian Policy Reform*. Albuquerque: University of New Mexico Press, 1983.

Kerber, Linda K. *Women of the Republic: Intellect and Ideology in Revolutionary America*. Chapel Hill: University of North Carolina Press, 1980.

Kern, Robert, ed. *Labor in New Mexico: Strikes, Unions and Social History Since 1881*. Albuquerque: University of New Mexico Press, 1983.

Kessler-Harris, Alice. *Out to Work: A History of Wage-Earning Women in the U.S.* New York: Oxford, 1982.

Kraditor, Aileen. *Ideas of the Women's Suffrage Movement, 1890–1920*. New York: Columbia University Press, 1965.

Leavitt, Judith Walzer, ed. *Women and Health in America: Historical Readings*. Madison: University of Wisconsin Press, 1984.

Leighton, Alexander H. and Dorothea C. Leighton, *The Navajo Door: An Introduction to Navajo Life*. Cambridge: Harvard University Press, 1945.

Lemons, J. Stanley. *The Woman Citizen: Social Feminism in the 1920s*. Urbana: University of Illinois Press, 1973.

Lerner, Gerda. *Black Women in White America*. New York: Pantheon Books, 1972.

Leuchtenburg, William E. *The Perils of Prosperity, 1914–1932*. Chicago: University of Chicago Press, 1958.

Limerick, Patricia Nelson. *Legacy of Conquest: The Unbroken Past of the American West*. New York: W. W. Norton & Company, 1987.

Litoff, Judith Barrett. *American Midwives: 1860 to the Present*. Westport, CT: Greenwood Press, 1978.

———. *The American Midwife Debate: A Sourcebook on Its Modern Origins*. Westport, CT: Greenwood Press, 1986.

Lord, Russell. *The Agrarian Revival*. New York: George Grady Press, 1939.

Love, Marian F. *The History of the Southwestern Association on Indian Affairs*. Santa Fe: Southwestern Association on Indian Affairs, 1974.

Lowitt, Richard. *The New Deal and the West*. Bloomington: Indiana University Press, 1984.

Lubove, Roy. *The Struggle for Social Security, 1900–1935*. Cambridge: Harvard University Press, 1968.

McCarthy, Kathleen D. *Noblesse Oblige: Charity and Cultural Philanthropy in Chicago, 1849–1929*. Chicago: University of Chicago Press, 1982.

Margolis, Maxine L. *Mothers and Such: Views of American Women and Why They Changed*. Berkeley: University of California Press, 1984.

Martin, Theodora. *The Sound of Our Own Voices: Women's Study Clubs, 1860–1910*. Boston: Beacon Press, 1987.

May, Elaine Tyler. *Homeward Bound: American Families in the Cold War Era*. New York: Basic Books, 1988.

Meining, D. W. *Southwest: Three Peoples in Geographical Change*. New York: Oxford University Press, 1971.

Meriam, Lewis. *The Problem of Indian Administration*. Reprint. New York: Johnson Reprint Corporation, 1971.

Mock, Charlotte K. *Bridges: New Mexican Black Women, 1900–1950*. Albuquerque: New Mexico Commission on the Status of Women, 1985.

Nash, Gerald D. *The American West Transformed: The Impact of the Second World War*. Bloomington: Indiana University Press, 1985.

———. *The American West in the Twentieth Century: A Short History of an Urban Oasis*. Albuquerque: University of New Mexico Press, 1973.

——— and Richard W. Etulain, eds. *The Twentieth-Century West: Historical Interpretations*. Albuquerque: University of New Mexico Press, 1989.

Norton, Mary Beth. *Liberty's Daughter: The Revolutionary Experience of American Women, 1750–1800*. Boston: Little, Brown, 1980.

Oppenheimer, Valerie Kincaide. *The Female Labor Force in the United States: Demographic and Economic Factors Governing Its Growth and Changing Composition*. Westport, CT: Greenwood Press, 1976.

Palmer, Phyllis. *Domesticity and Dirt: Housewives and Domestic Servants in the United States, 1920–1945*. Philadelphia: Temple University Press, 1989.

Parman, Donald L. *The Navajos and the New Deal*. New Haven: Yale University Press, 1976.

Pearce, T. M. *New Mexico Place Names: A Geographical Dictionary*. Albuquerque: University of New Mexico Press, 1964.

Philps, Kenneth R. *John Collier's Crusade for Indian Reform, 1920–1954*. Tucson: University of Arizona Press, 1977.

Prucha, Francis Paul. *The Great Father: The United States Government and the American Indians*. vol. 2. Lincoln: University of Nebraska Press, 1984.

Reeve, Kay Aiken. *Santa Fe and Taos, 1898–1942: An American Cultural Center*. El Paso: Texas Western Press, 1982.

Richardson, Barbara J., comp. *Black Directory of New Mexico: Black Pioneers in New Mexico*. Rio Rancho: Panorama Press, 1976.

Riley, Glenda. *The Female Frontier: A Comparative View of Women on the Prairie and the Plains*. Lawrence: University Press of Kansas, 1988.

Ross, Dorothy. *G. Stanley Hall: The Psychologist as Prophet*. Chicago: University of Chicago Press, 1972.

Rothman, Sheila M. *Woman's Proper Place: A History of Changing Ideals and Practices, 1870 to the Present*. New York: Basic Books, 1978.

Ryan, Mary P. *The Empire of the Mother: American Writing About Domesticity, 1830–1860*. New York: Haworth Press, 1982.

———. *Womanhood in America From Colonial Times to the Present*. New York: Franklin Watts, 1983.

Sandweiss, Martha A. *Laura Gilpin: An Enduring Grace*. Fort Worth, TX: Amon

Carter Museum, 1986.

Scadron, Arlene. *On Their Own: Widows and Widowhood in the American Southwest, 1848–1939*. Urbana: University of Illinois Press, 1988.

Scharf, Lois. *To Work and to Wed: Female Employment, Feminism, and the Great Depression*. Westport, CT: Greenwood Press, 1980.

Scopol, Theda, et al., eds. *The Politics of Social Policy in the United States*. Princeton: Princeton University Press, 1988.

Smith, Clarence Beaman and Meredith Chester Wilson. *The Agricultural Extension System of the United States*. New York: John Wiley & Sons, 1930.

Spidle, Jake W., Jr. *Doctors of Medicine in New Mexico: A History of Health and Medical Practice, 1886–1986*. Albuquerque: University of New Mexico Press, 1986.

Strasser, Susan. *Never Done: A History of American Housework*. New York: Pantheon Books, 1982.

Trattner, Walter I. *From Poor Law to Welfare State: A History of Social Welfare in America*. New York: The Free Press, 1974.

Trolander, Judith Ann. *Settlement Houses and the Great Depression*. Detroit: Wayne State University Press, 1975.

————. *Professionalism and Social Change: From the Settlement House Movement to Neighborhood Centers, 1886 to the Present*. New York: Columbia University Press, 1987.

Wandersee, Winnifred D. *Women's Work and Family Values, 1920–1940*. Cambridge, MA: Harvard University Press, 1981.

Ware, Susan. *Holding Their Own: American Women in the 1930s*. Boston: Twayne, 1982.

————. *Beyond Suffrage: Women in the New Deal*. Cambridge, MA: Harvard University Press, 1981.

Weiner, Lynn. *From Working Girl to Working Mother: The Female Labor Force in the U.S., 1820–1980*. Chapel Hill: University of North Carolina Press, 1985.

Westin, Jeanne. *Making Do: How Women Survived the 30s*. Chicago: Follett Publishing Co., 1976.

Wiebe, Robert H. *The Search for Order, 1877–1920*. Westport, CT: Greenwood Press, 1967.

Williams, Donald B. *Agricultural Extension: Farm Extension Services in Australia, Britain and the United States of America*. Carlton, Victoria: Melbourne University Press, 1968.

Wilson, Margaret Gibbons. *The American Woman in Transition: The Urban Influence, 1870–1920*. Westport, CT: Greenwood Press, 1979.

Wood, Mary I. *The History of the General Federation of Women's Clubs: For the First Twenty-Two Years of Its Organization*. Farmingdale, NY: Dabor Social Science Publications, 1978.

Articles

Anderson, Dorothy R. "Why New Mexico Nurses Cooperate in Maternity and Infancy Work." *American Journal of Public Health* 16 (May 1926): 473–75.

Anderson, Karen. "Western Women: The Twentieth Century Experience." In *The Twentieth Century West: Historical Interpretations*. Gerald D. Nash and Richard W. Etulain, eds. Albuquerque: University of New Mexico Press, 1989.

Antler, Joyce. "Female Philanthropy and Progressivism in Chicago: Essay Review." *History of Education Quarterly* 21 (Winter 1981): 461–69.

Armitage, Susan. "A Stereoptical View." *Western Historical Quarterly* 16 (October 1985): 381–95.

———. "Farmwomen and Technological Change in the Palouse, 1880–1980," n.d., unpublished paper.

———, Theresa Banfield and Sarah Jacobus. "Black Women and Their Communities in Colorado." *Frontiers* 11 (1979): 36–39.

Arrington, Leonard J. "The New Deal in the West: A Preliminary Statistical Inquiry." *Pacific Historical Review* 38 (August 1969): 311–16.

———. "The Sagebrush Resurrection: New Deal Expenditures in the Western States, 1933–1939." *Pacific Historical Review* 52 (February 1983): 1–16.

Baker, Paula. "The Domestication of Politics: Women and American Political Society, 1780–1920." *American Historical Review* 89 (June 1984): 620–47.

Beers, H. W., and I. T. Sanders. "Effective Communication in Agricultural Extension." In *United States Papers Prepared for United Nations Conference on the Application of Science and Technology for the Benefit of the Less Developed Areas, 1963.* Vol. III. Washington, D.C.: Department of Agriculture, 1962.

Brady, Marilyn Dell. "Kansas Federation of Colored Women's Clubs, 1900–1930." *Kansas History* 9 (Spring 1986): 19–30.

———. "Organizing Afro-American Girls' Clubs in Kansas in the 1920s." *Frontiers* 9 (1987): 69–72.

Bremner, Robert H. "The State of Social Welfare History." In *The State of American History.* Herbert J. Bass, ed. Chicago: Quadrangle Books, 1979.

Chambers, Clarke A. "Towards a Redefinition of Welfare History." *Journal of American History* 73 (September 1986): 407–33.

———. "Women in the Creation of the Profession of Social Work." *Social Service Review* 60 (March 1986): 1–33.

Conway, Jill. "Women Reformers and American Culture, 1870–1930." *Journal of Social History* 5 (Winter 1971–72) 164–77.

Cowan, Ruth Schwartz. "Two Washes in the Morning and a Bridge Party at Night: The American Housewife Between the Wars." *Women's Studies* 31 (1976): 147–71.

de Graaf, Lawrence B. "Race, Sex, and Region: Black Women in the American West, 1850–1920." *Pacific Historical Review* 49 (May 1980): 285–313.

DeMark, Judith L. "Chasing the Cure: A History of Health Seekers to Albuquerque, 1902–1940." *Journal of the West* 21 (July 1982): 49–58.

Dickson, Lynda F. "Toward a Broader Angle of Vision in Uncovering Women's History: Black Women's Clubs Revisited." *Frontiers* 9 (1987): 62–68.

DuBois, Ellen, Mari Jo Buhle, Temma Kaplan, Gerda Lerner, and Carroll Smith-Rosenberg. "Politics and Culture in Women's History: A Symposium." *Feminist Studies* 6 (Spring 1980): 26–64.

Dye, Nancy Schrom. "Mary Breckinridge, the Frontier Nursing Service and the Introduction of Nurse-Midwifery in the United States." In *Women and Health in America: Historical Readings.* Judith Walzer Leavitt, ed. Madison: University of Wisconsin Press, 1984.

——— and Daniel Blake Smith. "Mother Love and Infant Death, 1750–1920." *Journal of American History* 73 (September 1986): 329–53.

Fergusson, Erna. "Crusade From Santa Fe." *North American Review* 243 (December

1936): 377–87.

Fox, Stephen D. "Healing, Imagination, and New Mexico." *New Mexico Historical Review* 58 (July 1983): 213–37.

Freedman, Estelle. "Separatism as Strategy: Female Institution Building and American Feminism, 1870–1930." *Feminist Studies* 5 (Fall 1979): 512–29.

———. "The New Woman: Changing Views of Women in the 1920s." *Journal of American History* 61 (September 1974): 372–93.

Gilbert, Fabiola Cabeza de Baca. "New Mexican Diets." *Journal of Home Economics* 34 (November 1942): 668–69.

Gittell, Marilyn and Theresa Shtob. "Changing Women's Roles in Political Volunteerism and Reform of the City." *Signs* 5 (Spring 1980): 567–78.

Goldin, Claudia. "The Changing Economic Role of Women: A Quantitative Approach." *Journal of Interdisciplinary History* 13 (Spring 1983): 707–33.

Gordon, Linda. "Family Violence, Feminism and Social Control." *Feminist Studies* 12 (Fall 1986): 453–78.

Jameson, Elizabeth. "Toward a Multicultural History of Women in the Western United States." *Signs* 13 (Summer 1988): 761–91.

Jellison, Katherine. "Women and Technology on the Great Plains, 1910–1940." *Great Plains Quarterly* 8 (Summer 1988): 145–57.

Jensen, Joan M. "Crossing Ethnic Barriers in the Southwest: Women's Agricultural Extension Education, 1914–1940." *Agricultural History* 60 (Spring 1986): 169–81.

———. "Canning Comes to New Mexico: Women and the Agricultural Extension Service, 1914–1919;" " 'Disenfranchisement Is a Disgrace': Women and Politics in New Mexico, 1900–1940;" " 'I've Worked; I'm Not Afraid of Work': Farm Women in New Mexico, 1920–1940;" and "The Campaign for Women's Community Property Rights in New Mexico," all in *New Mexico Women: Intercultural Perspectives*. Joan M. Jensen and Darlis Miller, eds. Albuquerque: University of New Mexico Press, 1986.

———. "New Mexico Farm Women, 1900–1940." In *Labor in New Mexico: Strikes, Unions and Social History Since 1881*. Robert Kern, ed. Albuquerque: University of New Mexico Press, 1983.

———. "Pioneers in Politics." *El Palacio* 92 (Summer/Fall 1986): 2–19.

——— and Darlis A. Miller. "The Gentle Tamers Revisited: New Approaches to the History of Women in the American West." *Pacific Historical Review* 49 (May 1980): 173–213.

Knack, Martha C., "Philene T. Hall, Bureau of Indian Affairs Field Matron: Planned Culture Change of Washakie Shoshone Women." *Prologue* 22 (Summer 1990), 151–67.

Lemons, J. Stanley. "The Sheppard-Towner Act: Progressivism in the 1920s." *Journal of American History* 55 (March 1969): 776–86.

Link, Arthur S. "What Happened to the Progressive Movement in the 1920s?" *American Historical Review* 64 (July 1959): 833–51.

Loustaunau, Martha Oehmke. "Hispanic Widows and Their Support Systems in the Mesilla Valley of Southern New Mexico, 1910–1940." In *On Their Own: Widows and Widowhood in the American Southwest, 1848–1939*. Arlene Scadron, ed. Urbana: University of Illinois Press, 1988.

Meigs, Grace L. "Other Factors in Infant Mortality Than the Milk Supply and

Their Control." *American Journal of Public Health* 6 (August 1916): 847–53.

Melzer, Richard. "A Dark and Terrible Moment: The Spanish Flu Epidemic of 1918 in New Mexico." *New Mexico Historical Review* 57 (July 1982): 213–36.

Messner, Michael. "Review Essay: Women's Public Lives." *Social Science Journal* 25 (1988): 233–36.

New Mexico: Fifty Years as a Vital Registration State, 1929–1979. Santa Fe: New Mexico Health and Environment Department, 1979.

Petrik, Paula. "The Gentle Tamers in Transition: Women in the Trans-Mississippi West." *Feminist Studies* 11 (Fall 1985): 677–94.

Philps, Kenneth R. "Albert B. Fall and the Protest From the Pueblos, 1921–1923." *Arizona and the West* 12 (July 1970): 245–47.

Pickens, William Hickman. "New Deal in New Mexico." In *The New Deal: The State and Local Levels.* John Braeman, Robert H. Bremner, and David Brody, eds. Columbus: Ohio State University Press, 1975.

Schwartz, Bonnie Fox. "Social Workers and New Deal Politicians in Conflict: California's Branion-Williams Case, 1933–1934." *Pacific Historical Review* 15 (September 1987): 53–73.

Scott, James R. "Twenty-Five Years of Public Health in New Mexico, 1919–1944." *New Mexico Health Officer* 12 (December 1944): 13–14.

Shane, Karen D. "New Mexico: Salubrious El Dorado." *New Mexico Historical Review* 56 (October 1981): 387–99.

Sklar, Kathryn Kish. "Hull House in the 1890s: A Community of Women Reformers." *Signs* 10 (Summer 1985): 658–77.

Smith, Daniel Scott. "Family Limitation, Sexual Control and Domestic Feminism in Victorian America." In *Clio's Consciousness Raised.* Mary Hartman and Lois W. Banner, eds. New York: Harper & Row, 1974.

Smith-Rosenberg, Carroll. "The Female World of Love and Ritual: Relations Between Women in Nineteenth-Century America." *Signs* 1 (Autumn 1975): 1–29.

———. "Beauty, the Beast, and the Militant Woman," *American Quarterly* 23 (1971), 562–84.

Sturgis, Cynthia. " 'How're You Gonna Keep 'em Down on the Farm?' Rural Women and the Urban Model in Utah." *Agricultural History* 60 (Spring 1986): 182–99.

Swain, Martha H. " 'The Forgotten Woman': Ellen S. Woodward and Women's Relief in the New Deal." *Prologue* 15 (Winter 1983), 201–13.

Swentzell, Rina and Tito Naranho, "Nurturing the Gia at Santa Clara Pueblo," *El Palacio* 92 (Summer/Fall 1986), 35–39.

Underwood, June O. "Civilizing Kansas: Women's Organizations, 1880–1920." *Kansas History* 7 (Winter 1984/85), 291–304.

Weed, Helena Hill. "The New Deal That Women Want." *Current History* 41 (November 1934): 179–83.

Welter, Barbara. "The Cult of True Womanhood: 1820–1860." *American Quarterly* 18 (Summer 1966): 151–74.

Williams, J. Whitridge. "Medical Education and the Midwife Problem in the United States." *Journal of the American Medical Association* 58 (January 1912): 1–2.

Wills, Louise. "Instruction of Midwives in San Miguel County." *Southwestern*

Medicine 6 (July 1922): 276–79.

Ziegler, Charles Edward. "How Can We Best Solve the Midwifery Problem?" *American Journal of Public Health* 12 (May 1922): 403–13.

Theses and Dissertations

Borst, Charlotte G., "Catching Babies: The Change from Midwife to Physician-Attended Childbirth in Wisconsin, 1870–1930." Ph.D. dissertation, University of Wisconsin, 1989.

Chepaitis, Joseph B. "The First Federal Social Welfare Measure: The Sheppard-Towner Maternity and Infancy Act, 1918–1932." Ph.D. dissertation, Georgetown University, 1968.

Dickson, Lynda F. "The Early Club Movement Among Black Women in Denver, 1890–1925." Ph.D. dissertation, University of Colorado, 1982.

Emmerich, Lisa Elizabeth. " 'To Respect and Love and Seek the Ways of White Women': Field Matrons, the Office of Indian Affairs, and Civilization Policy, 1890–1938." Ph.D. dissertation, University of Maryland, College Park, 1987.

Foote, Cheryl J. " 'Let Her Works Praise Her': Women's Experiences in the Southwest, 1846–1912." Ph.D. dissertation, University of New Mexico, 1985.

Forrest, Suzanne. "The Preservation of the Village: The Origins and Implementation of New Mexico's Hispanic New Deal." Ph.D. dissertation, University of Wyoming, 1987.

Gaither, Jane M. "A Return to the Village: A Study of Santa Fe and Taos, New Mexico, as Cultural Centers, 1900–1934." Ph.D. dissertation, University of Minnesota, 1958.

Hamilton, Tullia Brown. "The National Association of Colored Women, 1896–1920." Ph.D. dissertation, Emory University, 1978.

Hubbard, Rose Ethel. "Infant Mortality in New Mexico." Master's thesis, Tulane University, 1924.

Johnson, Judith R. "Health Seekers to Albuquerque, 1880–1940." Master's thesis, University of New Mexico, 1983.

Mayhew, Robert William. "The New Mexico Association on Indian Affairs, 1922–1958." Master's thesis, University of New Mexico, 1984.

Pascoe, Peggy A. "The Search for Female Moral Authority: Protestant Women and Rescue Homes in the American West, 1874–1939." Ph.D. dissertation, Stanford University, 1986.

Pickens, William Hickman. "The New Deal in New Mexico: Changes in State Government and Politics, 1926–1938." Master's thesis, University of New Mexico, 1971.

Weiss, Nancy Pottisham. "Save the Children: A History of the Children's Bureau, 1903–1918." Ph.D. dissertation, University of California, Los Angeles, 1974.

Wladaver-Morgan, Susan. "Young Women and the New Deal: Camps and Resident Centers, 1933–1943." Ph.D. dissertation, Indiana University, 1982.

Miscellaneous

Bannan, Helen M. " 'True Womanhood' on the Reservation: Field Matrons in the United States Indian Service." Working paper no. 18. Tucson: Southwest Institute for Research on Women, 1984.

James, Pamela F. "The Junior League of Albuquerque: Not Just a Social Club." Seminar Paper, University of New Mexico, 1986.

Miller, Michael, comp. *Chronology of the U.S. Constitution and New Mexico Statehood.* Santa Fe: Office of Cultural Affairs, New Mexico State Library, 1986.

Newspapers

Albuquerque Journal
Albuquerque Tribune
Clovis Evening News-Journal
El Paso Herald-Post
Las Vegas Daily Optic
New Mexico Examiner
New York Tribune
Raton Daily Range
Salt Lake Tribune
Silver City Independent
Santa Fe *New Mexican*

Interviews

McMurry, Zenobia. Albuquerque, New Mexico, October 8, 1986.
Mayhew, Robert W. Santa Fe, New Mexico, October 15, 1986.
Meem, Faith. Santa Fe, New Mexico, September 16, 1986.
Mitchell, Ena Walter. Lordsburg, New Mexico, November 8, 1986.
Napoleon, Florence. Albuquerque, New Mexico, September 25, 1986.
Ruyle, Ruby. Albuquerque, New Mexico, July 14, 1987.
Thomas, Anita Gonzales. Santa Fe, New Mexico, August 28, 1986.
Tixier, Domecinda Vigil. Albuquerque, New Mexico, September 4, 1986.
Van Pelt, Esther. Albuquerque, New Mexico, May 18, 1987.
Vuicich, Mela. Santa Fe, New Mexico, August 27, 1986.
Webb, Laura. Albuquerque, New Mexico, October 6, 8, 1986.
Wood, Rose K. Santa Fe, New Mexico, October 3, 1985; August 6, 1987; and July 19, 1989.

INDEX